Whitehead's Philosophy

SUNY series in Constructive Postmodern Thought

David Ray Griffin, editor

Whitehead's Philosophy

Points of Connection

Edited by

JANUSZ A. POLANOWSKI
and
DONALD W. SHERBURNE

STATE UNIVERSITY OF NEW YORK PRESS

Published by
State University of New York Press, Albany

Printed in the United States of America

For information, address State University of New York Press, Albany, NY
www.sunypress.edu

Production by Kelli Williams
Marketing by Michael Campochiaro

Library of Congress Cataloging-in-Publication Data

Whitehead's philosophy : points of connection / edited by Janusz A. Polanowski and Donald W. Sherburne.
p. cm. — (SUNY series in constructive postmodern thought)
Includes bibliographical references and index.
ISBN 0-7914-6137-8 (hc : alk. paper)—ISBN 978-0-7914-6138-9 (pb : alk. paper)
1. Whitehead, Alfred North, 1861–1947. .I. Polanowski, Janusz A. II. Sherburne, Donald W. III. Series.

B1674.W354W54 2004
192—dc22

2004018560

10 9 8 7 6 5 4 3 2 1

In Memoriam

DAVID L. HALL died unexpectedly shortly after completing his chapter in this book. From the beginning he was an enthusiastic supporter of the project, offering helpful suggestions to the editors as the structure of the book unfolded. He was particularly pleased at the prospect of being united in this venture with five friends and contemporaries whose careers and interests overlapped so closely with his own—George Allan, John Cobb, Fred Ferré, Bob Neville, and Don Sherburne. We reciprocate the pleasure of his company and are sorely vexed that he is unable to celebrate with us the completion of our venture together.

Footnote 24 of chapter 2, authored by Bob Neville, gives a succinct overview of the contributions made by David during his long and fruitful career.

Contents

Introduction to SUNY Series in Constructive Postmodern Thought[1]

The rapid spread of the term *postmodern* in recent years witnesses to a growing dissatisfaction with modernity and to an increasing sense that the modern age not only had a beginning but can have an end as well. Whereas the word *modern* was almost always used until quite recently as a word of praise and as a synonym for *contemporary*, a growing sense is now evidenced that we can and should leave modernity behind—in fact, that we *must* if we are to avoid destroying ourselves and most of the life on our planet.

Modernity, rather than being regarded as the norm for human society toward which all history has been aiming and into which all societies should be ushered—forcibly if necessary—is instead increasingly seen as an aberration. A new respect for the wisdom of traditional societies is growing as we realize that they have endured for thousands of years and that, by contrast, the existence of modern civilization for even another century seems doubtful. Likewise, *modernism* as a worldview is less and less seen as The Final Truth, in comparison with which all divergent worldviews are automatically regarded as "superstitious." The modern worldview is increasingly relativized to the status of one among many, useful for some purposes, inadequate for others.

Although there have been antimodern movements before, beginning perhaps near the outset of the nineteenth century with the Romanticists and the Luddites, the rapidity with which the term *postmodern* has become widespread in our time suggests that the antimodern sentiment is more extensive and intense than before, and also that it includes the sense that modernity can be successfully overcome only by going beyond it, not by attempting to return to a premodern form of existence. Insofar as a common element is found in the various ways in which the term is used, *postmodernism* refers to a diffuse sentiment rather than to any common set of doctrines—the sentiment that humanity can and must go beyond the modern.

Beyond connoting this sentiment, the term *postmodern* is used in a confusing variety of ways, some of them contradictory to others. In artistic and literary circles, for example, postmodernism shares in this general sentiment but also involves a specific reaction against "modernism" in the narrow sense of a movement in artistic-literary circles in the late nineteenth and early twentieth centuries. Postmodern architecture is very different from postmodern literary criticism. In some circles, the term *postmodern* is used in reference to that potpourri of ideas and systems sometimes called *new age metaphysics,* although many of these ideas and systems are more premodern than postmodern. Even in philosophical and theological circles, the term *postmodern* refers to two quite different positions, one of which is reflected in this series. Each position seeks to transcend both *modernism,* in the sense of the worldview that has developed out of the seventeenth-century Galilean-Cartesian-Baconian-Newtonian science, and *modernity,* in the sense of the world order that both conditioned and was conditioned by this worldview. But the two positions seek to transcend the modern in different ways.

Closely related to literary-artistic postmodernism is a philosophical postmodernism inspired variously by physicalism, Ludwig Wittgenstein, Martin Heidegger, a cluster of French thinkers—including Jacques Derrida, Michel Foucault, Gilles Deleuze, and Julia Kristeva—and certain features of American pragmatism.[2] By the use of terms that arise out of particular segments of this movement, it can be called *deconstructive, relativistic,* or *eliminative* postmodernism. It overcomes the modern worldview through an antiworldview, deconstructing or even entirely eliminating various concepts that have generally been thought necessary for a worldview, such as self, purpose, meaning, a real world, givenness, reason, truth as correspondence, universally valid norms, and divinity. While motivated by ethical and emancipatory concerns, this type of postmodern thought tends to issue in relativism. Indeed, it seems to many thinkers to imply nihilism.[3] It could, paradoxically, also be called *ultramodernism,* in that its eliminations result from carrying certain modern premises—such as the sensationist doctrine of perception, the mechanistic doctrine of nature, and the resulting denial of divine presence in the world—to their logical conclusions. Some critics see its deconstructions or eliminations as leading to self-referential inconsistencies, such as "performative self-contradictions" between what is said and what is presupposed in the saying.

The postmodernism of this series can, by contrast, be called *revisionary, constructive,* or—perhaps best—*reconstructive.* It seeks to overcome the modern worldview not by eliminating the possibility of worldviews (or "metanarratives") as such, but by constructing a postmodern worldview through a revision of modern premises and traditional concepts in the light of inescapable presuppositions of our various modes of practice. That is, it agrees with deconstructive postmodernists that a massive deconstruction of many received concepts is needed. But its deconstructive moment, carried out for the sake of the presuppositions of practice, does not result in self-referential inconsistency. It also is not so totalizing as to prevent reconstruction. The reconstruction carried out by this type of postmodernism involves a new unity of scientific, ethical, aesthetic, and religious intuitions (whereas poststructuralists tend to reject all such unitive projects as "totalizing modern metanarratives"). While critical of many ideas often associated with modern science, it rejects not science as such but only that *scientism* in which only the data of the modern natural sciences are allowed to contribute to the construction of our public worldview.

The reconstructive activity of this type of postmodern thought is not limited to a revised worldview. It is equally concerned with a postmodern world that will both support and be supported by the new worldview. A postmodern world will involve postmodern persons, with a postmodern spirituality, on the one hand, and a postmodern society, ultimately a postmodern global order, on the other. Going beyond the modern world will involve transcending its individualism, anthropocentrism, patriarchy, economism, consumerism, nationalism, and militarism. Reconstructive postmodern thought provides support for the ethnic, ecological, feminist, peace, and other emancipatory movements of our time, while stressing that the inclusive emancipation must be from the destructive features of modernity itself. However, the term *postmodern*, by contrast with *premodern*, is here meant to emphasize that the modern world has produced unparalleled advances, as Critical Theorists have emphasized, which must not be devalued in a general revulsion against modernity's negative features.

From the point of view of deconstructive postmodernists, this reconstructive postmodernism will seem hopelessly wedded to outdated concepts, because it wishes to salvage a positive meaning not only for the notions of selfhood, historical meaning, reason, and truth as correspondence, which were central to modernity, but also for notions of divinity, cosmic meaning, and an enchanted nature, which were central to premodern modes of thought. From the point of view of its advocates, however, this revisionary postmodernism is not only more adequate to our experience but also more genuinely postmodern. It does not simply carry the premises of modernity through to their logical conclusions, but criticizes and revises those premises. By virtue of its return to organicism and its acceptance of nonsensory perception, it opens itself to the recovery of truths and values from various forms of premodern thought and practice that had been dogmatically rejected, or at least restricted to "practice," by modern thought. This reconstructive postmodernism involves a creative synthesis of modern and premodern truths and values.

This series does not seek to create a movement so much as to help shape and support an already existing movement convinced that modernity can and must be transcended. But in light of the fact that those antimodern movements that arose in the past failed to deflect or even retard the onslaught of modernity, what reasons are there for expecting the current movement to be more successful? First, the previous antimodern movements were primarily calls to return to a premodern form of life and thought rather than calls to advance, and the human spirit does not rally to calls to turn back. Second, the previous antimodern movements either rejected modern science, reduced it to a description of mere appearances, or assumed its adequacy in principle. They could, therefore, base their calls only on the negative social and spiritual effects of modernity. The current movement draws on natural science itself as a witness against the adequacy of the modern worldview. In the third place, the present movement has even more evidence than did previous movements of the ways in which modernity and its worldview *are* socially and spiritually destructive. The fourth and probably most decisive difference is that the present movement is based on the awareness that *the continuation of modernity threatens the very survival of life on our planet.* This awareness, combined with the growing knowledge of the interdependence of the modern worldview with the militarism, nuclearism, patriarchy, global apartheid, and ecological devastation of the modern world, is providing an unprecedented impetus for people to see the evidence for a postmodern worldview and to envisage postmodern ways of relating to each other, the rest of nature, and the cosmos as a whole. For these reasons, the failure of the previous antimodern movements says little about the possible success of the current movement.

Advocates of this movement do not hold the naively utopian belief that the success of this movement would bring about a global society of universal and lasting peace, harmony and happiness, in which all spiritual problems, social conflicts, ecological destruction, and hard choices would vanish. There is, after all, surely a deep truth in the testimony of the world's religions to the presence of a transcultural proclivity to evil deep within the human heart, which no new paradigm, combined with a new economic order, new child-rearing practices, or any other social arrangements, will suddenly eliminate. Furthermore, it has correctly been said that "life is robbery": A strong element of competition is inherent within finite existence, which no social-political-economic-ecological order can overcome. These two truths, especially when contemplated together, should caution us against unrealistic hopes.

No such appeal to "universal constants," however, should reconcile us to the present order, as if it were thereby uniquely legitimated. The human proclivity to evil in general, and to conflictual competition and ecological destruction in particular, can be greatly exacerbated or greatly mitigated by a world order and its worldview. Modernity exacerbates it about as much as imaginable. We can therefore envision, without being naively utopian, a far better world order, with a far less dangerous trajectory, than the one we now have.

This series, making no pretense of neutrality, is dedicated to the success of this movement toward a postmodern world.

David Ray Griffin
Series Editor

Notes

1. The present version of this introduction is slightly different from the first version, which was contained in the volumes that appeared prior to 1999.

2. The fact that the thinkers and movements named here are said to have inspired the deconstructive type of postmodernism should not be taken, of course, to imply that they have nothing in common with constructive postmodernists. For example, Wittgenstein, Heidegger, Derrida, and Deleuze share many points and concerns with Alfred North Whitehead, the chief inspiration behind the present series. Furthermore, the actual positions of the founders of pragmatism, especially William James and Charles Peirce, are much closer to Whitehead's philosophical position—see the volume in this series entitled *The Founders of Constructive Postmodern Philosophy: Peirce, James, Bergson, Whitehead, and Hartshorne*—than they are to Richard Rorty's so-called neopragmatism, which reflects many ideas from Rorty's explicitly physicalistic period.

3. As Peter Dews points out, although Derrida's early work was "driven by profound ethical impulses," its insistence that no concepts were immune to deconstruction "drove its own ethical presuppositions into a penumbra of inarticulacy" (*The Limits of Disenchantment: Essays on Contemporary European Culture* [London: New York: Verso, 1995], 5). In his more recent thought, Derrida has declared an "emancipatory promise" and an "idea of justice" to be "irreducible to any deconstruction." Although this "ethical turn" in deconstruction implies its pulling back from a completely disenchanted universe, it also, Dews points out (6-7), implies the need to renounce "the unconditionality of its own earlier dismantling of the unconditional."

Purpose of This Book

Persons who dip just a little bit into the works of Alfred North Whitehead are likely to have the uncomfortable feeling that they have slipped into a philosophical world that is quite foreign—isolated from the tradition and unconnected to anything happening in philosophy today. Those of us who have worked long and hard to master Whitehead's conceptuality, by contrast, experience his scheme of ideas, that is, his process philosophy, as deeply related to the tradition and helpfully relevant to contemporary philosophizing. Unfortunately, however, the initial sense of entering a foreign, isolated world often turns readers away before they have become familiar enough with Whitehead's work to appreciate its aptness to serve as a ground from which to approach the issues embedded in contemporary thought. The present volume seeks to address this problem: in it, philosophers with a double expertise in Whitehead's thought and some contemporary philosophical issue or some other important philosopher focus their bridging expertise on the topic/title, *Whitehead's Philosophy: Points of Connection.*

Whitehead found himself with a process vision in an intellectual world dominated by the notion of substance. He knew from the very beginning that he could not capture his process orientation in the language of substance, which has been dominant in philosophy as well as ordinary discourse. Whitehead, accordingly, quite deliberately set about creating a complex set of neologisms, and thereby a partially new language, designed to support his vision. He knew full well that the newness and the density of his language would cut him off from the casual reader, but he wrote for the long haul, for the time when a supporting scholarship would investigate, interpret, and develop his ideas and the language in which they were expressed, then struggle to make them more accessible to a wider community. That indeed has happened. Whitehead wrote his philosophical treatises in the 1920s and '30s. After a modest amount of discussion of his ideas in the 1940s and '50s, the 1960s brought an outpouring of books and articles devoted to clarifying and disseminating his ideas, an outpouring that shows no signs of abating. In 1970 a journal, *Process Studies,* began an uninterrupted stream of interpretive essays. The present volume is just the latest of a vast and growing secondary literature.

Given Whitehead's new language, which often makes his writings so forbidding, it would clearly be helpful if this volume were to start with an introduction to that idiosyncratic language. Fortunately, this task can be carried out in the context of an introductory essay that relates Whitehead's language to the familiar terms found in the writings of Descartes. This means that the introductory essay can follow the structure of the book as a whole by exhibiting a very central point of connection, that between Whitehead and the Father of Modern Philosophy. The essays that follow this introductory essay, written by Professor Sherburne, will be able to presuppose that the reader has at least a modicum of familiarity with Whitehead's vocabulary and orientation.

While the contributors to this volume are sympathetic with the Whiteheadian perspective, in the essays that follow the concern is with points of connection, not points to be made in polemical debate. The aim of this volume is to show various ways in which Whitehead's ideas are connected to the tradition and relevant to the contemporary scene, not that they are infallible.

As a final introductory thought, it is worth noting that this volume appears in a series devoted to "constructive postmodern thought." Whitehead, of course, never used the term *postmodern,* but in chapter IX of *Science and the Modern World* he did observe that he was putting "Descartes and [William] James in close juxtaposition" because "[t]hey each of them open an epoch by their clear formulation of terms in which thought could profitably express itself at particular stages of knowledge, one for the seventeenth century, the other for the twentieth century" (147; cf. 143ff). Descartes opened an epoch of thought that lasted for some two hundred and fifty years; James was a major player in opening a new epoch of thought just shortly before Whitehead came upon the scene. Without any doubt, Whitehead saw himself clearly as standing at the end of one era and at the beginning of the new one. It is certainly fair to characterize that passing era as "Modernism"—Descartes is, after all, the Father of *Modern* Philosophy! So Whitehead is certainly "postmodern," but, it must be noted, most assuredly "constructively postmodern" and not "deconstructively postmodern." While it is true that the term *postmodern* is most widely understood to connote a type of philosophy that emphasizes deconstruction, Whiteheadians believe that a properly "postmodern philosophy," while certainly containing heavy doses of deconstruction, must also engage in the task of reconstruction. It is here that Whitehead excels.

It is worth noting that many philosophers believe that, in spite of their very real differences, there are genuine "points of connection" between the orientation generally known as "deconstruction" and "constructive postmodern thought." There is, in fact, a recent volume in this series that has explored this claim in depth. It is titled *Process and Difference: Between Cosmological and Poststructuralist Postmodernisms* and is edited by Catherine Keller and Anne Daniell. We commend it to your attention.

Biographical Sketch of Alfred North Whitehead

Before moving to the introductory Whitehead/Descartes essay, it will be useful to have a brief summary of Alfred North Whitehead's distinguished career, a career that included election to England's Royal Society and as a Fellow of the British Academy on one side of the Atlantic, and to the presidency of the American Philosophical Association on the other.

Alfred North Whitehead was born in 1861 in the southeast corner of England at Ramsgate on the Isle of Thanet in Kent. The son and grandson of Church of England clergy, who were also educators, Whitehead prepped at the Sherborne School in Dorsetshire before entering Trinity College of Cambridge University in 1880 to study mathematics. In 1884 he received his degree in mathematics with first-class honors and was elected a Fellow of Trinity College, where he remained on the faculty until 1910.

Six years after Whitehead began his teaching career, the young Bertrand Russell arrived at Trinity as an undergraduate. Russell, too, had a brilliant undergraduate career that also led to an appointment to the faculty. As the century turned, the two colleagues traveled together across the channel to Paris, where they attended the Second International Congress of Mathematics. While there they listened to presentations concerning the foundations of mathematics delivered by the famous Italian mathematician, Giuseppe Peano. Back home they both discovered, in playing around with Peano's formulations, that inconsistencies could be derived from Peano's principles taken jointly.

Both Whitehead and Russell had written a book in the general area (*A Treatise on Universal Algebra* by Whitehead and *The Principles of Mathematics* by Russell), and each was planning a second volume that would dig more deeply into the issues involved. Quite reasonably they decided to write that next volume jointly. Whitehead originally projected that this new undertaking would require a year to complete; in fact, it consumed a decade and resulted in the publication, in 1910, 1912, and 1913, of their three-volume, groundbreaking masterpiece, *Principia Mathematica.*

Whitehead's move to London (which led to the chair of applied mathematics at the Imperial College of Science and Technology of the University of London) and quite different attitudes toward Britain's role in World War I led Whitehead and Russell to drift apart. In addition, Russell's interests remained largely formal in character, while Whitehead's interests broadened quite naturally toward the philosophy of science and then into metaphysics.

Whitehead had a long-standing interest in geometry. It was originally projected that he would write a fourth volume to *Principia Mathematica,* a volume on the foundations of geometry which never appeared, though materials that might have originally been intended for this volume could have ended up years later in Part IV of *Process and Reality.* Issues in the foundations of geometry, issues involving the nature of space and the relationships between space and whatever it is that is in space, constitute a natural bridge between mathematics and natural science. Whitehead spent the war years crossing that bridge and in 1919, 1920, and 1922 he published three volumes that explored issues in the philosophy of science: *An Enquiry Concerning the Principles of Natural Knowledge, The Concept of Nature,* and *The Principle of Relativity.*

By this time Whitehead was well known not only in England and Europe, but in America as well. He had had several invitations from Harvard and finally, in 1924 at age sixty-three, accepted a five-year appointment in the Department of Philosophy, an affiliation that continued until 1937 and resulted in thirteen extraordinarily productive years. As he finished writing his three books dealing with the philosophy of science in the early 1920s, Whitehead became convinced that writings in that area, including his own, were fatally flawed by their working assumption that mind could be bracketed out of nature, could be safely ignored as one studied nature. That assumption was built into the philosophical framework with which Descartes launched modern philosophy. If a substance required nothing but itself in order to exist, and if mind and matter were two totally different, independent substances, then philosophers and scientists were justified in ignoring mind when they explored the fundamental issues in the philosophy of science. That philosophical assumption had cleared the way for several hundred years of remarkable advances in science—it had been exactly the assumption needed at that moment in the history of ideas—but by the opening decades of the twentieth century, Whitehead had come to believe, that foundational assumption was no longer compatible with the huge advances in understanding that it itself had made possible. Shortly after his arrival at Harvard, in 1925, he published a remarkable book setting forth, and defending, this view. It was titled *Science and the Modern World.* It chronicled the negative impact of developing scientific views on the philosophical assumptions that made that progress possible and adumbrated some leading ideas describing a philosophical standpoint more in harmony with the new science. In 1929 he published his masterwork, *Process and Reality,* in which he took the suggestions for a new perspective presented in *Science and the Modern World* and developed them into a full-blown version of what he titled the philosophy of organism, or process philosophy. In a sentence, what Whitehead did in this book was to create a scheme of ideas that did justice to the richness and complexity of human being yet exhibited human being as an integral part of nature. In short, Whitehead had moved, as had Plato long before him, from being a mathematician to being a full-fledged metaphysician.

Other books appeared developing aspects and implications of these ideas. In 1926 he wrote *Religion in the Making,* followed in 1927 by *Symbolism: Its Meaning and Effect. The Function of Reason* was published in 1929, as was *The Aims of Education,* and in 1933 Whitehead produced another classic with *Adventures of Ideas,* a wise set of reflections on the philosophy of civilization that explored certain implications of his philosophy in less technical and more metaphorical terms than one finds in *Process and Reality. Modes of Thought,* in 1938, was the last of his books. He lived out his life in the new world Cambridge, often in rather fragile health. He died in December 1947.

One final reflection. Oxford and Cambridge Universities, in the nineteenth century, were extraordinary places, exquisitely tuned to the needs of the day. They provided the environment that prepared Gladstone and Disraeli to govern the Empire by earning double firsts in mathematics and greats. The intensity and richness of the intellectual atmosphere was remarkable. One may have formally studied "maths," yet the common room discussions and debates ranged over the entire intellectual landscape. Whitehead was elected a member of The Apostles. Formed early in the nineteenth century by Tennyson, this group, officially titled the Cambridge Conversazione Society, has been described by Victor Lowe as "the most elite discussion club in the English-speaking university world." Its members went on to become leading figures in the literary, artistic, and political life of the country. Later on, in his London years, Whitehead became a member of the Aristotelian Society, participating fully in its frequent programs. The intellectual breadth generated by these experiences served Whitehead well as he moved through the phases of his intellectual development.

Part One

An Introductory Essay

CHAPTER 1

Whitehead, Descartes, and Terminology

DONALD W. SHERBURNE

The first sentence of the Preface to Whitehead's magnum opus, *Process and Reality*, reads: "These lectures are based upon a recurrence to that phase of philosophic thought which began with Descartes and ended with Hume."[1] This sentence is certainly *prima facie* evidence that in Descartes's philosophy there lurks a basic "point of connection" with Whitehead's mode of philosophizing. Yet one must be careful here. The word *recurrence* is tricky. It might suggest that Whitehead is going back and embracing Descartes's standpoint. Nothing could be farther from the truth!

What, then, is Whitehead building into this notion of 'recurrence'? He is saying, from his viewpoint in the twentieth century, that Descartes really does deserve his title, Father of Modern Philosophy, because he laid out the assumptions that to a large extent dictated subsequent philosophical reflection and created the intellectual environment that helped clear the way for the enormously fruitful advances in science of the next several centuries. By the 1920s, however, science had progressed way beyond the framework supported by Cartesian principles and the philosophy itself had become bankrupt. The phrase "ended with Hume" is Whitehead's observation that the tradition that began with Descartes ended, or at least faced the beginning of the end, with Hume's articulation of a set of arguments that established that if one begins with Descartes's assumptions, then one ends up in a hopeless skepticism.

But some endings really drag out. Whitehead noted that Hume's "sceptical reduction" was "reissued with the most beautiful exposition by Santayana in his *Scepticism and Animal Faith*." That "reissue" came after almost two hundred years. More recently than that, some persons, most notably Richard Rorty, have announced, not the end of "a phase of philosophic thought," but the very end of philosophy itself! In this latest scenario Sellars, Quine, and Davidson take on the role of Hume and Santayana. Suddenly a lot is at stake—the very future of philosophy itself! In the twenty-first century, recurring to the Descartes/Hume era happens in a context more urgent even than was Whitehead's context in the 1920s.

In the modern era it is those Cartesian assumptions that demand reconsideration. Whitehead is announcing right at the opening of *Process and Reality* that he is returning to the beginnings of modern philosophy to review the assumptions of Descartes for the purpose of locating the weak spot in those assumptions, the spot that, if accepted, leads to the Humean reduction. Whitehead will repudiate certain of those assumptions and replace them with new assumptions, with just those assumptions that undergird his process philosophy. This is a point of connection of the first order. If we can grasp it clearly we are well on our way to grasping the relevance of Whitehead's philosophy to current issues and discussions.

Descartes's problems are epistemological problems, problems about knowing. If we as knowers are mental substances, requiring, as substances, nothing other than ourselves in order to exist, how do we really know there is anything "out there" beyond us? When we say that we see an object, do we really directly see the object itself, or do we rather infer that there is an object out there of which we entertain some sort of representation or appearance? Descartes held that we really do not perceive such external objects at all, but merely "representations," which are subjective occurrences in our minds. Maybe these representations relate in some way to external objects, but we cannot know how, or even that, they do. This is a hugely abbreviated statement of the problem, but this is the basic philosophical architecture, drafted by Descartes, from which Hume et al. proceed to draw their skeptical conclusions.

This philosophical architecture is anathema to Whitehead! Contemplating it moves him to write some pretty blunt prose. "All modern philosophy," he writes, meaning by this the tradition with its roots in Descartes, "hinges round the difficulty of describing the world in terms of subject and predicate, substance and quality, particular and universal. The result always does violence to that immediate experience which we express in our actions, our hopes, our sympathies, our purposes, and which we enjoy in spite of our lack of phrases for its verbal analysis. We find ourselves in a buzzing [This epithet is, of course, borrowed from William James.—*Whitehead's footnote*] world, amid a democracy of fellow creatures; whereas, under some disguise or other, orthodox philosophy can only introduce us to solitary substances, each enjoying an illusory experience: 'O Bottom, thou art changed! what do I see on thee?'" (PR 49–50—the quote will be recognized as from Act III of Shakespeare's *A Midsummer-Night's Dream,* where Bottom has been transformed by fairy magic so that he has the head of an ass). In another passage Whitehead makes the point more directly: "[C]ommon sense is inflexibly objectivist. We perceive other things which are in the world of actualities in the same sense as we are. Also our emotions are directed towards other things. . . . These are our primary beliefs which philosophers proceed to dissect" (PR 158).

Here, then, is the point of connection, and the point of departure—the notion of "solitary substances" must be abandoned! But how does one defend such a move? With what does one replace the notion of substance? These are not easy questions, as Whitehead is quite aware—he will have to introduce new concepts and a new vocabulary to support the philosophical perspective he intends to submit as an alternative to the philosophy of substance.

I begin this summary of Whitehead's response to Descartes by introducing a terse passage from PR that sets the stage for Whitehead's fundamental moves. "All metaphysical theories which admit a disjunction between the component elements of individual experience on the one hand, and on the other hand the component elements of the external world, must inevitably run into difficulties over the truth and falsehood of propositions, and over the grounds for judgment. The former difficulty is metaphysical, the latter epistemological. But all difficulties as to first principles are only camouflaged metaphysical difficulties. Thus the epistemological difficulty is only solvable by an appeal to ontology" (PR 189).

The first point to focus on here is the claim that if your epistemological problems seem intractable, you had better scout around in the neighboring fields of the metaphysical assumption or assumptions that may well be generating your problem. Put more directly in terms of Descartes's epistemological problem, we can focus Whitehead's point by translating it thusly: if you have problems re know*ing*, you had better go back and check out your assumptions about the nature of the know*er*. Questions about the know*er* are questions in the domain of ontology, questions about assumptions in the undergirding metaphysical theory.

Descartes's knower is a mind, which means, in his terms, that it is a mental substance requiring nothing but itself in order to exist. Even if there were nothing out there beyond it in a spatial world it could continue to exist in its "solitary" splendor, continuing to entertain a stream of mental events originating perhaps, as suggested by Berkeley, with God. This is the fundamental assumption that Whitehead repudiates. In its place he puts the notion of a "knower" that is totally dependent for its existence upon other, preceding entities of the same sort that it is and which are internally related to it so that it could not be, and could not be just that entity it becomes, without appropriating, that is, prehending, those entities in its immediate past. Whereas Descartes continues and deepens Aristotle's systematic commitment to the primacy of the category of substance, Whitehead reaches down to Aristotle's category of relation and promotes it to the position of honor—to be is to be in relation.

In the penultimate sentence the word *knower* was placed in quotes to warn that it is very misleading to carry over the term to its new Whiteheadian context. Descartes embraces a dualism of mind and matter; Whitehead digs below that dualism and in its place establishes what might best be called a neutral monism. Whitehead's "knower" is not a mind at all; neither is it a bit of matter. It is what he labels an actual entity, or actual occasion. It is critically important that we begin by establishing just what an actual entity is as well as what it is not.

So, if an actual entity is not a mind, what is it? My answer is going to sound paradoxical, but hang with me—in a few paragraphs we can work this out. An actual entity, then, is not a mind but is, rather, a momentary drop, or bud (to use William James's word) of "experience" that pulls the actual entities that constitute its immediate past, its actual world, into the unity (of "experience") that it is. Okay, you say, what is accomplished by putting the word *experience* in quotes, as, indeed, Whitehead does? How do the quotes get us beyond the Cartesian notion of mind?

I reply by noting that at one point in PR (p. 176) Whitehead invites us to "descend the scale of organic being." This is a thought experiment. As we move from dogs and horses down to the amoeba and the jellyfish, various dimensions of human consciousness drop out of what remains of "experience," but such animals, and even vegetables, retain some aspect of a relation to the environment. A jellyfish advances and withdraws and an amoeba moves its pseudopodia in response to the prick of a pin, as we all discovered in junior high science class. A vegetable grows down to the point of dampness in the earth and upward to the sun, growing out of the shade of other plants if need be to get into the light. Most assuredly the amoeba and the plant do not possess anything like the properties of a Cartesian mind, yet, as Whitehead notes, there is "some direct reason for attributing [to them] dim, slow feelings of causal nexus" (PR 176–77). Normally Whitehead puts the term *feelings* in quotes in such a context, matching his use of "experience." His point is that even at that level there is some primitive mode of taking account of the environment, some basic way of "feeling," or being in relation with, other actual entities. The amoeba is clearly not a mind and its "experience" is clearly nothing like conscious human experience. Yet it, in some very primitive way, "takes account of" its environment. Even in the inorganic world magnets "attract" filings and gravity "pulls" objects. Just so, when we reach the bottom of the scale of organic being, Whitehead says, it is the case that "[a]s we pass to the inorganic world, causation never for a moment seems to lose its grip. What is lost is originativeness, and any evidence of immediate absorption in the present. So far as we can see, inorganic entities are vehicles for receiving, for storing in a napkin, and for restoring without loss or gain" (PR 177).

Let us step back and ask what has happened here. We have been reviewing the considerations in terms of which Whitehead accuses Descartes of having committed the Fallacy of Misplaced Concreteness. Descartes claims that mental substances and material substances are the two final, fully concrete realities. Whitehead denies this claim, maintaining that minds and bodies are both abstractions from that which is fully, concretely real, viz., actual entities. In Whitehead's words: "'Actual entities'—also termed 'actual occasions'—are the final real things of which the world is made up. There is no going behind actual entities to find anything more real. They differ among themselves: God is an actual entity, and so is the most trivial puff of existence in far-off empty space. . . . The final facts are, all alike, actual entities; and these actual entities are drops of experience, complex and interdependent" (PR 18). Of course there are minds and bodies in the world, but every mind and every body is a grouping of actual entities. Such groupings of actual entities are called societies. A society is not a final actuality; it is, rather, an abstraction that has its reality in virtue of the full and final concreteness of the actual entities that make it up.

The interdependence of actual entities is critical. As Whitehead says, "Actual entities involve each other by reason of their prehensions of each other" (PR 20). This word *prehensions* relates to the business of putting the word *experience* in quotes as one moves down the scale of organic being. "Prehension" is cut off from the word *apprehension.* "Apprehension" refers to the fully conscious grasping of something; the attenuated version of that word, that is, "prehension," refers, for Whitehead, to the primitive, unconscious, primordial, attenuated way that, way down at the bottom of the scale of organic and then inorganic being, one actual occasion takes account of another. The becoming of an actual entity is its process of prehending the actual entities in its immediate past, in what Whitehead labels its actual world, and then harmonizing those prehensions into the unity of being which that concrescing actual entity becomes. It is helpful to note that the word *concrescence* means a growing together—in this case the growing together of the prehensions that constitute the actual entity which is in the process of becoming.

Actual entities happen very quickly; they appropriate their actual world, concresce, reach their final unity, and then become part of that actual world which gives rise to the next generation of actual entities. They exist (their being is their becoming) very briefly as "subjects" and then take up their role as objects, as brute facts that the future must take into account.

These last few paragraphs have introduced a good many technical terms, terms that Whitehead uses to support his process vision and which are therefore an alternative to the terminology that Descartes uses to support his substance vision. Since one cannot get from Descartes's terminology to Whitehead's vision (any more than one can get from Whitehead's terminology to Descartes's vision), it will be worth our while to explore Whitehead's language a bit more in order to clarify some of the philosophical implications of this unusual and unique mode of expression.

A first, very important point about this unusual philosophical language can be made by pointing out that Whitehead sometimes referred to his orientation as The Philosophy of Organism. In the early pages of chapter III of *Science and the Modern World* Whitehead notes that the philosophy of the seventeenth century was "dominated by physics," meaning that the vocabulary to be used to shape the most general ideas of the era as they were bedded in philosophy were derived from the language of physics. In a most suggestive passage, Whitehead states: "[T]he root ideas of the seventeenth century were derived from the school of thought which produced Galileo, Huyghens and Newton, and not from the physiologists of Padua."[2] In a somewhat longer, very illuminating passage near the end of chapter I of SMW, Whitehead provides a very clear description of these "root ideas":

> There persists, however, throughout the whole period the fixed scientific cosmology which presupposes the ultimate fact of an irreducible brute matter, or material, spread throughout space in a flux of configurations. In itself such a material is senseless, valueless, purposeless. It just does what it does do, following a fixed routine imposed by external relations which do not spring from the nature of its being. It is this assumption that I call 'scientific materialism.' Also it is an assumption which I shall challenge as being entirely unsuited to the scientific situation at which we have now arrived. It is not wrong, if properly construed. If we confine ourselves to certain types of facts, abstracted from the

> complete circumstances in which they occur, the materialistic assumption expresses these facts to perfection. But when we pass beyond the abstraction, either by more subtle employment of our senses, or by the request for meanings and for coherence of thoughts, the scheme breaks down at once. The narrow efficiency of the scheme was the very cause of its supreme methodological success. For it directed attention to just those groups of facts which, in the state of knowledge then existing, required investigation. (SMW 17)

Whitehead makes it absolutely clear in his discussions that while scientific materialism was just what the world needed in the seventeenth and subsequent centuries, today it is a disaster of the first order. The day of those researchers at the University of Padua has arrived! Whitehead is very deliberately grounding the "root ideas" of his philosophy in the language of biology, not the language of physics. A Whiteheadian actual entity is an organism, not an inert bit of physical stuff.

What can be said in support of this monumental shift of perspective? A great deal, Whiteheadians will assure you. It was Pierre Teilhard de Chardin who observed that from the twentieth century forward no one could philosophize responsibly without giving Darwin due consideration. Whitehead was not familiar with the writings of his somewhat younger contemporary, Teilhard, but it is almost as though one could imagine that Whitehead, on the model of Darius having a servant say "Remember the Athenians" before every meal, chanted "Remember Darwin" each morning upon arising! It seemed axiomatic to Whitehead that you could not get from inert material stuff, "senseless, valueless, purposeless," to the richness of human experience. Something analogous to the barest, simplest structures apparent in human experience has to go all the way down to the level of the most fully concrete reality, to the level of the simplest actual occasions, if evolution is ultimately to be a coherent concept.

Whitehead is confident that his doctrine of actual entities and the prehensions that link them is grounded in the immediate human experience of memory. If I set myself the task of remembering something—what I had for breakfast, for instance—memory floods in upon, and shapes, my experience in an immediate, direct way. I encounter brute fact, that is, I immediately encounter certain given structures and attendant meanings that bear in upon my experience and constitute my recollections. This, Whitehead would maintain, is one instance of my direct encounter with the experiences that underlie the categories and concepts that he uses to give the most general description of the real, viz., actual entities undergoing their own becoming as they prehend the structures dominating their actual worlds and reproduce those structures in the warm subjectivity of their immediate concrescence.

Very simple actual entities are considered by Whitehead to be pulses of physical causation, appropriating their immediate past and passing it on to the next generation pretty much intact as received—as already quoted above, Whitehead describes such simple actual entities as "vehicles for receiving, for storing in a napkin, and for restoring without loss or gain." Evolution, however, proceeds as clusters of actual entities, termed societies, emerge and provide ever more sophisticated structures that channel prehensive inheritance into richer and richer patterns, patterns that, in their richness, allow for the emergence of increasingly ordered and meaningful experience. In short, complex and sophisticated actual entities emerge at the nodal points of complex societies, complex societies such as those that constitute animals and human beings, for instance. But while sophisticated actual entities, like simple ones, do inherit the structures of their immediate past through their prehensions, they also, due to the richness of their inheritance, have the possibility of reacting to their environment in innovative ways.

These last paragraphs are meant to suggest that Whitehead's starting point can deal with the subject matter of the physical sciences in terms of simple actual entities and yet can also deal with the subject matter of the biological sciences in terms of his account of the emergence and functioning of complex societies of actual entities. The scientific materialism against which Whitehead is protesting notoriously suffers from the difficulty of dealing with human experience given the assumptions with which it starts. And the dualism of Descartes, isolating knowing substances from the external world, encounters, as we saw above, enormous difficulties in articulating the character of the interaction of its two different sorts of substances. Hence Whitehead would argue that his position, rooted in the biological sciences, is the better way, better because it can do justice to the richness of human experience while still presenting human beings as an integral part of nature. Of course, as the saying goes, the Devil is in the details, and the account I have been able to provide is most admittedly short on details. But I hope that this overview, brief as it has been, is sufficient to orient the reader unfamiliar with Whitehead's thought so that he/she can follow the comparisons, introduced in the remaining essays in this book, between Whitehead's philosophy and various other philosophical positions.

There is, however, one more topic that needs to be introduced before this terminological overview is complete. This topic/term is 'God'. Whitehead observed that Christianity has been a religion in search of a metaphysics (whereas Buddhism has been a metaphysics in search of a religion). Augustine and Plotinus utilized Platonism to ground and give meaning to Christianity; St. Thomas utilized Aristotle's writings for the same purpose; and many contemporary Christian thinkers have adopted Whitehead's metaphysics because they see it as capable of supporting a kinder Christianity that can be made compatible with twentieth/twenty-first century sensibilities and understandings of the world about us. The result has been the emergence of Process Theology as a significant presence in the domain of philosophical theology. The good news emerging from this is that many, many very sharp theological/philosophical minds have turned their attention to Whitehead's metaphysics, clarifying and developing his philosophical, as well as theological, categories. Indeed, it is fair to say that a great deal of the work done in process metaphysics has been done, and in most instances done very well, by persons whose ultimate concern is with shaping that metaphysics to adapt it more adequately to the theological concerns that they bring to their philosophical studies.

The bad news, the downside to all this, is that the dominant mood in the philosophical community at large is nonreligious. Certainly this secular mood is in part an inheritance from the recent decades that saw analytic philosophy, with its overwhelming lack of interest in matters religious, totally dominate philosophy in the Anglo-American world. But it is more than just that. Developments in astronomy, in theoretical physics, and in the mapping of the human brain combined with the use of DNA analysis to confirm the reliability of ever richer archeological evidence clarifying the origins and development of the human species have contributed immensely to the creation of an intellectual climate within which religious concepts seem to many within the philosophical community to have less and less relevance to our self-understandings and to our understandings of the way the world works and of how we as human beings fit into the general world scheme. In this intellectual climate a widespread perception among philosophers that Whitehead's accomplishments are primarily in the domain of religious understandings serves as a put off, serves immediately to marginalize Whitehead in the philosophical community.

Religiously oriented Whiteheadians are quite aware of this "downside," but in most cases, I suspect, they shrug it off as a phenomenon that does not interfere with their work or really bother them all that much. Other Whiteheadians, however, for whom the religious hypothesis is not a live option, are struck by the sophistication and relevance of Whitehead's philosophical categories and are a bit sad that the religious dimension of his work may be a barrier to wider philosophical interest in what he has to say. I myself fall in this last group and have written articles with titles such as "Whitehead Without God" and "Decentering Whitehead" with the hope that arguments in favor of the thesis that the concept 'God' is not essential to the coherence or viability of Whitehead's philosophy might encourage an interest in Whitehead's writings by the more secularly inclined.

These, then, are some of the wider issues surrounding Whitehead's process philosophy and process theology. I turn now to a look at how the concept 'God' functions in Whitehead's metaphysics. Because Whitehead considers God to be an actual entity, and therefore because a discussion of Whitehead's God will illuminate the structures of actual entities in general, this analysis will provide additional background that will be helpful to bring to the articles that follow in this book. In this regard it is worth noting that Whitehead insists that God not be brought forward as an exception to the normal principles of his philosophy in order to solve philosophical problems, but, rather, that the concept exhibit the regular categories of the system in an exemplary way.

Like all actual entities, God inherits the input provided by the past actual world. At any given moment, then, God experiences the totality of the structures embodied in the immediately past phase of the entire sweep of all that which is—what separates God from us, as finite human prehenders of the past, is that whereas each of us is relatively limited in what constitutes the actual world for us, God's prehensive vision encompasses everything. Whitehead identifies that aspect of God that takes account of the totality of the actual world as the consequent nature of God.

But in addition to a consequent nature, God also has what Whitehead terms a primordial nature. God's primordial conceptual visualization is God's grasp of the realm of potentiality. The realm of potentiality is constituted by the infinitely extended relatedness of the forms of definiteness that may, or may not, attain realization in the actual world.

As functioning as an element in the universal process, God begins by, using Whitehead's word, "weaving" the divine consequent nature upon the divine primordial nature. This gives God a vivid grasp of the many different ways that present concrescences might move from the givenness of the past into the emerging concreteness of the future. The key point is that God is not neutral as to how the process of growth from past to future works out. On some scenarios the future works out "better" than on some alternative scenarios. Here "better" means that those scenarios are such that when the new future emerges and then becomes the immediate past for yet another instance of creative advance, the consequent nature of God will have an experience of that newly emergent past that is more harmonious, more vivid, more satisfying than it would have been had other alternatives prevailed.

This raises the question of whether or not God can influence the way that the creative process unfolds into the future. Whitehead's answer is affirmative. But it is crucial to note that for Whitehead God does not operate as an efficient cause upon the world. Rather, God "lures" the process from the front, if you will, rather than pushing it from the rear. This happens, Whitehead suggests, because God functions for every actual entity as part of its given actual world. In the prehensive experience of each relatively sophisticated actual entity there is a sense of the possibilities relevant to the future of just that past, and there is also a sense that some of those possibilities are more desirable than are others. This, in human experience, is an encounter with God that is experienced as a lure for feeling that can take the form of a nagging sense of "ought" that attaches to certain possibilities and not to others. Whitehead suggests that this sense of ought can be an encounter in experience with God's preference for how things should work out. This preference on the part of God can be accepted, or can be ignored, by actual entities that encounter it. And sometimes events have worked themselves into such a mess that no option is really good. In such a situation, Whitehead opines, "God can be personified as Até, the goddess of mischief. The chaff is burnt" (PR 244).

To recapitulate, God plays a role in the unfolding process of the world that is strongly analogous to the role played by each and every actual entity. Just as each finite actual entity prehends its actual world, so God prehends the actual worlds of each and every entity as it appears. Each finite actual entity then enjoys its own process of concrescence whereby it achieves the definiteness that will constitute an aspect of the actual world of the next generation of actual entities. God does not concresce to a completion, as do temporal, finite actual occasions, but continues to prehend each new generation of settled, completed finite actual entities as it arises and then project possibilities relevant to the future of each such generation upon the gathering experience of those entities that will shape that future by means of their concrete decisions. Whitehead refers to God in this role as the fellow sufferer who understands.

The portrait of God painted by Whitehead is not that of a being with a plan worked out in advance for the universe as a whole. To the contrary, he holds that

> Tennyson's phrase [in the final lines of *In Memoriam*],
> . . . one far-off divine event
> To which the whole creation moves,
> presents a fallacious conception of the universe. (PR 111)

Whitehead's image, rather, is that God is the Eros of the universe, luring it forward toward what God envisions as a definiteness that will produce the most intense satisfaction for the actual entities that will experience that particular definiteness as they prehend their actual worlds. God will also prehend those very same actual worlds, so it is in this sense that God is the fellow sufferer who understands. Insofar as actual entities in the world accept God's lure, they *and* God will enjoy richer, more harmonious experience as the process unfolds. But there is in Whitehead's thinking no final end, no point at which the process aims; rather, the process is without end, advancing through the rise, and then the decline, of a fundamental order which defines a cosmic epoch and then moving to new orders and new cosmic epochs undreamed of in epochs past.

It is worth noting here that Whitehead finds no justification for affirming a notion of personal immortality. Each actual entity emerges in the process, concresces into its particular form of concrete definiteness, and then perishes after having functioned as an element in the actual world of the next unfolding generation of actual entities. We human beings are very complex societies of entities. It is societies that endure over time, some, such as mountains or stars, enduring for huge stretches, others, such as mosquitoes or human beings, enduring over far more modest stretches. That in us that is analogous to the traditional notion of soul, or to the Cartesian notion of mental substance, is what Whitehead refers to as the regnant nexus in this complex hierarchy of societies which each of us is. The regnant nexus is a string of actual entities, each one of which inherits its experience from the actual entity preceding it in the string as well as from some of the subordinate societies that make up the animal body. The regnant nexus is often conscious and is experienced by each of us as the self that we most truly are. The question of immortality is the question of whether or not the regnant nexus can exist apart from the complexly interwoven societies that underlie and support it. Whitehead notes: "We do not know of any living society devoid of its subservient apparatus of inorganic societies" (PR 103).

With this conclusion we have come full circle in our comparison of Whitehead and Descartes. We have seen that Descartes conceives of each substance as requiring nothing but itself in order to exist, a philosophical position that makes immortality an easy notion to defend but which creates insoluble problems in the domain of epistemology. Whitehead's actual entities *are* their relations, *are* their absorption, via prehensions, of their actual worlds into the being that they are becoming, which obviates the epistemological issue but has the added effect of placing in question any notion of immortality. Descartes's language draws its inspiration from the world of the physicists and not surprisingly has a profound problem with the "mind-body" relationship, whereas Whitehead's language has its roots in the discourse of those physiologists of Padua and consequently is at home with evolution and the idea that a philosophical position must not only do justice to human nature, but must at the same time incorporate humanity firmly into that nature studied by the physicists. The contrast between Descartes and Whitehead is stark, as is the contrast between the languages in which they express their deepest convictions about the nature of that which is, including their convictions about human nature. It is my hope that this introductory presentation, brief as it has been, will make it much easier for the reader unfamiliar with Whitehead's writings to grasp the drift of what transpires in the essays that follow.

Notes

1. Alfred North Whitehead, *Process and Reality* (corrected edition edited by David Ray Griffin and Donald W. Sherburne; New York: The Free Press, 1978), xi. This book will hereafter be cited in the text as PR.

2. Alfred North Whitehead, *Science and the Modern World* (New York: The Free Press, 1967), 41. This book will hereafter be cited in the text as SMW.

Part Two

Whitehead and Classical American Philosophy

CHAPTER 2

Whitehead and Pragmatism

ROBERT CUMMINGS NEVILLE

Pragmatism and process philosophy should not be viewed as alien schools of thought at all but as tangled with one another in many common causes throughout twentieth-century philosophy. At Harvard from 1924 until his death, Whitehead was in the academic and cultural home of Charles Peirce, William James, Josiah Royce (the Absolute Pragmatist as he called himself),[1] Ralph Barton Perry, C. I. Lewis, William Ernest Hocking, and Willard Quine. Among his most important graduate students were Charles Hartshorne and Paul Weiss who edited the *Collected Papers of Charles Sanders Peirce* at Harvard while he was teaching there. Hartshorne says that his move to the University of Chicago from Harvard put him in close personal and intellectual touch with Dewey and Mead. Dewey, from the pragmatists' side, was enthusiastic about Whitehead's philosophy, reviewed it, and contributed a major article to the Library of Living Philosophers volume on Whitehead. George Lucas has traced many of the entanglements of Whitehead with the pragmatists.[2]

In many respects, pragmatism and process philosophy, especially in the early years, worked the same side of the street, defending:

- realism against idealism,[3]
- realism in the other sense against nominalism,[4]
- the importance of experience in a broader sense than British empiricism,[5]
- the possibility of metaphysics in the grand tradition though in revolutionary forms critical of the tradition,[6]
- the importance of philosophy for public life rather than as an academic subject alone (as it tended to be on British, German, and French models of philosophy),[7]
- the meaning of truth as correspondence,[8]

- the criteria of truth as pragmatic (some pragmatists are more careful with this distinction than others),[9]
- fallibilism and the method of hypothesis over against foundationalism,[10]
- all of the above in considerable self-conscious cooperation over against both Anglo-American analytic philosophy and Continental philosophy which were dominant in the English-speaking academic world throughout the last two-thirds of the twentieth century, with the result that pragmatism and process philosophy together were marginalized in academic philosophy from the 1960s onward.[11]

This having been said, there are some crucial *cultural* and *class* differences in the origins and trajectories of process thought and pragmatism. Although these may not be politically correct to mention, they are important for understanding the distinctions between the schools, especially in the minds of recent representatives. Whitehead was an upper-class Anglican, and so is Hartshorne; Harvard seemed their due.[12] If that religious upper-class sense of intellectual place has slipped a bit in process-Methodists such as John B. Cobb Jr. and myself, it should be remembered that Methodists are fallen-away Anglicans with more spirit but less class. Although not all process philosophers are theists by any means (consider the important anti-process-theism work of Donald W. Sherburne),[13] most process philosophers are also philosophers of religion or theologians. The ambiance of Whitehead's thought is that of high civilization in which religions play defining roles. The "adventure of ideas" relates to civilization, not society.

The pragmatists related more to society than to civilization. This is least true of William James, a true Boston Brahmin, though it is still true of him. Charles Peirce was an utter cultural failure at the Boston Brahmin role, despite being an Episcopalian, deeply religious, theologically imaginative, and filled with as much Greek and Latin as Whitehead.[14] Of the other Harvard philosophers who might be called pragmatists, Royce was also an idealist and is usually classified that way rather than as a pragmatist, and the same was true later of Hocking.[15] Perry was too close to James to reach out fully to the naturalism and social reform interests of pragmatists of his generation such as Dewey and Mead. Lewis and Quine narrowed pragmatism toward logic, not social relevance.[16] Pragmatism in mid-century flourished in the unpolished Midwest, and in New York with all its immigrants, including especially Jews such as Ernst Nagel and Sidney Hook. Thinkers who want to change the world through social reform and education can quickly latch on to pragmatism in some form or other but have a hard time thinking of process philosophy as a practical guide for change-agents.

Although some pragmatists have been theists, and Dewey's *A Common Faith* is an important positive theological contribution,[17] pragmatists have generally thought of themselves as naturalists. To many who came from Orthodox Jewish or low-church conservative Christianity, naturalism means anti-supernaturalism which in turn means antireligion.[18] Whereas process thinkers have tended to identify religion with its very sophisticated expressions, pragmatists have tended to identify it with its least sophisticated expressions. Both are motivated by sensibilities of class background, I suspect, as much as by philosophical considerations; therefore on the whole they have had opposite responses to theism and religion. Properly to understand the origins and trajectories of pragmatism and process philosophy, it would be important to pursue these cultural issues in much greater detail, though I shall not do that here.

One more introductory remark needs to be made here, namely, that both process philosophy and pragmatism are products of the early twentieth century and a great deal has changed since then. First, both of those schools inspired major thinkers who would not identify with the school itself but would claim their own philosophies in which the schools have impact but not determining identity. Paul Weiss was Whitehead's most important student in the same sense that Aristotle was Plato's; he started from the possibilities Whitehead gave him for speculative thought and has gone his own unique and brilliant way.[19] So too, Justus Buchler was a Peircean pragmatist, but surely went far beyond Peirce.[20]

Then the evolution of generations within the schools has produced such novelty that even those closely associated with the lineages have gone far beyond the original motifs. Think of the multivolume systems now being published by Frederick Ferré,[21] George Allan,[22] and Joseph Grange[23]—all process thinkers in some sense, but far from orthodoxy. Think of the philosophy of culture of David L. Hall,[24] or the aesthetics of Elizabeth Kraus[25] and Judith Jones.[26]

The pragmatist side is harder to identify in a consistent lineage, although the marvelous system of Sandra Rosenthal in *Speculative Pragmatism*[27] and various essays is a clear extension of Dewey and Peirce, and also James and Mead. The lineage of pragmatism is hard to track in part because it ramified itself so quickly outside of academic philosophy into social and political theory and practical educational theory.

But an even more important block to tracking the pragmatic lineage is the current popularity of Richard Rorty's neo-pragmatism which rejects the systematic or metaphysical elements in pragmatism both in principle and in nearly all the points listed above it has in common with process philosophy.[28] Thus, instead of a realistic philosophy of nature it has an idealism of conversation,[29] instead of a realism of generals or habits it has what David Hall calls "default nominalism,"[30] and instead of truth's nature as correspondence and criteria as pragmatic it holds to a kind of persuasive-coherence theory of rhetoric.[31] Instead of opposing analytic philosophy's evisceration of experience as interaction, neo-pragmatism builds on the "linguistic turn."[32] Instead of opposing Continental philosophy's tendency to translate experience into narratives and texts rather than nature, it builds a super-narrative of Western philosophy, justifying "strong misreadings."[33] About all that's left of classical pragmatism in neo-pragmatism is anti-foundationalism, an expansion of British empiricism to include (not nature, but) other points of view, and a strong commitment to philosophy as a contributor to public life.[34] The great irony is that neo-pragmatism deletes nearly everything from classical pragmatism except its epistemology, and the very heart of pragmatic epistemology is a criticism of the Western tradition for being too epistemological.[35] Moreover, without its realism (in both senses) and its speculative metaphysics to help correct bias, pragmatic epistemology focusing on fallible knowledge vulnerable to experiential correction degenerates into rhetoric and the power of convincing narratives. That is a decisive rejection of pragmatism's naturalism and appreciation of science. This is not to say that neo-pragmatism is wrong—I believe it is mainly wrong whereas David Hall in this very collection believes it is mainly right—only that it skews understanding the lineage of classical pragmatism. The above points have been footnoted so obsessively to prove a point: where pragmatism has any interesting connection with Whitehead is precisely in the elements of pragmatism rejected by neo-pragmatism. Rorty writes:

> I myself would join Reichenbach in dismissing classical Husserlian phenomenology, Bergson, Whitehead, the Dewey of *Experience and Nature,* the James of *Radical Empiricism,* neo-Thomist epistemological realism, and a variety of other late nineteenth- and early twentieth-century systems. Bergson and Whitehead, and the bad ("metaphysical") parts of Dewey and James, seem to me merely weakened versions of idealism—attempts to answer "unscientifically" formulated epistemological questions about the "relation of subject and object" by "naïve generalizations and analogies" which emphasize "feeling" rather than "cognition."[36]

As to Peirce, Rorty says his "contribution to pragmatism was merely to have given it a name, and to have stimulated James."[37] What I am concerned about in this chapter is the relation of Whitehead to classical pragmatism, perhaps even better called "paleo-pragmatism" to avoid confusion with neo-pragmatism.[38]

One more element of the philosophical situation needs to be mentioned that has changed since the founding days of process philosophy and pragmatism, namely, that the philosophical public now includes the traditions of South and East Asia, as well as (though to a lesser extent) Islam. Although both Whitehead and Dewey wrote about Asian thought, and Dewey made an important visit to China, although both schools' idioms have been used extensively to translate Asian philosophy for Westerners, and although both of those authors would heartily approve of the more nearly global public for philosophy, it was not their public. Their ideas were not shaped in dialogue with Confucianism or Nyaya. Contemporary process philosophers and pragmatists operate within that larger public, even if not so well as they should in all cases. David Hall's philosophy, especially in the books written with the Sinologist Roger Ames—*Thinking Through Confucius, Anticipating China,* and *Thinking from the Han,* is an outstanding example of process philosophy (and neo-pragmatism?) elaborated in a context including East Asian thought in terms Whitehead never thought about.

Finally, our present situation includes many thinkers who have developed their own positions, showing deep indebtedness to both process and pragmatic thought, but who would never be thought to "belong" to either school, contemporary heirs of the independence of style of Weiss and Buchler if not of their philosophies. One thinks of Steve Odin whose first book[39] used process philosophy to engage Hua-yen Buddhism critically on the issue of time and whose second book[40] used the pragmatism of George Herbert Mead to engage the Japanese conception of the self. Or one thinks of the system of scientific naturalism of David Weissman who draws equally on Whitehead, Dewey, and Wittgenstein, but not to the satisfaction of any defenders of orthodox lineage.[41] Or Robert S. Corrington, a Whiteheadian, Heideggerian, Peircean "ecstatic naturalist":[42] no Deweyan pragmatist would be ecstatic, no Heideggerian would be a naturalist, and no Whiteheadian would accommodate the strong rejection of final causes in ecstatic naturalism.[43] For an interesting analysis of thinkers such as these, see George Lucas's "Outside the Camp: Recent Work on Whitehead's Philosophy."[44]

The moral to draw from this long introduction with a gazillion footnote citations is that Whitehead's process philosophy and Peirce's pragmatism together have produced a vital group of philosophers who cannot be identified as merely process thinkers or pragmatists. Although many in the group have interacted also with analytic philosophy, Continental philosophy, and neo-pragmatism, by and large the group enlarges on the general areas of agreement between process and pragmatism cited at the beginning.[45] It is out of a strong sense of appreciation and continuity with these heirs of process and pragmatism that I raise the following issues to extend the debate.

My purpose in the remainder of this chapter is to engage a contemporary debate concerning continuity and time that might well illustrate some of the integral tensions between Whitehead and pragmatism. Then I shall argue that those tensions illustrate a deeper intuition about time and eternity that both Whiteheadians and pragmatists fail to grasp. And finally I shall explore the implications of this intuition (into creation *ex nihilo*) for assessing pragmatism and process philosophy on time and its significance.

Sandra Rosenthal has argued in several places that the decisive difference between pragmatism and process philosophy lies in their treatments of the continuity of time.[46] Both schools stress process over substance, to use the old polemical categories. They emphasize the temporality of all things (well, maybe not eternal objects) and reject idealist themes such as an eternal absolute or a Whole inclusive of all time. Rosenthal points out, however, that their metaphysical analyses of temporal continuity are different, and arise from fundamentally different intuitions of things.

To summarize a well-known process theory, Whitehead held that an emerging occasion comes into being, defining its present/here temporal/spatial scope, and when it is fully definite with regard to its extension and all other possibilities, it stops becoming and simply is, past. Whitehead was ambiguous regarding the status of a finished occasion. Perhaps it simply is what it is, with an achieved actual reality in itself, such that any subsequent occasion has to take account of it; I hope that is what Whitehead meant. Or perhaps a past occasion has no reality except insofar as it is prehended by a subsequent present occasion, with the result that all reality is either in God or is present reality, residing objectively in an emerging prehending. The latter view has a somewhat weakened sense of continuity because everything gets packed into the present somehow or other, with the past occasions losing any sense of independent or in-themselves reality. This latter view is attractive to people who emphasize relationship to the point of saying that things have no reality except their relations. But I think in the end it will fall back to an idealist notion of *totum simul*.[47] The process analysis of time that Rosenthal examines is the former view, that there is a continuity between present emerging occasions and past, finished, fully definite occasions, a continuity that consists in the past being prehended into the present.

How the past is prehended into the present to provide continuity is not an easy doctrine for which there is consensus among process thinkers. Jorge Nobo has the most detailed examination of this question, though his own answer is not the popularly received account.[48] Rosenthal is a master of these debates and her articles are to be consulted on the topic. With regard to continuity in the process view of time, however, she focuses on two central points common to all the approaches.

First, for all interpretations of the process account of continuity, the past is prehended into the present by, and hence continuous with, the present concrescence which harmonizes the many past elements into one. As she puts it in all her articles cited, continuity in the process model is a matter of "the coming together of" diverse past elements. The basic Whiteheadian "intuition," as she calls it, is that process consists of harmonization, beginning with diversity and adding to the diversity with a new harmonizing entity. This is, of course, the Category of the Ultimate in *Process and Reality* as expressing itself in the issues of temporal continuity.

The second point central to all Whiteheadian positions is the interpretation of time's directional arrow in terms of the definiteness of the past. A present occasion is present and emerging precisely because it is not fully definite, and "when" it achieves full definiteness the urge for definiteness is "satisfied" and the occasion becomes past. Within an emergent present occasion there are no earlier and later stages, though a genetic analysis of the occasion can give logical stages. Only when the occasion is past does it have a definite temporal (and spatial) dimensionality. Only when it is past can it be prehended, and there must be finished definite past things to prehend in order for a present moment to emerge ("subjective unity" in Whitehead's categoreal terms). Time's arrow is defined by the order of prehension. Anything that can be prehended is in the past of the prehender, anything that can prehend an occasion is in the future of that occasion, and all the things that neither can be prehended by an occasion nor can prehend it are simultaneous with it. Thus, there is a sharp discontinuity between fully definite prehendable occasions and emergent prehending occasions, and a total indeterminateness of temporal relation among occasions where no order of prehending-prehended exists. Rosenthal's question, relative to pragmatism, is whether the continuity of prehension is sufficient to overcome the discontinuity of the prehended-prehending relation when it comes to accounting for the actuality of time's passage.

The pragmatic theory, she points out, takes such a different tack as to be attributable to a different fundament intuition. Whereas the process intuition is "the coming together of," the alternative pragmatic intuition is "the emerging out of." For pragmatists in various ways present time is characterized by the growth or extension of what has been into what is emerging and will continue to emerge. For Peirce, this is at the heart of the doctrine of Thirdness.[49] It appears in James, Dewey, and Mead in their biological metaphors and a great many other elements, as Rosenthal lays out. On the pragmatic analysis, emergence has no sharp breaks. It is a process of infinitesimal growth or accretion, and the direction of causal action is from the past to what emerges from the past's burgeonings. This contrasts with the Whiteheadian reversal of the classical direction of causation: for Whiteheadians, it is the causal power of the emerging present that integrates into actuality the diversity of past potentials.

The pragmatic theory of infinitesimal continuity in emergence contrasts also with the Whiteheadian discontinuity in the order of time's flow. For the pragmatists, Rosenthal points out, the past is only relatively definite, and indeed can change as what emerges from it gives it new overall character. Pragmatism therefore entertains a rather extended specious present in which the orders of earlier and later are not fully set. Present nature might not be entirely "blooming, buzzing, confusion," to use James's phrase, but neither does it exhibit a sharp distinction between finished and new. Rather, present time for pragmatism, on Rosenthal's accurate account, is the reality of the act of emerging, wherein there is no discontinuity or even distinction regarding definiteness between that from which the emergence comes and that which emerges as new. Within the extended moment of present time, what emerges comes from what is sometimes not settled. Whereas for process philosophy, continuity requires separate and discontinuous acts of concrescence to bring the past together in continuity with the present, for pragmatism the very meaning of present emergence is a continuity of creativity.

Rosenthal rightly says that, despite my other protestations of pragmatic allegiance, I am on the process side in this "great divide," as she calls it. There are several reasons for this. One is that, agreeing with both process philosophy and pragmatism that the present involves (indeed requires) novelty, I believe that novelty consists in part in a reaction to the past. The past must be fixed, wholly definite, in order to be objectified in reaction. A later thing cannot come after something unless there is something definite to come after. The arguments for reaction come from Peirce's theory of Secondness. But Whitehead had the better theory to show how reaction is possible. It requires, among other things, energy in the reactor over against the object of reaction, hence a discontinuity in time's moment's acts of creativity or concrescence.

Another reason I am on Whitehead's side are all the sentiments in existentialism now validated in critical theory about the importance of otherness. Consider some kinds of otherness. Present time is not really a swarmy reaching out into the past and future, Husserl's retention and protention notwithstanding, but rather a time when the past is dead and gone and the future is not yet. Self-conscious realization of present time should be filled with amazement, and helplessness, and loneliness. I don't agree with those who say that only the present is real. On the contrary, the past is very real in determining parameters for the present, in having a value that is obligatory for the present to respect, especially in human terms, and in being normative for continuing identity and moral life. The future too is real as determining the stage in which our present actions have consequences, and thus lays its own kind of norms upon present action. Though real, neither past nor future are presently real, and the present does not inhabit them as it does its own arena.[50] Augustine's ontological shock at this was right on.

Another sense of otherness is that there are really different things in the past, each with their own integrities and somewhat autonomous careers. These things often have contemporary otherness as well, and have future stories not to be reduced to any present experience. So I reject the pragmatic sense of a monolithic past unfolding emerging elements, though that perhaps is an unfair characterization. Rather, the diversity of things is given and ought to be acknowledged, and the integration or harmonizing of the diversity is an achievement and sometimes doesn't happen. The deep tragic element in passing time is that so many things are distorted when harmonized in the present or lost altogether when the harmony fails.[51] The pragmatic idiom fails to catch that metaphysical tragedy. The process intuition of "the coming together of," which sometimes does not come together, or does so at an oppressive price, is far better.

Nevertheless, there is a deeper intuition in these matters than either the pragmatic "emerging out of" or the process "coming together of," namely, the intuition of making, "creation *ex nihilo*." Creation *ex nihilo* is something like a reversal of the "coming together" theme, for it denotes a creative act which results in a determinate plurality of things that are really different from one another and are interdefined so as to be different. Each created thing has its own essential features, and it also has the features by which it is conditioned by or conditionally defined by the other things, so that the different things are determinately different from one another. As products of creation *ex nihilo,* created things are determinate and partly defined in terms of one another, but radically new: without the creative act there is nothing, and with it there is the plural world.[52]

Creation *ex nihilo* picks up on the pragmatic intuition that something new emerges in present process. But pragmatism fudges the issue of whether the new is already contained in the old. If it is, as Aristotle argued in saying that process is the reduction of potency to act by the act in efficient causes (a point carried on in early modern popular science), then there is nothing really new.[53] But if there is something new, whatever is new was not contained in the old and its appearance necessarily is *ex nihilo.* Pragmatism should acknowledge a continuous input of creation *ex nihilo* if emergence is continuous. "Emergence" really means *"ex nihilo"* because what emerges is not in that "from which" it emerges. The "from which" is a fake except in the sense of denoting the earlier state plus those elements in the present that are not new. As mentioned, however, pragmatism has difficulty distinguishing the new from the old in present time. In his famous "Neglected Argument for the Reality of God," Peirce clearly adopted the creation *ex nihilo* hypothesis to account for the togetherness of the three realms of reality, Firstness, Secondness, and Thirdness, thus seeing the point of this critical advance.[54]

The advantage of process philosophy in locating the causal power of harmonization or "coming together of" in the present is that it underscores the novelty in the emergence of a new occasion. There is a new individuated harmony that did not exist before; before there was only a disjunctive harmony. Each new occasion combines the old, namely the data prehended, with the new, namely new subjective forms individuated to the new satisfaction. Without something new, there is only the old disjunction. But if there is something new, the new is combined with the old, and whatever is new was not there before. The new in every occasion, insofar as it is not among the data prehended, is *ex nihilo.* Every occasion is an instance of some new creativity *ex nihilo.* Process philosophy is in a good position to indicate the experiential cash for this in its general interpretations of the subjectivity of human experience. Ordinarily, process philosophy, however, has emphasized that experience is the creation of new *order* out of the old prehended things. It would bring out its existential potential, however, by emphasizing the experience of the creation of *new* order, with the *ex nihilo* surprise of the new in the spotlight.

Process philosophy and pragmatism are together in not grasping the implication of creation *ex nihilo* in their emphasis on novelty in process. Why? I believe there have been two reasons. The first is a kind of failure of nerve, if I might put it bluntly, in the face of the insight into novelty: it would seem that novelty is intelligible only as derivative from something old or higher, the Aristotelian point generalized. So most Whiteheadians think that what explains has to be some high principles, a rationalist position.[55] The creation *ex nihilo* theory by contrast says that ultimately what explains is locating the creative decisions or acts of makings: understanding is not reduction to principle but grasp of an act that makes. If philosophers do not admit that grasp of a making-act is explanatory, then every novelty will be a mystery on top of determinism, whether emergent or concrescent.

The other reason pragmatism and process philosophy draw back from creation *ex nihilo* is the theistic history of the notion. The idea of creation *ex nihilo* here is highly refined, but it arises out of a distinctive theological tradition. That theological tradition is directly opposed to the theory of God in process philosophy, and so I clearly and systematically reject process theology in its classic forms.[56] Process philosophy's polemic against God as creator being coercive blinds it to any serious notion of divine creation, and also to the brute creativity in the bitsy novelty in individual actual occasions. For its part, pragmatism has generally been allergic to serious theology that owns up to an institutionalized tradition, as noted above. The exception is Peirce, who was a theist and defended creation *ex nihilo.*

So I propose that creation *ex nihilo* is a deeper intuition than either "the coming together of" or "emerging out of," and indeed is necessary to acknowledge the novelty both process philosophy and pragmatism want to affirm.

Large matters remain to be settled, however, to sort the functions of creation *ex nihilo* within continuous temporal process and the characterization of it as giving rise to a plurality of different though related things. Here the theological resonance of the concept comes to time's flow. My hypothesis is that the theory best expressing the deepest intuition is that everything determinate is created in a single creative act. "Everything determinate" is a loaded phrase. I define determinateness in terms of the essential and conditional features of things mentioned above.[57] To be a thing is to be a harmony of essential and conditional features. To be created is to be in a context of mutual relevance with everything with respect to which a creature is determinate; mutual relevance means that things not only can condition one another but can integrate their conditioning features with their respective essential features which are not mutually conditioning.

Think of just one instance of the generality of this claim. The modes of time, the past, present, and future, are different from one another but obviously determinate with respect to those differences. Process philosophy and pragmatism give somewhat different accounts of the three modes, but would agree with the general point. The togetherness of past, present, and future cannot be temporal. That is, the past is not earlier than the present, nor the future later. Temporal things are earlier or later than one another because of the nontemporal togetherness of the modes of time. The modes of time all have essential features and also conditional features defining their relations. So, to review briefly only a process philosophy model, the past is essentially fixed actuality, the present essentially spontaneous creativity, and the future essentially pure form. The past has form (and value) as a condition from the future, and it has increasing growth or extension as a condition from present temporality. The present has actualized things as potentials for new actuality from the past, and structured possibilities as conditions from the future. The future has actualized things from the past that give conditional structure to its form, and has a continually differentiating kaleidoscope of possibilities as the condition resulting from present decisions. This quick theory does not have to be swallowed whole for the point to be seen that the togetherness of the temporal modes is very definitely not temporal but eternal.[58] Eternity, as the ancient Western tradition and I use the term, does not mean static form but that ontological togetherness that makes the passage of time possible for temporal things. The singular act of creation *ex nihilo* does not take place in time at all but rather creates time itself, a theological position as old as Origen and Augustine.

Pragmatism and process philosophy are quite right, within this view, to say that time unfolds in a creative process with indeterminacy and novelty. Because it is not temporal, the singular act of creation *ex nihilo* does not determine anything in advance except in ways that the past partially determines the present which has its own novelty. This obviates the process criticism that a creator-God predetermines what happens. Within a present moment, supposing a process model, creation *ex nihilo* is finitized to be the creation of something new out of the prehended past, a new combination of old and new. Supposing a pragmatic model, creation *ex nihilo* is finitized to effect the emergence of novelty out of the rest of the emergent process. Although these remarks do not settle a theory of novelty within time, they at least indicate that such a theory needs to account for bits of creation *ex nihilo* functioning to bring the old and new together into something that has continuity but is also novel.

For all its emphasis on creativity, process philosophy has fallen into the idiom of time's flow as the ingression of order. Rosenthal's image of "the coming together of" describes this accurately. There is no metaphysical necessity in this, of course. Each occasion is a prehensive unification of its world in utter independence from its contemporaries, and it might well be that the only subsequent occasions that can harmonize the contemporaries are of trivial importance—things lost in a puff.[59] But the effect of the process conception of God has been to emphasize continuous, or at least repeated, inputs of order, a hedge against entropy. Even Lewis Ford's great reconception of process theology conceives God as future, only inputting order.[60] Peirce shared this confidence in creeping Thirdness.

Yet is not chaos as deep a feature of the cosmos as order? Creative novelty so often seems blind, to go nowhere. How do we reconcile the trajectory of order that results in the human habitat with the billions of failed experiments with life, the species lost, the planets blasted, the stars gone to supernovae? How do we face the fundamental realities of human life, a species not in a garden but cast in the wilderness to scrabble brief lives through work and pain, with a God who is an order-monger? Creation *ex nihilo* recognizes the unregulated, free, divine act whose lifeboats of order in oceans of chaos are leaky just like our own lives. The God of process theology is too small for real religion, too domestic. Creation *ex nihilo* represents a God whose power is infinite and whose character is constituted by the creating, a God shown as much by chaos as by order.[61] Perhaps pragmatism rejects the too-small God of order and fears the Creator *ex nihilo* who cannot be controlled because it hopes to control events that emerge from what we manage. Peirce alone of the pragmatists subordinated the managerial impulse to wonder and awe, and he did so because he had a semiotic theory open to chaos as well as order.

In sum, I have argued that process philosophy and pragmatism share much, disagree over the fundamental intuitions regarding continuity in time, as Rosenthal has shown, and both miss out on a deeper intuition about the true infinite scale of creativity. As a result, though their common ground and internal debates might be the place to begin in the current philosophical situation, their outcomes are tragically superficial. How can we have survived the twentieth century and entered the Third Millennium without knowing that our being is grounded in the Act that creates our cosmic doom as well as destiny, whose name is Chaos along with Order, and with whom is to be absolutely lonely as well as loving and beloved?

Notes

1. On Royce as a pragmatist and absolute idealist, see John E. Smith's *Royce's Social Infinite* (New York: Liberal Arts Press, 1950), 46–61 and *passim.* For Royce's own informal discussion of his relation to pragmatists, see his *Metaphysics,* the notes of his undergraduate course edited by Richard Hocking and Frank Oppenheim (Albany: State University of New York Press, 1998), especially the first several lectures.

2. See George R. Lucas Jr., *The Genesis of Modern Process Thought* (Metuchen, N.J.: Scarecrow Press and ATLA, 1983) and *The Rehabilitation of Whitehead: An Analytic and Historical Assessment of Process Philosophy* (Albany: State University of New York Press, 1989). See also Whitehead's biographical remarks and Dewey's essay in *The Philosophy of Alfred North Whitehead,* edited by Paul Arthur Schilpp (Library of Living Philosophers, vol. 3; New York: Tudor, 1941). See the discussions of Whitehead, process philosophy, and pragmatism in *The Philosophy of Charles Hartshorne,* edited by Lewis Edwin Hahn (Library of Living Philosophers, vol. 20; LaSalle, Ill.: Open Court, 1991), especially in Hartshorne's Intellectual Biography and Donald Lee's article. See the same topics discussed in *The Philosophy of Paul Weiss,* edited by Lewis Edwin Hahn (Library of Living Philosophers, vol. 23; LaSalle, Ill.: Open Court, 1995), especially in Weiss's biographical remarks and in the essays by Sandra Rosenthal, Kevin Kennedy, and Jay Schulkin.

3. Whitehead, expressing appreciation for Bradley's notion of *feeling,* asks whether his own thought might not be "a transformation of some of the main doctrines of Absolute Idealism onto a realistic basis," in *Process and Reality* (corrected edition edited by Donald W. Sherburne and David Ray Griffin; New York: Free Press, 1978), xiii. See also Whitehead's discussion of idealism and realism in *Science and the Modern World* (New York: Macmillan, 1926), 131-ff. Hartshorne might well be accused of idealism because of his panpsychism; nevertheless, he accepted Whitehead's argument that an actual occasion when finished is no longer conscious but a physical entity to be prehended as such, a realistic position. As to the pragmatists, Peirce did argue that the character of evolution behaves more like mind than like dead mechanical matter, and said that matter could be regarded as "frozen mind." See for instance *The Collected Papers of Charles Sanders Peirce,* vols. 1–6 edited by Charles Hartshorne and Paul Weiss (Cambridge: Harvard University Press, 1931–35; cited by volume and paragraph number), CP 6.238–86. But his complaint was with the mechanistic conception of matter and his own conception of mind was wholly naturalistic. His criticism of idealism focused on the fact that Hegel let Thirdness swallow Secondness, to use Peirce's categories, resulting in degenerate Secondness such that bumping real nature is not seen to be a corrective; see CP 6.218, 305; 1.521–29. Part of Peirce's Scotistic realism is his defense of the over-againstness of nature relative to mind, for which he cites Scotus's idea of haecceity (CP 1.405). On James against idealism see *Pragmatism* (New York: Longmans, Green, 1907), especially chapter 2, "On Some Hegelianisms," in *The Will to Believe* (New York: Henry Holt, 1912), and *A Plural-*

istic Universe (New York: Longmans, Green, 1909), chapters 2–3. James's most effective rejection of idealism is shown in the photograph of him and Royce in which he cried, "Royce, you're being photographed! Look out! I say *Damn the Absolute,*" in *The Letters of William James,* edited by his son Henry James (Boston: Atlantic Monthly Press), volume 2, opposite page 134. Dewey, of course, avowed idealism in his early period, but rejected it for pragmatic realism; see his "Experience and Objective Idealism," in *The Influence of Darwin on Philosophy* (New York: Henry Holt, 1910). George Herbert Mead set pragmatism and realism alongside one another as opponents of idealism in *Philosophy of the Act,* edited by Charles W. Morris (Chicago: University of Chicago Press, 1938), 360 ff. There were many kinds of realism in early twentieth-century American philosophy besides the pragmatic, including neo-realism and critical realism; they agreed in affirming that nature can correct our views in ways that the rational coherence of thought cannot, and that this is because things somewhat are as they seem to be. For subtle interpretations of the ways pragmatism sought to be realistic without any kind of copy theory of knowledge, and how Royce appreciated this to some extent, see John E. Smith's *The Spirit of American Philosophy* (revised edition; Albany: State University of New York Press, 1983), chapters 3–4. For a good survey of many of the kinds of realism and idealism in the heyday of classical pragmatism, see Andrew J. Reck's *Recent American Philosophy* (New York: Random House, 1964), which treats Ralph Barton Perry, William Ernest Hocking, George Herbert Mead, John Elof Boodin, Wilbur Marshall Urban, Dewitt H. Parker, Roy Wood Sellars, Arthur O. Lovejoy, Elijah Jordan, and Edgar Sheffield Brightman.

4. Whitehead was a strong Platonic realist in his defense of eternal objects; see *Science and the Modern World,* chapter 2, and *Process and Reality,* part 2, chapter 1. Peirce was a Scotistic realist in another sense from that in the previous note in defending the reality of what Scotus called "common natures" and Peirce called Thirdness or generals or vagues; see CP 1.337–415, 6.102–317. Peirce thought nominalism has been the root of all evils in modern philosophy; see CP 1.15–26, 6.619–24. Peirce's notion of habit, the embodiment of universals, is taken up and developed by James, Dewey, and Mead.

5. See Whitehead's discussion of civilized experience in the first chapter of *Process and Reality,* and throughout *Adventures of Ideas* (New York: Macmillan, 1933) and *Modes of Thought* (New York: Macmillan, 1938); see also his technical discussions of symbolic reference in *Symbolism* (New York: Macmillan, 1927) and the revised subjectivist principle in *Process and Reality,* part 2, chapter 7. James's *Essays in Radical Empiricism,* edited by R. B. Perry (New York: Longmans, Green, 1912) is the most polemical pragmatic critique of British empiricism, but all the pragmatists developed that critique and the pragmatic alternative. This point has been one of the chief themes of the work of John E. Smith in *The Spirit of American Philosophy, Religion and Empiricism* (Milwaukee: Marquette University Press, 1967), *Themes in American Philosophy* (New York: Harper, 1970), *Purpose and Thought: The Meaning of Pragmatism* (New Haven: Yale University Press, 1978), and *America's Philosophical Vision* (Chicago: University of Chicago Press, 1992).

6. Whitehead began *Process and Reality* with the following, which amounts to a rejection of the objections to metaphysics in the grand tradition:

> These lectures will be best understood by noting the following list of prevalent habits of thought, which are repudiated, in so far as concerns their influence on philosophy:
>
> (i) The distrust of speculative philosophy.
> (ii) The trust in language as an adequate expression of propositions.
> (iii) The mode of philosophical thought which implies, and is implied by, the faculty-psychology.
> (iv) The subject-predicate form of expression.
> (v) The sensationalist doctrine of perception.
> (vi) The doctrine of vacuous actuality.
> (vii) The Kantian doctrine of the objective world as a theoretical construct from purely subjective experience.
> (viii) Arbitrary deductions in *ex absurdo* arguments.
> (ix) Belief that logical inconsistencies can indicate anything else than some antecedent errors.
>
> By reason of its ready acceptance of some or all of these nine myths and fallacious procedures, much ninteenth-century philosophy excludes itself from relevance to the ordinary stubborn facts of daily life. (*Process and Reality,* xiii)

Whitehead, of course, is the great speculative metaphysician of the twentieth century whose use of categoreal schemes as hypotheses gets around both the empiricist and Kantian objections to metaphysics; I have studied this in some detail in *The Highroad around Modernism* (Albany: State University of New York Press, 1992), chapter 3. The method of hypothesis as a way around empiricism and Kant, of course, was invented by Charles Peirce much earlier; the neatest statement is in CP 6.452–93, and that whole volume illustrates it; I have examined and extended the argument in *Normative Cultures* (Albany: State University of New York Press, 1995). James had little flair for metaphysics but he made a valiant effort in *Some Problems of Philosophy,* edited by Henry James Jr. (New York: Longmans, Green, 1911). Dewey's great metaphysical works are *Experience and Nature,* in vol. 1 of *John Dewey: The Later Works,* edited by Jo Ann Boydston (Carbondale and Edwardsville: Southern Illinois University Press, 1981; first edition, 1925, second edition revised, 1929) and *The Quest for Certainty,* in vol. 4 of *John Dewey: The Later Works.* Whitehead praised Dewey's metaphysics in "John Dewey and His Influence," in *Essays in Science and Philosophy* (New York: Philosophical Library, 1948). Of all the pragmatists, Dewey gave the most sustained criticism of the prior Western metaphysical tradition, in *Reconstruction in Philosophy* (New York: Henry Holt, 1920).

7. See Whitehead's *Science and the Modern World,* chapters 9, 12, and 13, and *The Function of Reason* (Boston: Beacon, 1929); Whitehead's influence in this re-

gard has been extended directly to William M. Sullivan's *Reconstructing Public Philosophy* (Berkeley: University of California Press, 1982), a title also reflective of Dewey, and *Work and Integrity: The Crisis and Promise of Professionalism in America* (San Francisco: Harper, 1995); Sullivan analyzes Whitehead on the public use of philosophy in his "The Civilizing of Enterprise," in *New Essays in Metaphysics*, edited by Robert C. Neville (Albany: State University of New York Press, 1987). Of the pragmatists, Peirce was the least concerned with public roles for philosophy, though he responded to William James's advocacy of public philosophy with his subtle essay, "Vitally Important Topics," CP 1.616–77. James talked about vitally important topics all the time—see the essays collected together by Ralph Barton Perry in *Essays on Faith and Morals* (New York: Longmans, Green, 1942). Dewey's great work on public philosophy was *The Public and Its Problems*, vol. 2 of *John Dewey: The Later Works* (original edition; New York: Henry Holt, 1927).

8. For Whitehead truth is the correspondence of propositions with their objects through symbolic reference, defined technically in *Process and Reality*, part 2, chapter 8, and colloquially in chapter 1; in *Adventures of Ideas*, at the beginning of chapter 16, he says, "Truth is the conformation of Appearance to Reality." For Peirce's discussion of truth as correspondence, see CP 5.549–73; his theory of truth was closely allied with his theory of signs, such that a sign is true or false of its indicated object as interpreted; his definition of reality was that it is the object of the representation or opinion that has been infinitely corrected (CP 5.405–10). Dewey defined truth as "warranted assertability," which was in fact to define it by its criteria; but the criteria he employed served to make our representations agree with reality so far as that is relevant to our purposes; he rejected the rhetoric of correspondence insofar as that meant an internal mirroring of reality; see his *Logic: The Theory of Inquiry* (New York: Henry Holt, 1938).

9. In his theory of truth as symbolic reference, Whitehead said, "Symbolism can be justified, or unjustified. The test of justification must always be pragmatic" (*Process and Reality*, 181); see also the chapter on truth in *Adventures of Ideas*. The pragmatists, of course, take the criteria of truth to be pragmatic. Some such as James do not distinguish very carefully between the meaning of truth and the criteria. Dewey has a fully developed theory of nature, within which are to be found truth-seeking human beings; so he defines truth in terms of its successful achievement as a natural phenomenon. I have advanced Dewey's theory of truth as an element within nature, borrowing somewhat from Whitehead's theory of nature, to allow for a clear distinction again between the meaning of truth as correspondence and the criteria of truth as making pragmatic cases; see *Recovery of the Measure* (Albany: State University of New York Press, 1989).

10. See Whitehead's famous discussion in chapter 1 of *Process and Reality*. See Peirce's attacks on intuition and defense of fallibilism in the several published papers in CP 5.213–463. See my analyses of fallibilism in *The Highroad around Modernism*, chapters 1 and 6, and in *Normative Cultures*, chapters 1–4.

11. See John E. Smith's "The New Need for a Recovery of Philosophy" in the revised edition of *The Spirit of American Philosophy*, and *The Recovery of Philosophy*

in America: Essays in Honor of John Edwin Smith, edited by Thomas P. Kasulis and Robert Cummings Neville (Albany: State University of New York Press, 1997).

12. Hartshorne expresses some bitterness at not being kept on at Harvard, but the University of Chicago where he spent the bulk of his career is itself about as Episcopalian as a Baptist university can get. See *The Philosophy of Charles Hartshorne,* 26.

13. See Sherburne's "Whitehead without God," in *Process Theology and Christian Thought,* edited by Delwin Brown, Ralph E. James Jr., and Gene Reeves (Indianapolis: Bobbs-Merrill, 1971), 305–28.

14. See the biography by Joseph Brent, *Charles Sanders Peirce: A Life* (Bloomington: Indiana University Press, 1993).

15. See Reck's *Recent American Philosophy.*

16. C. I. Lewis's *Mind and the World Order* (corrected edition; New York: Dover, 1956; original edition 1929) is not about what President George Bush wanted a new one of, but about ordering knowledge of the world by epistemological elements of givenness, the apriori, and hypothesis.

17. John Dewey, *A Common Faith* (New Haven: Yale University Press, 1934). See Steven C. Rockefeller's *John Dewey: Religious Faith and Democratic Humanism* (New York: Columbia University Press, 1991).

18. Justus Buchler is a case in point. One of the great systematic metaphysicians of our time, he says very little about God except that God would have to fit within his system as a natural complex just like everything else; and he says less about religion. A recent set of essays about his work, *Nature's Perspectives: Prospects for Ordinal Metaphysics,* edited by Armen Marsoobian, Kathleen Wallace, and Robert S. Corrington (Albany: State University of New York Press, 1991), has about twenty articles on Buchler, only two of which deal at all with God. One, by John Ryder and Peter Hare, says it might not be too bad to be a natural complex and the other, by Robert S. Corrington, uses Buchler's categories to advance a theory of divinity within nature. The God of Aristotle, Plotinus, Augustine, Thomas, Spinoza, Hegel, or Peirce is not even a topic. Religion is not mentioned, as if it were not as important as art and politics which are Buchlerian topics.

19. Weiss's first book, *Reality* (Princeton: Princeton University Press, 1939), was an explicit argument against Whitehead's emphasis on process and in defense of substance, although it is dedicated to Mrs. Whitehead. His most recent book is *Being and Other Realities* (LaSalle, Ill.: Open Court, 1995), and his *Emphatics* (Nashville: Vanderbilt University Press, 2000) is forthcoming at the time of this writing while *Surrogates* is growing in his computer.

20. See Buchler's *Charles Peirce's Empiricism* (London: Kegan Paul, Trench, Trubner, 1939), *Metaphysics of Natural Complexes* (New York: Columbia University Press, 1966), and *The Main of Light* (New York: Oxford University Press, 1974).

21. *Being and Value* (Albany: State University of New York Press, 1996) and *Knowing and Value* (Albany: State University of New York Press, 1998).

22. *Importances of the Past* (Albany: State University of New York Press, 1986).

23. *Nature: An Environmental Cosmology* (Albany: State University of New York Press, 1997) and *The City* (Albany: State University of New York Press, 1999).

24. *The Civilization of Experience* (New York: Fordham University Press, 1973) is his Whitehead book, and Whitehead's philosophy is apparent in *The Uncertain Phoenix* (New York: Fordham University Press, 1982) and *Eros and Irony* (Albany: State University of New York, 1982). His first three books with Roger T. Ames develop a philosophy of culture that enables him to contrast the Western with the Chinese tradition, with the latter looking somewhat Whiteheadian in its aesthetic emphases; see *Thinking Through Confucius, Anticipating China,* and *Thinking from the Han* (Albany: State University of New York Press, 1987, 1995, 1998). His most recent book with Ames, *Democracy of the Dead* (LaSalle: Open Court, 1999) is a straightforward defense of pragmatism as the philosophy with which to engage China.

25. Her *The Metaphysics of Experience* (New York: Fordham University Press, 1979) is a commentary on Whitehead's *Process and Reality* but presents its own aesthetic interpretation of Whitehead.

26. *Intensity: An Essay in Whiteheadian Ontology* (Nashville: Vanderbilt University Press, 1998).

27. Sandra B. Rosenthal, *Speculative Pragmatism* (Amherst: University of Massachusetts Press, 1986; reprint edition, Open Court).

28. See his *Philosophy and the Mirror of Nature* (Princeton: Princeton University Press, 1979), *Consequences of Pragmatism* (Minneapolis: The University of Minnesota Press, 1982), *Objectivity, Relativism, and Truth* (Cambridge: Cambridge University Press, 1991), and *Essays on Heidegger and Others* (Cambridge: Cambridge University Press, 1991). The best general study of Rorty is David L. Hall's *Richard Rorty: Prophet and Poet of the New Pragmatism* (Albany: State University of New York Press, 1994).

29. See Rorty's *Philosophy and the Mirror of Nature,* chapter 8.

30. See Hall's *Richard Rorty,* 202 ff.

31. *Philosophy and the Mirror of Nature,* chapters 6–8.

32. See Rorty's edited volume, *The Linguistic Turn: Recent Essays in Philosophical Method* (Chicago: University of Chicago Press, 1967), editor's introduction.

33. See the brilliant analysis in Hall's *Richard Rorty,* chapter 3.

34. See Rorty's powerful *Achieving Our Country: Leftist Thought in Twentieth Century America* (Cambridge: Harvard University Press, 1997).

35. See Dewey's *Reconstruction of Philosophy.*

36. *Consequences of Pragmatism,* 213 ff.

37. *Consequences of Pragmatism,* 161. Rorty's criticism of Peirce was that Peirce seems to believe philosophy can find a foundationalist ahistorical context for philosophy. I have no idea how he can find that in Peirce unless he made the mistake of thinking that a hypothesis about basic things, *signs* according to Rorty, has to be itself foundational. Peirce and Whitehead agree that all metaphysical hypotheses are historically contextual, ideas adventuring.

38. I have discussed Rorty's attack on metaphysics in much more detail in *The Highroad around Modernism,* the introduction and chapters 1 and 6.

39. *Process Metaphysics and Hua-Yen Buddhism* (Albany: State University of New York Press, 1982).

40. *The Social Self in Zen and American Pragmatism* (Albany: State University of New York Press, 1996).

41. See Weissman's *Eternal Possibilities* (Carbondale: Southern Illinois University Press, 1977) for the Wittgenstein roots, and then *Intuition and Ideality* (Albany: State University of New York Press, 1987), *Hypothesis and the Spiral of Reflection* (Albany: State University of New York Press, 1989), and *Truth's Debt to Value* (New Haven: Yale University Press, 1993) for his system that engages process philosophy and pragmatism.

42. See his *An Introduction to C. S. Peirce: Philosopher, Semiotician, and Ecstatic Naturalist* (Lanham, Md.: Rowman and Littlefield, 1993), *Ecstatic Naturalism: Signs of the World* (Bloomington: Indiana University Press, 1994), *Nature and Spirit: An Essay in Ecstatic Naturalism* (New York: Fordham University Press, 1992), and *Nature's Self* (Lanham, Md.: Rowman and Littlefield, 1996).

43. And what am I? I think of myself as a pragmatist, most others call me a process philosopher, and my critics blame my inadequacies in either allegiance on my teacher Paul Weiss. See the collection of wonderful essays in *Interpreting Neville,* edited by J. Harley Chapman and Nancy Frankenberry (Albany: State University of New York Press, 1999).

44. George R. Lucas Jr., "Outside the Camp: Recent Work on Whitehead's Philosophy," Part I in *Transactions of the Charles S. Peirce Society,* 21, no. 2 (Winter 1985): 49–75 and Part II in the same journal, 21, no. 3 (Summer 1985): 327–82.

45. See John E. Smith's responses to the papers in *The Recovery of Philosophy in America.*

46. See her "Contemporary Process Metaphysics and Diverse Intuitions of Time: Can the Gap Be Bridged?" in *The Journal of Speculative Philosophy* (New Series) 12, no. 4 (1998): 271–88, and "Neville and Pragmatism: Toward an Ongoing Dialogue," in *Interpreting Neville,* edited by J. Harley Chapman and Nancy K. Frankenberry (Albany: State University of New York Press, 1999). These essays contain some overlap of material, with the former analyzing Whitehead in more detail, and the latter pragmatism and my own work. See also her "Continuity, Contingency, and Time: The Divergent Intuitions of Whitehead and Pragmatism," in *Transactions of the Charles S. Peirce Society* 32 (1996): 542–67.

47. This conclusion is fully drawn by Harold H. Oliver, for instance, in his *Relatedness: Essays in Metaphysics and Theology* (Macon, Ga.: Mercer University Press, 1984).

48. See his *Whitehead's Metaphysics of Extension and Solidarity* (Albany: State University of New York Press, 1986).

49. The point is discussed throughout his work. The most extended discussion is probably in CP 6.101–213.

50. I have analyzed this point in detail in *Eternity and Time's Flow* (Albany: State University of New York Press, 1993), part 2. See also my essay in the Library

of Living Philosophers volume on Hartshorne, and *Recovery of the Measure,* chapters 9–10.

51. See Elizabeth Kraus's poignant essay on this, "God the Savior," in *New Essays in Metaphysics,* edited by Robert C. Neville (Albany: State University of New York Press, 1987).

52. I have analyzed creation *ex nihilo ad nauseam,* and essential and conditional features too, beginning with *God the Creator* (new edition; Albany: State University of New York Press, 1992; original edition, University of Chicago Press, 1968), with updatings in *Recovery of the Measure* and *Eternity and Time's Flow.*

53. The classic criticism of this view, in defense of novelty, is Paul Weiss's in *Modes of Being* (Carbondale: Southern Illinois University Press, 1958), chapter 3.

54. CP 6.452 ff.

55. I have discussed this with a dialectic of arguments in *Creativity and God* (New edition; Albany: State University of New York Press, 1995; original edition The Seabury Press, 1980).

56. This is much of the reason I think of myself as a pragmatist rather than a process philosopher, despite process commitments on continuity in time, because the theology is so central to much of process thinking.

57. See my *God the Creator,* chapter 3, or *Eternity and Time's Flow,* part 3.

58. See *Eternity and Time's Flow.*

59. Trivial things lose the details and the contrasts of the things they prehend, and hence most of their intrinsic value.

60. See his essay in *New Essays in Metaphysics.*

61. I'm preaching here. See my *The God Who Beckons: Theology in the Form of Sermons* (Nashville: Abingdon Press, 1999), for more sermons on this point.

CHAPTER 3

Whitehead and Dewey: Religion in the Making of Education

GEORGE ALLAN

Romance

In a 1908 essay, "Religion and Our Schools," Dewey assails a proposal that religion be taught as part of the public school curriculum. Proponents see it as a way to instill in students the moral character prerequisite to good citizenship, but Dewey thinks "education in religion" is an oxymoron, the didactic promulgation of parochial irrationalisms. American education is already plagued by a tradition of "dogmatic, catechetical and memoriter methods" of instruction (172). Its problems would only be exacerbated by including instruction in that most dogmatic of all subject matters.

Dewey is equally hostile, however, to those secularists who argue that character and citizenship are best inculcated by teaching students to revere science and democracy rather than God and the Church. They invest science with "the same spiritual import as supernaturalism" and think that the social conditions for democracy are the same as for feudalism, imagining that they are enlightened moderns because of a few "slight changes of phraseology," giving marginally "new shades of meaning" to old symbols. "Such beliefs testify to that torpor of imagination which is the uniform effect of dogmatic belief" (167). Genuine science is a method of inquiry open to critique and requiring empirical verification, not a set of dogmatic conclusions, and genuine democracy is a mode of association based on equal access and shared responsibility, not on hierarchical authority.

What Americans need is a new "intellectual attitude," a new "interpretation of the world" that carries with it a new approach to social interaction and hence a new sense of what constitutes the moral life. We ought "to labor persistently and patiently," says Dewey, "for the clarification and development of the positive creed of life implicit in democracy and in science, and to work for the transformation of all practical instrumentalities of education till they are in harmony with these ideas" (168).

We cannot teach superstitious people to think rationally nor unjust people to act justly unless there is "an accompanying thorough reorganization of social life and of science" (171). Unless we reconceive religion in a way compatible with the methods of science and the ideals of democracy, it will only be an obstacle to the liberation of persons from ignorance, prejudice, and suffering. Religion if rightly understood, however, if taken as "a natural expression of human experience," as the "natural piety" persons should cultivate toward their potential for achieving fulfillment through "a broader and more catholic principle of human intercourse and association," can be "the fine flower of the modern spirit's achievement" (176,177).

Dewey argues that, if teachers foster the values implicit in scientific inquiry and democratic association, students will develop this natural piety, committing themselves to the ideal of human betterment as a concretely realizable possibility. They will understand that they are natural creatures able to improve their lives by taking seriously their "implication" with other natural entities "in a common career and destiny" (176). Religion, interpreted in this way, should be integral to an educational system that aims to help people become skilled in the uses of experimental intelligence for the enhancement of human goods.

Alfred North Whitehead asserts at the conclusion of a 1916 essay on "The Aims of Education" that "the essence of education is that it be religious," for instruction is educational only insofar as it "inculcates duty and reverence." Reverence arises from the perception that "the present holds within itself the complete sum of existence, backwards and forwards, that whole amplitude of time, which is eternity"; duty, from recognizing that "our potential control over the course of events" comprises that present (AE 14).

Earlier in the essay, Whitehead contrasts "inert ideas" with "understanding." Ideas are inert, a student thereby suffering "mental dryrot," if they "are merely received into the mind without being utilized, or tested, or thrown into fresh combination" (1). Understanding, however, is the active appropriation and integration of ideas, ideas "illumined" by "the spark of vitality" because seen as "useful" (2). Understanding is "of an insistent present." It involves "knowledge of the past" not as an end in itself but with respect to its constraints and possibilities, its usefulness as a way "to equip us for the present" (3). Teachers encourage a reverence for life when they help students understand their world, their cultural heritage, in terms of its concrete relevance to the attainment of the good. The present is where values are made and unmade, where we honor past achievements by putting them to work in the fashioning of new ones. No where else but now can we actualize good, and to understand that this is so, that the present and the sacred are the same, that the present "is holy ground; for it is the past, and it is the future" (3), is for us to have attained a religious sensibility.

Realizing this, we therefore also recognize that what we know or could have known has bearing on what we can do, and how well we utilize what we know will determine the quality and character of what in fact is done—or not done. We are responsible for the good we could have accomplished. "Where attainable knowledge could have changed the issue, ignorance has the guilt of vice" (14). Education inculcates duty insofar as it brings students to this awareness of the role that they can, and therefore that they should, play in the shaping of present value.

Whitehead calls the practice of attempting to fulfill our duty "the sense for style": an "admiration for the direct attainment of a foreseen end, simply and without waste" (12). The point of action is to attain a goal, whatever it be, and to that extent any means is justified that harnesses the power necessary to produce the desired results. But a poor choice of means can have unintended consequences, give rise to unfortunate "side issues," create "undesirable inflammations." With style, says Whitehead, "you attain your end and nothing but your end" (12). We restrain the power we have harnessed so that our actions become "calculable," our means suited to our ends, tailored to the task for which they were designed. Power, by being thus restrained, is not curtailed but augmented. "With style your power is increased, for your mind is not distracted with irrelevancies, and you are more likely to attain your object." Foresight, the fruit of style, "is the last gift of gods to men" (13).

Thus, a proper education for Whitehead is one that teaches students their duty by making them aware that they have the power to alter the present for the better, by helping them understand what the resources are relevant to their task, and by encouraging them to find a stylish way to its accomplishment. Because it is the keystone to achieving what is best in the most elegant available manner, "style is the ultimate morality of mind" (12). Developing in students this sense of duty toward the holy ground where whatever good there might be must be made is the moral imperative that good teaching should communicate, and it is in this sense that the essence of education can be said to be religious.

So both Dewey and Whitehead argue that genuine education is religious education, that the aim of the teacher should be to develop a student's religious sensibilities. But they understand religion as natural piety, a faith in the potential humans have for creating together the conditions of mutually fulfilling lives. And hence the education they both advocate is practical, having to do with how students can be taught the skills by which that potential can be cashed out, that fulfillment realized. Dewey and Whitehead reject an approach to education that takes the accomplishments of the past as accesses to timeless truth, but they also reject an approach that dismisses those accomplishments as irrelevant. Both are forms of dogmatism and are idolatrous because they take the highest human values to be either transcendent or private whereas values should be understood as made by the efforts of persons working cooperatively with the limitations and opportunities provided by the natural resources, both cultural and physical, available to them.

This characterization of Dewey's views paints an expected portrait, except possibly for the surprisingly early evocation on his part of the themes famously articulated a quarter century later in *A Common Faith*. The portrait painted of Whitehead is not so familiar, however, since the importance in *Process and Reality* of God, as source of novelty and preserver of good, has given a transcendental cast to what are usually considered the key features of his philosophy. Yet in these brief and comparatively early essays, both Dewey and Whitehead are strikingly humanistic in their orientation. The good is contingent and creaturely, its creation a this-worldly task, and education the only way by which new generations can learn to use well what their predecessors have wrought so as to enhance rather than degrade the quality of their common life.

The question immediately becomes how we should take these two essays. Are they merely occasional pieces, ephemeral bouquets of passing interest, or do they mirror accurately and adequately each man's fully developed philosophical system? I shall argue that they are the latter, that they are miniatures of the theories of education each advocates and that those theories are integral to their views of person, value, and nature—to their metaphysical ontologies. If so, then Dewey's pragmatism and Whitehead's organicism are birds of the same feather, both philosophies of process. And we should take seriously their warnings in concert that ignoring a process interpretation of religion, and hence of its proper relation to the aims and methods of education, can have disastrous results.

Dewey, always indefatigably optimistic, warns of the dangers of an uneducated citizenry in order to call us to the tasks required for their overcoming:

> We need . . . to accept the responsibilities of living in an age marked by the greatest intellectual readjustment history records. There is undoubted loss of joy, of consolation, of some types of strength, and of some sources of inspiration in the change. . . . Yet nothing is gained by deliberate effort to return to ideas which have become incredible, and to symbols which have been emptied of their content of obvious meaning. (168)

Whitehead sounds less sanguine in his roll call of "the broken lives, the defeated hopes, the national failures" that are a result of the current "frivolous inertia" among his fellow citizens with regard to improving how the nation's youth are educated:

> It is difficult to restrain within oneself a savage rage. In the conditions of modern life the rule is absolute, the race which does not value trained intelligence is doomed. Not all your heroism, not all your social charm, not all your wit, not all your victories on land or at sea, can move back the finger of fate. To-day we maintain ourselves. To-morrow science will have moved forward yet one more step, and there will be no appeal from the judgment which will then be pronounced on the uneducated. (14)

Precision

In attempting to compare the views of Dewey and Whitehead with regard to education, we immediately run up against a problem of centrality. Dewey's philosophy is fundamentally an ethics, a set of claims concerning the optimal conditions for achieving our aims and for determining what they should be. Truth is a function of practices that satisfy those conditions, practices best exemplified in natural science research and formalized by Dewey as the method of experimental intelligence. A theory of educational practices must be the core of any adequate philosophy because schooling is at the core of any society, the institutional manner by which people attempt to assure the continuance from generation to generation of the conditions for achieving goods.

For Whitehead, however, education is far removed from the concerns that drive his metaphysical reflections. The only references to education in his systemic works are brief asides, a single paragraph in *Process and*

Reality, for instance, extolling the importance of cultivating a student's imagination (PR 338). Education was a topic he wrote about frequently, but always in the form of addresses given on specific occasions for a general audience. Educational theorists quote Whitehead constantly because these essays are filled with stimulating insights pithily expressed, but he made no effort to connect those observations to his metaphysics, to show the relevance of the categoreal scheme to the experience of learning and the proper forms of schooling. He proposes no theory of ethics and hence provides no explicit grounds for making normative judgments about educational practices and the role they should play in the attainment of individual and societal goods.

An obvious strategy for permitting a comparison between Dewey and Whitehead is either to elicit a metaphysical framework from Dewey's thought or an educational theory from Whitehead's. But a formidable obstacle immediately blocks the latter route: the problem of connecting Whitehead's two kinds of process. At the microcosmic level, process is the becoming of what occurs; at the macrocosmic, of what endures. Micro becoming is explicated in terms of actual occasions, processes of concrescence that are the making of space-time quanta. Macro becoming explicates how certain features of these quanta come to be replicated in the features of their successors.

There are no direct connections among the enduring macro features. An actual occasion in its coming to be characterizes a particular determinate moment, and this achievement with its character influences what then comes to be as characterizing a successor determinate moment. One actual occasion constrains another; the result is a similarity that reflects that constraint. The extensive continuum is a way of taking sequences of discrete micro processes as a single macro totality by disregarding their coming to be and attending only to the determinate features they fashion, treating episodic similarities as enduring identities. "There is a becoming of continuity, but no continuity of becoming" (PR 35).

Most things human beings think important are middle-sized enduring objects of some sort, regions of the macrocosmic extensive continuum that display what I shall call mesocosmic features. Describing the coming to be and perishing of enduring meso objects in terms of the coming to be and perishing of their constituent actual occasions is awkward, however, just as it is difficult in the natural sciences to describe molar events such as teaching a student how to read by referring only to molecular events. It can be done, and perhaps even done nonreductively, but what seems important is drowned by the details.

The technical terms Whitehead uses for describing meso and macro events are designed to highlight their micro foundations: nexūs of actual occasions, societies of nexūs, defining characteristics of societies. When he uses nontechnical meso terms—steam and barbarians, art and adventure, importance and expression—they refer to modes of civilization or kinds of thought, not to individual human beings and their day to day concerns as persons in communities. Philosophers of education therefore prefer the sturdy mesocosmic directness of Dewey's terms: problematic situations, ends in view, experimental logic, warranted assertions, meliorative goods. They find this directness in Whitehead's education essays, but the words used there are given no systematic import.

One way to give them import is by means of Whitehead's famous "flight of an aeroplane," the "method of discovery" which takes off from the ground of "particular observation" and soars into "the thin air of imaginative generalization," abstracting from all particularity. The originating ground is not a matter of bare unvarnished experience, however, but of "particular factors discerned in particular topics of human interest," among which he mentions "ethical beliefs." Thereby, the resulting metaphysical principles are assured of at least "some important application" (PR 5): at least they apply to the areas of interest from which they were generalized.

The airplane must eventually return to earth. The "scheme of philosophic categories" is used to derive "true propositions applicable to particular circumstances" other than those from which it was generalized (PR 8). By this means "some synoptic vision" is gained; the metaphysical system is taken as adequate as well as applicable (PR 5). The ways in which its categories recast our understanding and reorient our actions are then explored—until they prove inadequate and some new flight of the imagination, some new "experimental adventure" (PR 9), is launched into the thin philosophic air.

Hence, it is not only permissible but obligatory for us to generalize the concepts at work in Whitehead's comments on education until they have become metaphysical categories. Insofar as they are the same or similar to the scheme found in *Process and Reality,* the claim that Whiteheadian process philosophy is applicable to education will have been demonstrated. Conversely, Whitehead's metaphysical categories can be used as a matrix from which to derive concepts relevant to education, and if those concepts prove compatible with the familiar ones from his own education essays, the adequacy of Whitehead's philosophy is confirmed for yet another region of experience.

Traveling by the adequacy route, it is tempting to take Whitehead's theory of actual occasions as an application of his categoreal scheme to events at the meso as well as micro level. The best articulation of this strategy is Nathaniel Lawrence's. He argues that we should understand actual occasions as having "concrescent periods" of varying duration, ranging from fractions of a second to minutes and days, even to the whole of a human lifetime. One popular version of this approach is in educational theory, where the phases of learning are taken as phases of concrescence. Such moves simply won't do, however, since in order to claim that concrescent processes take time, that they can endure, we must abandon them as space-time constituents. But Whitehead insists that this atomism is the one "ultimate metaphysical truth" (PR 35). To turn actual occasions into enduring objects is to turn Whitehead into Bergson.

We are impaled on a frustrating dilemma: either abandon mesocosmic concrescences or abandon Whitehead. The way between the horns is the way of metaphor. If the notion of actual occasions is an interpretation of the categoreal scheme, applying it in such as way as to explain the cosmos in terms of basic constituting events, then that scheme can be otherwise interpreted for other purposes. If the scheme is a general matrix of abstract concepts, then we can give it more than one interpretation, including one that applies to mesocosmic events. The categoreal scheme so instantiated would share certain structural features with the scheme as instantiated by microcosmic actual occasions but not other features. In particular, there would be no claim that the dynamic patterns by which determinate individual and social values are wrought from the initial multiplicity of one's cultural heritage and personal experiences is a process constitutive of space-time realities. The categoreal scheme applied to the mesocosm of human activities, or to a subregion where those activities have educational significance, would presuppose but offer no account of its underlying constitutive atomism.

Metaphors function in exactly this way. They exploit the isomorphic features of reality in order to link one of its regions or levels or aspects to another. The aim of the linkage may be to reveal neglected features of the one by means of familiar features of the other. Or the aim may be to show the link itself, to propose that what had seemed quite disparate should henceforth be taken as similar in form and maybe therefore as identical in origin or orientation or destiny, or as causally connected. If normative educational practices can be shown to have the same shape as an actual occasion's concrescence, if this meso and that micro region can be taken as two interpretive applications of the same abstract systemic form, then it is legitimate to use the language of one to describe features of the other. But the language must be understood as metaphorical. No actual occasion comes to be by means of an expert style and no pupil's experimental inquiry results in a determinate satisfaction, for expertise and inquiry require duration and what enduring objects achieve are changes in their defining characteristics.

The metaphors, if they disclose illuminating similarities between micro and meso processes, support the further claim that although the cosmos may be composed of differing levels and regions, and although the meso and macro levels of order are dependent on the order of their micro processes, nonetheless they all exemplify the same structure. The structure exemplified is abstract and general, however. It is not that human beings are actual occasions writ large or the macrocosmos writ small, but that each in its own way instantiates the same schematic order. The many become one actual occasion specifically, but they are one metaphysical totality only vaguely.

Thus, I propose taking Whitehead's theory of actual occasions as the "root model" for his philosophy. I take it to be applicable primarily to microprocesses of becoming, but also to human beings in the sense just discussed. The root model for Dewey's philosophy is his theory of inquiry, the primary application of which is to normative scientific method, with a secondary application to human interactions and social institutions. I mean "root" here in the same sense Stephen Pepper uses it in *World Hypotheses:* with respect to a philosophical system, a "root metaphor" is the "original area" of "commonsense fact" upon which the system is based, in terms of which "structural characteristics" and "basic concepts of explanation and description" are developed for interpreting "all other areas of fact" (91). My root models are these structural characteristics that formalize a root metaphor.

I propose that Dewey and Whitehead be understood as working from the same root model, that actual occasions and experimental inquiries be taken as having the same fundamental shape. Dewey would seem to agree, if it is clear this shape is "genetic-functional" and not merely "morphological" (1937, 151–53). When applied to human beings, both root models are of the shape of action. They each stipulate the same dynamic form for praxis, its necessary conditions. Aristotle's four causes function identically as the conditions by reference to which a thing, in this case an action, can be understood to be what it is. So by mapping the root models of Dewey and Whitehead onto Aristotle's root model, their systems can be seen to be of the same species (see Allan 1990, ch. 1). If so, we have a categoreal justification for talking about how Dewey's and Whitehead's views on education critique and complement each other.

For Dewey, "the antecedent conditions of inquiry" are the natural forces—inorganic and organic, human and nonhuman—that encompass a person, that comprise what is for her an "indeterminate situation" (1938, 109). This situation may in the past have been a resource satisfying her needs and desires, but it is dynamic—"disturbed, troubled, ambiguous, confused, full of conflicting tendencies, obscure" (109)—and so indeterminate "with respect to its issue," to its "significance," to the "import and portend" of her interactions with it (110). This unsettling indeterminacy of the very things one is dependent upon is the material condition for inquiry.

Whitehead's material condition for concrescence is similar. The emergence of an actual occasion begins with "the mere reception of the actual world as a multiplicity of private centers of feeling, implicated in a nexus of mutual presupposition" (PR 212). This reception is through a process of "abstraction," however. It is not at all a "mere reception" but rather one shaped by its potentiality for relevance. The initial data are "felt under a 'perspective' which [for each initial datum] is the objective datum of the feeling" (231). The objective data, the resources out of which the actual occasion will become, need to be taken account of. But it is unclear how; they are indeterminate with respect to their issue.

When, in Dewey's account, a person's needs and desires cease being satisfied, when the significance of what is going on seems to threaten the continued success of his interactions, the situation becomes "problematic." This shift marks the "evocation of inquiry," for "to see that a situation requires inquiry is the initial step in inquiry" (111). A contrast has emerged between the person's situation as it is and as he wants it to be, and this want orients him within that situation toward its alteration. His goal is to eliminate this contrast, the possibility of doing so functioning as a final condition or outcome aspiration that governs his behavior. The factual and conceptual constituents of the situation will be henceforth "entertained" or "dismissed" because of assessments of their "relevancy and irrelevancy" to this goal, his effort to resolve the contrast, to return his situation to a nonproblematic status (112).

In Whitehead's system, the equivalent to the human organism's continual need to satisfy its desires is the "creative advance," the requirement that the perishing of the multiplicity of determinate entities comprising present actuality give rise to successors that are each "other than the entities given in disjunction" (21). Thus, the actual occasion must have a "subjective aim" which is also its "initial aim," an orientation toward some definite outcome, such that right from the first its character is not just that of a process but a process of becoming a determinate unity. If there is to be a solution to the problem of transforming a multiplicity of initial data, the perspective from which those data are prehended must be one that includes their potential for integration. They are "compatible for synthesis" because an aim at synthesis governs the actual occasion from its inception: "the one subject is the final end which conditions each component feeling" (223).

Such an outcome, however, is vague with respect both to its character and to how it might be actualized. So the person in Dewey's model of inquiry formulates a plan, a course of action that she thinks will solve the problem. Any such plan has two aspects: "facts" and "suggestions." "The facts in the case" are the "settled" constituents of the problematic situation, the observable "conditions that must be reckoned with or taken account of in any relevant solution that is proposed" (113). A "suggestion" is a vague possibility—an "idea," or "meaning," or "hypothesis" are its more focused successors—for how the observed facts might be linked together into a more complicated fact, "examined with reference to its functional fitness; its capacity as a means of resolving the given [problematic] situation" (114). The person's plan thus involves taking her situation not in terms of its immediately given features but with respect to a structure those features are taken as illustrating. Her suggested structure, her idea for how things relevant to her problem hang together meaningfully, is the formal condition for achieving the ends she desires, because it links what is actually given to possible alternatives by means of a general form that points to how the given can be reformed, how it can be reordered so as to provide what she wants of it.

For Whitehead also, the final condition is initially vague. The aim of the actual occasion is at "some" outcome, and so is always a "lure for feeling" (85), an always functioning evocation of prehensions that can contribute to a resolution of the occasion's indeterminateness. But what its aim might be changes as the "subjective forms" that are the formal conditions of the concrescence alter. A subjective form is a pattern, and when it functions as a structure of how it might be possible for available data, both physical and conceptual, to be harmonized, it is a "proposition": "a manner of germaneness of a certain set of eternal objects to a certain set of actual entities" (188). Propositional feelings reorder the data with respect to their mutual relevance, such that a multiplicity of data can be treated either as one datum or as contrasts, as coherent and consistent despite, or rather because of, their differences. "The process of concrescence is a progressive integration of feelings controlled by their subjective forms" (232). These integrations increase the degree of determinateness characterizing the concrescent process, clarifying and constraining both the ways of reconciliation still available and hence the likely result.

"Reasoning" for Dewey is the process of connecting meanings to other meanings, formulating a "proposition" that "indicates operations which can be performed to test its applicability" (115). The facts and ideas taken as relevant to the problem are made "operational," linked up "in the definite ways that are required to produce a definite end" (117). A pathway toward a solution is devised, and appropriate "existential operations" then "bring about the re-ordering of environing conditions required to produce a settled and unified situation" (121). But it is not that the reasoning comes first, followed by the existential operations, for as the environing conditions alter so also the facts and ideas taken as relevant alter. The facts are always "trial facts" (117), the ideas always tentative propositions, the character of the problematic situation and hence its resolution always at issue. Elsewhere, Dewey calls this whole transformational process "thinking": "that mode of serial responsive behavior to a problematic situation in which transition to the relatively settled and clear is effected" (1929, 181). Thinking is the efficient condition for success, the process of practical reasoning by which the person's hypothesis is concretized. Thinking is the trajectory of his interactions with his situation, as guided by his ideas, as he effects the changes proposed.

In Whitehead's ontology, the efficient condition of this transformation, this making from a multiplicity of atomic accomplishments a new accomplishment, is "creativity." For each process of concrescence is the creative advance canalized, sheer cosmic energy ordered by the determining functions of data, aim, and form into a concrete actuality. Past actual occasions are not efficient causes, even though Whitehead often refers to them as such. They provide the only resources available for concrescence and so condition what results, but they do not account for why there is a result. This vector character to the cosmos is beyond explication because presupposed by every explanation, every attainment, and every obligation. It is "in the nature of things" that through the power of creativity "the many, which are the universe disjunctively, becomes"—again and yet ever again—"the one actual occasion, which is the universe conjunctively" (244).

A given material situation, an ideal of it as more satisfactory, a corrective reforming possibility, the effecting of a new situation: this fourfold of conditions, endlessly iterated, constitutes a general model of human action implicate in both Dewey's and Whitehead's root models. Dewey's summative definition is that "inquiry is the controlled or directed transformation of an indeterminate situation into one that is so determinate in its constituent distinctions and relations as to convert the elements of the original situation into a unified whole" (1938, 108). This definition could just as well be describing the phases of concrescence that explicate Whitehead's notion of an actual occasion.

Generalization

The cash value of this long excursus into the root models structuring the thought of Dewey and Whitehead is that we can now understand better why both philosophers should think religion so important educationally. I have argued their root models are functionally identical, and that therefore the theory of inquiry and the theory of concrescence can be taken as metaphors of each other and of the form of human action. Their approaches to educational issues should therefore be similar because the interpretive frameworks of those approaches are metaphorically linked. Their views are mutually illuminating, not by accident but for fundamental systemic reasons.

The root models when interpreted with respect to human beings characterize their activities as always concretely situated. Religion has to do with ultimate ends and ideals, with meanings that fundamentally orient our lives, and so it functions as a final condition of action. If education is a societal institution the aim of which is to develop adults able to act effectively, to resolve individual and communal problems, to improve their situation so that it better supports their potential for self-fulfillment and better provides for the common weal, then it must have a religious dimension.

Natural piety, for Dewey, is the vague orienting confidence that in any given situation there are realizable possibilities for human betterment. It is the belief that the problems we face are addressable through human effort, that our making a positive difference is a reasonable guiding principle for belief and action. Seeking to meliorate the human condition is in this sense a moral imperative that we need to feel and accept in order to become good persons. For Whitehead, reverence for the present is the confidence that our physical surroundings and cultural heritage are relevant for actions able to reshape the present so that it might better fulfill human needs. It is the realization that we have a duty to take up this challenge as best we can. Developing the skill to use ideas effectively needs to become an aspiration essential to our sense of who we are, to our character.

Thus, the importance both philosophers accord religion is not a rhetorical gesture but exactly what follows from understanding the world as a natural process in which humans are situated organisms. Our actions are always contextual, arising over against that context as an urge toward possibilities for achievement the context does not provide or does not guarantee. To be pious or reverent is to take such possibilities seriously, to be committed to the difficult task of finding a way to make them into worthwhile ends and workable means. Religion is about ideals that should be at work in the world, enhancing the quality and character of what gets done. It is a factor in things being accomplished in a manner that is properly intelligent or civilized.

The method of scientific inquiry, according to Dewey, is thus the most important thing that students need to learn because it echoes their nature normatively. *Homo sapiens* has evolved as an organism with the capacity to interact intelligently with its environment. Thinking is the Darwinian tool by which humans can optimize the conditions for their survival and flourishing. The capacity to think may be genetic but its exercise is learned, and students can only learn to inquire intelligently if they are situated in inquiry-oriented learning environments. For inquiry is a practice not a fact, a set of skills to exercise not a body of information to possess.

Good teaching, therefore, means not lecturing on the nature and function of inquiry but surrounding students with contexts worth inquiring about. The teacher should find or invent a situation students find problematic, encourage them to explore ways the problem might be resolved, then critique with them the results of their effort. By reiterating this pattern of experiment and critique, students will develop their ability to discern what ends are best in a given situation and what means most appropriate. "Every subject and lesson [should be] taught in connection with its bearing upon creation and growth of the kind of power of observation, inquiry, reflection and testing that are the heart of scientific intelligence" (1958, 168). That is, subjects "should be treated in their social bearings and consequences—consequences in the way, on one side, of problems and on the other side of opportunities" (182).

It is not enough for us to learn how to be good problem solvers, to become clever technicians. We need also the confidence that our efforts are functionally worthwhile, that the hypothesizing and the effecting are not their own justification. We need the meliorative confidence that a fully functioning person is a genuine possibility and that it is in the nature of being human to aspire to realize such a possibility. "The religious attitude," says Dewey, involves both "a sense of the possibilities of existence" and "a devotion to the cause of those possibilities" (1929, 242). So the task of education is to nurture the development of good people by helping them learn to appreciate their natural capacity for doing good and to exercise it intelligently.

A democracy needs intelligent citizens; it is only as good as its people are good. For when in the making of public policies those affected by a policy are genuinely involved in its determination, the laws of the land and their implementation will be for the common weal only if the society's citizens are able to distinguish between their desires and their needs and only if they understand their own well-being to involve that of others. The context for human action is always a social context, involving a shared heritage of accomplishments institutionalized in attitudes, customs, rituals, and law. Aspirations for social change or for resisting change arise in response to the perceived limitations and the fragility of that heritage. Public and private efforts to secure those dreams lead to conflicting goals, strategies, and tactics, to conditions of instability in which both established and proposed values are put at risk.

These conditions call for citizens who are able to advocate interests without reducing them to factional dogmas, keeping them interlaced with the general interest and the long-term viabilities, seeking compromise where possible while avoiding recurrent exclusions and other modes of continuing dominance by a given majority. Likening it to "the method of effecting change by means of empirical inquiry and test," Dewey argues that "the very heart of political democracy is adjudication of social differences by discussion and exchange of views" (1958, 157). Citizens in a democracy have a religious vision insofar as they seek reconciliation and healing not merely as pragmatic responses to immediate problems but also as practices that will reconstruct how their society functions. They aspire to fashion a good society, one in which the citizens use their differences and disagreements as a resource for cooperatively making a way of life that enhances the quality of the goods each can and does enjoy. A good society is one that functions intelligently and so makes it possible for its members to live good lives. Just as much as good citizens are prerequisite to the making of a good society, so also they are only as good as their societies make it possible for them to be.

Whitehead's version of the human action model, because its root is cosmological rather than ethical, helps us notice features that Dewey's version tends to neglect. For instance, and I think most importantly, a meliorist faith should not be utopianist. Actual occasions, and hence actual persons whose actions have the same functional form as concrescences, will always find their situation problematic. Successful applications of the method of experimental inquiry may improve things, but meliorations of this sort do not entail any eventual utopian outcome. The resolution of a problem is never more than a temporary expedient, because it is impossible to include all that has been prehended and nonetheless fashion it into a maximally intense unity. Breadth must be sacrificed to gain intensity, and intensity to preserve breadth. The best bread baked for a situation is always half a loaf, no matter how promising or how meager its ingredients.

Whitehead's thought is susceptible to an utopianist interpretation, however. He introduces as a "derivative notion" to his scheme of metaphysical categories a primordial actual entity, God. One of God's functions is to provide each actual occasion with an initial aim, the originative orienting final condition of its becoming (PR 108). Whitehead explicitly insists that the aim is relative to the particular givenness the new occasion supersedes: the aim is "at the best for that *impasse,*" which in certain situations can be so meager a finality as to make God seem "ruthless," "remorseless," the "goddess of mischief" (244). But it is an easy enough mistake to extend God's provision of the best possibility for that situation to include the coordination of all such parochial bests into a best possibility for the whole. Were this the case, God's orienting lures would always have an ultimate totalized good in view, persuasively bending the world progressively toward its realization. The related notion of God's consequent nature then encourages a transcendent version of this interpretation. The bests that the many occasions manage to accomplish severally are integrated with "tender care" into God's nature. They are objectively immortalized as aspects of a single, time-space surpassing, Good in which "nothing that can be saved" is lost (346). The differing goods of worldly achievement are reconciled in an all-encompassing totality, if not in some omega point at history's end, then at least in the everlasting totality of the divine life.

Dewey's critique of all forms of nontemporality should alert us to the likely incoherence of attempting to interpolate into the philosophy of organism characteristics of divinity that are tied inextricably to notions of eternal realities. But Whitehead needs no God to account for the originative orientation of each particular concrescence. If the desires of mesocosmic organisms can be applied metaphorically not only to organic behaviors of every sort but also to actual occasions, then the past is resource enough. Dewey shows how situations can be experienced as insufficient, and how energy can be oriented toward their improvement, without having recourse to anything other than the features of that situation. No deus ex machina is required to explain the capacity of temporal things to idealize their given world and so be lured toward a better one.

In the absence of such transcendent powers, with their potential for visions and lures of unlimited scope, we are less in danger of imagining erroneously that a temporally ultimate and all-encompassing best world is possible. For if all aims are ineluctably situational then all outcomes are unavoidably limited. No matter how successful they may be deemed when seen from one perspective, there are necessarily other perspectives that will show them as less successful or even as failures. Indeed, the endemic inadequacy of every achieved good is why the cosmos is essentially dynamic, its actuality always surpassing itself toward new actuality.

Whitehead expresses this counter-utopian point at the macro level by distinguishing in *The Function of Reason* between appetition and entropy, and with respect to the discipline of appetition between speculative and practical reason. In *Adventures of Ideas,* he makes his point by a series of contrasts: Barbarians and Christians, Steam and Democracy, Instinct and Intelligence, Theory and Method, Beauty and Truth. The first of each pair are the forces of novelty: conscious or senseless agencies that expand the scope of what counts as experience, as interpretable fact, as the given. They are, or they are urges toward, adequacy, the world prehended in all its discordant, confusing, often senseless, multiplexity. The contrasting members of each pair are forces of order, effecting some sort of unity from things, making the relative chaos into an intelligible world, a meaningful and well-wrought harmony of components. This result can be achieved only if the components and the modes of their relationships are clarified, but this means limiting how they are defined and functionally determined. Adequate scope of detail must be sacrificed in order to obtain intensity of integration.

On the one hand, the problem with speculation is that it cannot distinguish between the important and the trivial; novelty becomes a narcotic that makes it insensitive to the practicalities involved in achieving and sustaining genuine values. On the other hand, the problem with systematization is that its success blinds it to what those achievements have had to exclude, blinding it—ironically—to the practicalities requisite for successful adaptation as the conditions for genuine value change. Neither speculation nor systematization by itself suffices. Whitehead warns against both the "dogmatic fallacy" and "the fallacy of discarding method" (AI 223), extolling in their stead "the almost incredible secret" that speculative thinking can be "itself subject to orderly method," that it can be divested of "its anarchic character without destroying its function of reaching beyond set bounds" (FR 66).

This interplay of speculative and practical reason is, of course, scientific inquiry in the reformed sense Whitehead advocates, a style of thinking he finds as appropriate to metaphysics and the social sciences as to the natural sciences. So Whitehead echoes Dewey's emphasis on the centrality of inquiry, and his pedagogical observations thus emphasize students in active situations using ideas with imaginative freedom and then testing those uses rigorously. The results of any inquiry, however, are necessarily—in principle—inadequate, because the method required to attain the result has framed the situation selectively. In excluding what was irrelevant to the task at hand, inquiry lets slip away what might be crucial for the next situation. Students, learning how to think experimentally, need to learn the limits as well as enjoy the fruits of their success.

Whitehead's three "stages of mental growth," famously outlined in the two chapters of *The Aims of Education* following the one discussed in the first part of this essay, need to be interpreted in this light. Romance and Precision are incommensurable activities, the one valuing adequacy the other coherence. Romance is a grasp after the importance of a thing, "the excitement consequent on the transition from the bare facts to the realisations of the import of their unexplored relationships, whereas in Precision "width of relationship is subordinate to exactness of formulation" (18). The import of a thing, the width of its possible connections to other things, awaiting our exploration, fades into the background as we set about actually working out a way to determine what any of those connections might be.

Unfocused raucous inclusiveness and focused frameworks of ordered relevance: thesis and antithesis. Generalization, the final stage of mental growth, is thus "Hegel's synthesis. It is a return to romanticism with added advantage of classified ideas and relevant technique" (19). The synthesis is not a procrustean Precision imposed on the Romance, nor a protean Romance shrugging off such impositions. Synthesis is the harmonization of both Romance and Precision: the breadth of a thing's possibilities deepened by their ways of relatedness being evaluated, the resulting insight into the precise nature of the thing enlarged by being taken as the focal center of a context.

To understand by means of Generalization "is always to exclude a background of intellectual incoherence" while at the same time "confronting [that] intellectual system with the importance of its omissions" (AI 47). Generalization is thus inherently unstable because it both achieves its goal and recognizes the goal's insufficiency. Hence "education should consist in a continual repetition of such cycles" and "we should banish the idea of a mythical, far-off end of education" (AE 19). The meliorism belongs to Romance: a religious confidence in the importance of ideals because they are realizable as ends and are useful as tools for achieving those ends. Precision is how tools are sharpened that give those ideals a cutting edge, but when the tools are put to use in Generalization, clearly defined ends wrought by clearly stipulated methods, the limiting focus this honing required can be saved from dogmatism only if kept always in the context of the initiating religious vision—so that Generalization's effectiveness is always understood as incomplete.

Hence, for Whitehead social intelligence in a democracy is Sisyphean, endlessly addressing the problematic in the hope of achieving a workable solution, but never expecting, nor even yearning for, a final solution. The Art of reconciling Truth and Beauty is an Adventure the successes of which are unavoidably partial and failure endemic. The values we have achieved are always at risk, those we seek always just beyond our grasp. Peace not Utopia is the religious vision: that even failure and loss can have a use, can be redeemed by becoming relevant data for subsequent efforts.

The greatest educational challenge for anyone committed to a process understanding of the Dewey-Whitehead variety is how to teach students a method of inquiry, a strategy for concrescent achievement, that is imbued with religious vision but avoids utopianism of either a progressivist or transcendental variety. The allure of Utopia detracts from the problems of men and women by denying that ideals are only regulative principles by which to assess the intelligence of our efforts to redeem in some momentary way an ever-perishing present. Utopianism makes ideals into constitutive principles that draw our interest and energy away from holy ground toward the chimeral idolatry of an imperishable reality objectively immortal beyond our world or still to come as its apotheosis.

The counter-utopian religious humanism advocated by Dewey and Whitehead is the better way, but also the more difficult. For it promises "undoubted loss of joy, of consolation, of some types of strength," and disvalues our "heroism," our "social charm," and all our "victories on land or at sea." We ought to heed their advice and make of education a place where natural piety and reverence for life's possibilities lure students to acquire the stylish intelligence required of citizens in a democratic society. If we fail to do so, our common lot is not likely even to be meliorating but rather, as with all obscurantisms, to be a slow or not so slow descent into situations that are ever more narrowing in the opportunities they provide for human accomplishment.

Works Cited

Allan, George. 1990. *The Realizations of the Future: An Inquiry into the Authority of Praxis.* Albany: State University of New York Press.

Dewey, John. 1908. "Religion and Our Schools." In *Essays on Pragmatism and Truth 1907–1909: The Middle Works of John Dewey 1899–1914, Volume 4,* ed. Jo Ann Boydston. Carbondale and Edwardsville: Southern Illinois University Press, 1977, 165–77. Originally published *Hibbert Journal* 6 (1908): 796–809.

———. 1929. *The Quest for Certainty: A Study of the Relation of Knowledge and Action.* In *The Later Works of John Dewey 1925–1953, Volume 4: 1929,* ed. Jo Ann Boydston. Carbondale and Edwardsville: Southern Illinois University Press, 1984. Originally published New York: Minton, Balch and Co., 1929.

———. 1937. "Whitehead's Philosophy." In *The Later Works of John Dewey 1925–1953, Volume 11: 1935–1937,* ed. Jo Ann Boydston. Carbondale and Edwardsville: Southern Illinois University Press, 1987, 146–154. Originally published *Philosophical Review* 46 (1937): 170–77.

———. 1938. Logic: The Theory of Inquiry. In *The Later Works of John Dewey 1925–1953, Volume 12: 1938,* ed. Jo Ann Boydston. Carbondale and Edwardsville: Southern Illinois University Press, 1986. Originally published New York: Henry Holt and Co., 1938.

———. 1958. *Philosophy of Education.* Paterson, N.J.: Littlefield, Adams and Co. Originally published as *Problems of Men.* New York: The Philosophical Library, 1946. Its chapters are scattered across Boydston, ed., *The Later Works of John Dewey 1925–1953,* volumes 11, 13–15.

Lawrence, Nathaniel. 1961. "Time, Value, and the Self." In *The Relevance of Whitehead,* ed. Ivor Leclerc. London: George Allen and Unwin, 145–66.

Pepper, Stephen C. 1961. *World Hypotheses: A Study in Evidence.* Berkeley: University of California Press.

Whitehead, Alfred North. 1916. "The Aims of Education: A Plea for Reform." In *The Aims of Education and Other Essays,* chapter 1:1–14. Originally published *Mathematical Gazette* 8 (1916): 191–203.

———. AE. *The Aims of Education and Other Essays.* New York: The Free Press, 1967. Originally published New York: The Macmillan Company, 1929.

———. AI. *Adventures of Ideas.* New York: The Free Press, 1967. Originally published New York: Macmillan Publishing Co., 1933.

_________. FR. *The Function of Reason.* Boston: Beacon Press, 1958. Originally published Princeton: Princeton University Press, 1929.

———. PR. *Process and Reality: An Essay in Cosmology,* corrected edition, ed. David Ray Griffin and Donald W. Sherburne. New York: Free Press, 1978. Originally published New York: Macmillan Publishing Co., 1929.

CHAPTER 4

Spirit and Eternity in Whitehead and Santayana

PATRICK SHADE

[O]ur visions are usually not only our most interesting but our most respectable contributions to the world in which we play our part.

—William James

Alfred North Whitehead and George Santayana stand out among twentieth-century philosophers in virtue of their embrace of the eternal. In distinction from those who regard it as a hypostatization of the temporal,[1] both Whitehead and Santayana consider the eternal to be logically prior to existence. Although neither neglects time, each distinguishes what is eternal from what exists temporally and argues that it plays a significant role in the systematic analysis of our experience. Santayana, for instance, celebrates the realm of essence as "an eternal background of reality, which all minds when they are truly awake find themselves considering together."[2] Essences contrast with all existence in that each is what it is and remains forever unaffected by the flux of matter. Whitehead identifies a similar realm, God's primordial envisagement of eternal objects, which is necessary for, yet whose nature is also completely free of influence from, the becoming of actual entities. Essences and eternal objects alike are eternal qualities that are what they are apart from the adventures of the temporal world.

Writing in the early decades of the twentieth century, neither philosopher was unaware of the other's work. Indeed, Santayana identifies Whitehead as a contemporary who corroborates his own view of essences, noting that his colleague not only recognizes essences but also distinguishes them from events or existents. He adds that "[i]f there are impurities in Whitehead's description, they arise, not from his conception of the field of essence itself, where his mathematical expertness gives him an enviable scope and fertility, but rather from refraction in the thicker atmosphere through which he approaches it" (RB 171). Although Whitehead does not explicitly address Santayana's doctrine of essence, he critically notes the skeptical reduction Santayana makes in *Scepticism and Animal Faith.* Whitehead explains that "the exact point where Santayana differs from the organic philosophy is his implicit assumption that 'intuitions themselves' cannot be among the 'data of intuition,' that is to say, the data of other intuitions. This possibility is what Santayana denies and the organic philosophy asserts."[3] Although both philosophers embrace similar views of the eternal, their comments about one another suggest the relevance of other positions which uncover deeper differences.

How strong, then, is the kinship between Whitehead and Santayana?[4] Close examination of their accounts of the eternal ("eternal objects" for Whitehead and "essences" for Santayana) reveals considerable agreement. Each identifies a similar nature as well as a "realm" to which the eternal belongs. Yet while attributing independent reality to the eternal, neither subscribes to a Platonic view that gives it ontological priority. Indeed, each philosopher subordinates the eternal to the temporal in at least one important respect. In the process, both criticize attempts to attribute efficacy and inherent value to the eternal.

Although Whitehead and Santayana share a common view of the nature and efficacy of the eternal, the role it plays in the overall system of each differs and reveals the significantly unique *vision* of each thinker. In particular, Whitehead's treatment of eternal objects is consistent with his organic philosophy's emphasis on the interweaving of elements, which secures a processive but interconnected world, while Santayana's treatment of essence helps him articulate a specific view of the nature of spiritual life. The former gives us an interactive world in which we are intimate contributors; our conscious experience adds to the novelty and complexity that condition the actual world. The latter gives us a bustling world which generates a conscious experience that may be enjoyed but that fails to exert its own efficacy. The life of spirit makes possible a unique perspective on the world that is freed from the normal concerns of our animal existence. Whitehead and Santayana agree about the origin of consciousness but disagree about its function, role, and significance. My project here is to examine how each philosopher provides a detailed account of the eternal and gives it a significant place that highlights the distinctive character of his respective system. My goal in the following discussion, then, is to explore Whitehead and Santayana's treatment of the eternal especially as it illuminates the unique vision of each philosopher.

Santayana and the Realm of Essence

Santayana treats essences in both epistemological and metaphysical contexts. When he "discovers" essences as a consequence of his skeptical reduction in *Scepticism and Animal Faith,*[5] his primary focus is epistemological. Here Santayana drives skepticism to its most radical end. His central argument is that the deliverance of intuition[6] cannot corroborate belief in the existence of things, for all that is given in intuition is an appearance, the datum of which is an essence that in itself bears witness to nothing other than itself. Only essences, understood as any discriminable or conceivable character, are given in intuition. Santayana argues that it is animal faith which interprets essences given in intuition as signs of facts and thus moves beyond appearance to belief in existing things. Santayana gives a more exhaustive treatment of the nature of essence in his later, more metaphysical work, *The Realms of Being.*[7] Here his goal is to explore the unique realm of essence in distinction from the realms of matter, truth, and spirit. Each realm embodies a distinctive mode of being we uncover when exploring the rich and complex contours of human life. Santayana explains that one of his chief concerns is to describe each realm without introducing considerations appropriate to the others. In particular, since essence is distinct from existence, our description of the realm of essence must not be tainted by reference to the selection, valuation, and alteration characteristic of the realm of matter. The realm of essence lacks animal purpose and preference as well as activity and susceptibility. In it, peace and perfect democracy reign.

The chief characteristics of essences, according to Santayana, are that they are self-identical, individual yet universal, eternal, and infinite in number. The realm of essence is "the unwritten catalogue, prosaic and infinite, of all the characters possessed by such things as happen to exist, together with the characters which all different things would possess if they existed. It is the sum of mentionable objects, of terms about which, or in which, something might be said" (SAF 77). Each essence—whether a quality or pattern—is a fully determinate character that is self-identical with itself, for it is just *that* specific character which it is. Alizarin crimson is a definite form distinct from cadmium red, even though we call both red. Santayana argues that no essence "is vague in itself, or other than just what it is" (SAF 68). Each essence is complete in itself; none waits upon the adventures of existence for its completion.[8] Consequently, an essence defines itself or is "grounded in itself without reference to any other" (RB 78). Each is what it is in virtue of being the positive determinate character that it is, and so each essence is individual. Its individuality consists in "being perfectly self-contained and real only by virtue of its intrinsic character" (RB 18). As Santayana explains, "Had each term no private, indefinable, positive essence of its own, it could not justify those exclusions by which we define it, nor could it fill its anointed place and spread out its eternal intrinsic relations in the realm of essence" (RB 56). Every essence excludes every other essence, for no essence, as individual, is another.

The individuality of an essence remains unaffected by where or how many times it may appear. Santayana argues that an essence may be manifested in existence repeatedly without limit, for nothing external to it can alter or otherwise affect its identity. Existence neither adds to nor detracts from what it is in itself. Each essence is thus universal, that is, capable of, though not requiring, repetition or multiple manifestation in material existence. Santayana urges, however, that we correctly understand the *basis* of this universality; he explains that "[e]very essence is universal not because there are repeated manifestations of it (for there need be no manifestations at all) but because it is individuated internally by its character, not externally by its position in the flux of nature . . ." (RB 36). An essence's universality indicates that it may have many instantiations or none at all; in either case, it remains wholly available for, but unaffected by, material selection.

Clearly, then, essences do not *exist,* as do things in the realm of matter. While an existing thing wears one determinate character followed by another, the character of an essence does not and cannot change. Santayana thus contrasts essence, which is compacted of internal relations, with existence, which suffers the adventures of external relations. Each essence is static, complete, and self-identical; existing entities are in flux and incomplete, awaiting the next step in the dance of time to further characterize them. Moreover, essences are eternal. This is not because they persist through time and change, but rather because each is self-identical with itself. This self-identity cannot be altered by time or anything else; otherwise an essence would not be *that* essence. Change in the realm of essence, then, is impossible. Essences remain eternally what they are, without the threat of destruction or the promise of fulfillment endemic to every temporal existent. Being nonexistent, they cannot be affected by existence. Moreover, they are equally incapable of affecting anything existent. Santayana argues that "it is only by being distributed in the field of action that essences can add for a moment external and variable relations to those which their proper nature involves" (RB 276). Since they are themselves nonexistent, however, "[i]t is matter, impatient of form, that fills form with a forward tension, and realises one essence after another" (RB 286). Essences thus lack the power and efficacy that belong to material existents. Acknowledging this, however, is no derogation of essences, for such inertness belongs to them *qua* essences. While they do not exist, essences nevertheless have a mode of being proper to themselves. The capacity for change and efficacy belongs to the realm of matter; perfect unchanging being belongs to that of essence.

Finally, Santayana explains that each essence is primary. None is more or less basic or real than any other. Although we might think a complex essence depends on more simple essences for its determinate character, simple essences are not constituents of complex essences. Every essence is an *individual* essence in its own right. Santayana argues that "the essence of the whole is not compounded of the essences of the parts, but is a new essence, a summary unity, perhaps simpler, at any rate original" (RB 139). We might object that if the simple essence of blue and the complex essence of blue sky were not fundamentally the same, we could not relate them. Santayana insists, however, that each is a distinct individual essence in the realm of essence. Through discourse, we make them the same; that is, we *call* them the same and so *identify* them. But two essences, *qua* essences, cannot be identified, for each has its own self-identity. In the realm of essence, every essence is primary; "every degree of complexity is as calmly enthroned as every other: none is more primitive or natural or safe than the rest, since all are necessary and eternal" (RB 142). Every discriminable character, then, is a single individual essence. Additionally, no essence possesses a value that gives it a privileged position in the realm of essence, for value, selection, and privilege are the result of the animal perspective, belonging to the realm of matter. The realm of essence, then, is a perfect democracy of an infinite number of individual essences.

Unlike Plato who casts his favorite essences as normative paradigms, Santayana contends that essences are both metaphysically and morally neutral. Indeed, he argues that the realm of essence, properly understood, lacks any of the prioritizations or valuations that philosophers typically impute to it. He argues that "[i]n the realm of essence no emphasis falls on these favourite forms which does not fall equally on every other member of that infinite continuum" (SAF 79). The good, the true, and the beautiful are genuine essences, but so too are the bad, the false, and the ugly. Each is an essence with equal impotence in affecting the world, and each in itself is equally lacking in value. One essence may be valued by a living organism, but this emphasis is due to material selection and not to anything belonging to the essence *qua* essence. Santayana thus sweeps aside animal selection, admitting every character into the realm of essence and so expanding the traditional realm of forms into an infinite realm of essence. Moreover, Santayana denies that any essence is the intrinsic essence of all existence; no intuition of an essence probes more deeply into the nature of things than any other. In contrast to such traditional thinkers as Plato and Augustine, the novelty and unique insight of Santayana's account of essence lies in his recognition of the infinity, neutrality, and parity of essences that populate this realm. As shall see below, Santayana attributes the same neutrality and inefficacy to spirit, that product of psyche which enjoys essences.

Eternal Objects in Whitehead's Organic Philosophy

Though his language differs, Whitehead's basic characterization of eternal objects bears a strong resemblance to Santayana's account of essence. In his later thought (represented especially by *Process and Reality*), Whitehead introduces these qualities under the designation of "Eternal Objects, *or* Pure Potentials for the Specific Determination of Fact, *or* Forms of Definiteness" (PR 22).[9] Examples include a definite shade of a color, a specific emotion, a number, or a geometrical shape. Whitehead's explicit goal in discussing eternal objects is to uncover their role as constituents of what is fully real, that is, the actual entity. He identifies actual entities as "the final real things of which the world is made up. There is no going behind actual entities to find anything more real" (PR 18). Whitehead's metaphysics explains the process whereby actual entities become the entities that they are. He describes each as an interdependent drop of experience which *prehends* its past actual world (including both what is temporal and eternal) to become what it is.[10] Through prehension, eternal objects are said to have *ingression* in actual entities. Their ingression helps to account for the permanence, identity, and solidarity of the world. Actual entities *alone,* however, are fully real; Whitehead captures this doctrine in his ontological principle that states that "actual entities are the only *reasons;* so that to search for a *reason* is to search for one or more actual entities" (PR 24). Everything in the universe must have reference to some actual entity or another, for "in separation from actual entities there is nothing, merely nonentity—'The rest is silence'" (PR 43). As we shall see,

Whitehead's ontological principle plays a key role in distinguishing his philosophy from Santayana's.

Nevertheless, Whitehead describes eternal objects as self-identical and individual, just as Santayana does. He explains that "each eternal object is an individual which, in its own peculiar fashion, is what it is. This individuality is the individual essence of the object, and cannot be described otherwise than as being itself."[11] Nothing can alter the identity of an eternal object, for as Whitehead notes, "There can be no distortion of the individual essence without thereby producing a different eternal object" (SMW 171). As their name suggests, these objects are eternal, that is, temporality is not relevant to them. Though each is a form of definiteness which is a potential ingredient in the becoming of actual entities, neither time nor selection by a temporal entity affects the being of an eternal object. In light of this consideration, Whitehead formally defines an eternal object as "[a]ny entity whose conceptual recognition does not involve a necessary reference to any definite actual entities of the temporal world" (PR 44). Much like Santayana, then, he contrasts the eternal with what is temporal, existing, and actual. Eternal objects escape the vicissitudes of time and change which are central to the being of actual entities. A color is eternal and, as Whitehead says, "haunts time like a spirit. It comes and it goes. But where it comes, it is the same colour" (SMW 87). Each color is a form of definiteness which an existing event may wear, but the fact that it is worn does not affect the quality of the color *qua* color.

Further, Whitehead describes eternal objects as universal, in the sense of being repeatable, since an essence may have ingression in any number of actual entities without thereby altering its character. Whitehead thus agrees with Santayana that eternal qualities are both universal and individual. He makes, however, two significant additional points about eternal objects, both of which are consequences of important principles in his organic philosophy. The first follows from the ontological principle and stipulates that eternal objects are abstract; the second point, a consequence of the principle of relativity, requires a reconceptualization of the relation between universals and particulars. As we shall see, each of these points serves to distinguish Whitehead's vision from Santayana's.

First, Whitehead argues that eternal objects are by their very nature abstract. He explains that by "abstract" he means "that what an eternal object is in itself—that is to say, its essence—is comprehensible without reference to some one particular occasion of experience" (SMW 18). Consequently, *qua* potential forms, eternal objects lack the full concreteness of the actual entities they characterize. Moreover, eternal objects are neutral with respect to their ingression; Whitehead thus agrees with Santayana that what is eternal lacks the power of selection that belongs to actual, existing entities. As a consequence of his ontological principle, Whitehead explains that, though distinct from actual entities, eternal objects nevertheless must have relevance to those entities. A central tenet of his process philosophy is that "[t]he things which are temporal arise by their participation in the things which are eternal" (PR 40). Relevance requires decision and order, both of which are impossible without the agency of an actual entity. Whitehead secures relevance for *all* eternal objects by arguing that they subsist in the primordial nature of one actual entity, namely God. God's primordial nature is his "conceptual valuation of the entire multiplicity of eternal objects" (PR 31). Whitehead explains that "[t]he general relationships of eternal objects to each other, relationships of diversity and of pattern, are their relationships in God's conceptual realization. Apart from this realization, there is mere isolation indistinguishable from nonentity" (PR 257). Actualization is selection among these objects, but it is a selection that requires limitation and gradation. God's primordial nature brings order to the aboriginal multiplicity of eternal objects and renders selection among them possible.

Whitehead thus parts company with Santayana by ultimately subordinating the realm of eternal objects (his analogue to the realm of essences) to God. Santayana would disagree with this move, since essence *qua* essence is not deficient of anything appropriate to its being. Essences in themselves lack value, but value belongs to animal life with its inherently temporal and selective nature. Also, while essence lacks the being of actuality or material existence, actuality is also less than the self-identical complete being of essence. Each essence truly *is* in the sense that it cannot be otherwise. The actual changes and suffers the vicissitudes of time; nothing truly and fully abides in actuality as it does in the realm of essence. Consequently, essence does not lack anything proper to its mode of being. Santayana argues that essences are abstract "only by accident and in function" (SAF 94), not in themselves.

Moreover, Santayana would argue against Whitehead's subordination of essence to existence by noting that the realm of essence has its own primacy over the other realms. Without its forms, spirit, truth, and material existence would lack the definite characters that make them identifiable. We need not conclude, however, that Santayana therefore subordinates the actual to the eternal, and in fact he does not do this. Instead, Santayana presents each realm as an irreducible perspective which emphasizes unique features of our world and experience. He explains that "[t]he Realms of Being are only kinds or categories of things which I find conspicuously different and worth distinguishing" (RB vi). Each realm enjoys primacy from a certain perspective. For instance, relative to time and existence, the realm of matter is primary. The realm of spirit has primacy relative to knowledge, while from the perspective of history the realm of truth has priority.[12] Santayana thus treats his realms as descriptive categories, tools relevant from different perspectives. The realm of spirit is significant, as we shall see, in articulating an insight not available from the perspective of the other realms. Nevertheless, Santayana argues, "[i]t is perfectly possible for any one who will consider the realms of being together, to honour each in its place and to disregard the scorn which those who have eyes for one only must needs pour upon the others" (RB 63).

Despite these points, it is important to note that Santayana himself acknowledges the primacy of existence from our *own* animal perspective. He does not, however, give it the sort of ontological priority that Whitehead does. Nevertheless, Santayana's recognition of the centrality of matter is the basis of his naturalism and so of his attempts to avoid attributing to essence what properly belongs to matter. Santayana and Whitehead both agree that power, value, and selectivity all belong properly to existing things and not to what is eternal. The difference is that Whitehead's main concern is to adumbrate the eternal as a formative element in the order and (as we shall see) novelty of the world. This is not to attribute power to eternal objects, but rather to recognize that they are ingredients interwoven with actual entities to constitute and explain our experience.[13]

A second distinctive point Whitehead makes about eternal objects further underscores his commitment to the interconnectedness of things; it also highlights additional differences between his philosophy and Santayana's. While he recognizes that eternal objects are repeatable and thus fit the traditional characterization of universals, Whitehead takes pains to distinguish the former from the latter.[14] On his account, the traditional distinction between universal and particular does not match that between eternal object and actual entity. He explains that "[t]he term 'universal' is unfortunate in its application to eternal objects; for it seems to deny and in fact was meant to deny that actual entities also fall within the scope of the principle of relativity" (PR 149). This principle stipulates that "it belongs to the nature of a 'being' that it is a potential for every 'becoming'" (PR 22). The principle of relativity lies at the heart of Whitehead's organic philosophy and applies not only to eternal objects but also to actual entities. No actual entity can be exhaustively described by eternal objects; other actual entities are also disclosed in the analysis of each actual entity. Whitehead explains that

> [a]n actual entity cannot be described, even inadequately, by universals; because other actual entities do enter into the description of any one actual entity. Thus every so-called "universal" is particular in the sense of being just what it is, diverse from everything else; and every so-called "particular" is universal in the sense of entering into the constitution of other actual entities. (PR 48)[15]

Whitehead's entire system aims to overcome what he contends is the traditional error of uncritically accepting Aristotle's view that a substance is *not* present in a subject. Especially when it is conjoined with the sensationalist doctrine of modern philosophy,[16] this belief undermines the interconnectedness or solidarity of the actual world.

Whitehead argues that acceptance of the sensationalist doctrine renders our experience fundamentally disconnected from the world. The dichotomization of the universal and the particular is what leads to this disconnection. If the universal is identified exclusively with eternal objects, and if the particular is identified solely with the actual entities that constitute the basic units of experience, no actual entity can be a constituent of any other. This violates Whitehead's principle of universal relativity, for then only eternal objects can be repeatable. In this case, only universals can be given; actualities cannot be given, and so the experienced *togetherness* of actual entities is not possible. Whitehead argues that such a position results from the fallacy of misplaced concreteness, for the discreteness distinctive of perception in the mode of presentational immediacy is taken to be the fundamental and *only* mode of perception. Whitehead rejects such a view, arguing that the "withness" of the world *is* given in perception in the mode of causal efficacy (PR 81). Causal efficacy is that mode of perception by means of which a concrescing entity prehends the actual entities in its past actual world. Past actual entities are objectified in the entity through its prehension of them; they are thus "present in" the entity and condition what it will become. Whitehead argues that failure to acknowledge causal efficacy has led philosophers to assume that our experience is primarily cognitive and constituted of universals. Our knowledge of and connection with the external world thereby becomes problematic, and skepticism is the natural result.

As noted in the previous section, Santayana himself embraces skepticism and pushes it to its radical extreme. He concludes, however, that skepticism (the admission that nothing *given* exists) is compatible with animal faith (the belief in things not given). Whitehead is not altogether hostile to Santayana's position. Indeed, he grants that "[i]f we allow the term 'animal faith' to describe the kind of perception which has been neglected by the philosophic tradition [i.e., perception in the mode of causal efficacy], then practically the whole of Santayana's discussion [in *Scepticism and Animal Faith*] is in accord with the organic philosophy" (PR 142). The crucial difference, though, is Santayana's acceptance of the sensationalist doctrine; he denies that intuitions themselves may be among the data of intuition—that is, that other actual entities are prehended and so "present in" the experience of concrescing entities. From Whitehead's perspective, this doctrine isolates human cognitive experience from reality such that knowledge becomes exclusively symbolic in nature and hence indirect. This also makes problematic a systematic account of our interconnectedness with other beings. Whitehead seeks to avoid both problems by means of his principle of relativity.

At this point, we begin to see how distinct Whitehead and Santayana's visions are. By pushing philosophy to its skeptical extreme, Santayana concludes that all that is given in intuition are discrete essences. This does not mean that he denies the possibility of knowledge; rather, he argues that knowledge of the world is rooted in animal faith, which renders the data of intuition a symbol that signifies. In developing this view, Santayana strips superstition away from essences:[17] he argues that essences are just what they are. They lack inherent value, they are incapable of causality, and by themselves do not select or limit anything. They can be taken as signs or instruments for use in animal life, but in themselves they simply are what they are. Thus, while animal faith may readily interpret the intuition of red to signify the heat of the stove, the essence that is the datum of that intuition is redness. Selection, signification, causation, and valuation properly belong to matter, not essence.

Whitehead agrees with this general characterization of the eternal and of its difference from existence. His ontological principle renders it impossible for the eternal to be the ground of any value, causality, or selectivity. The reason he must ground the realm of eternal objects in God's primordial envisagement is that only an *actual entity* can be the seat of selection. Eternal objects tell no tales of their ingression. Whitehead thus agrees with Santayana in refusing to attribute to the eternal functions that properly belong to another "realm of being," namely, that of matter or actuality. Whitehead's goal, however, is not to take skepticism to its natural end but to question the assumptions that make skepticism an inevitable conclusion. He wants to refashion philosophy so that we can avoid the skeptical conclusion. This requires rethinking our categories to explain what is apparent to common sense: that what is given is not just essences, but things. To account for our experience of "withness," to explain our knowledge of the external world, and to adequately describe the solidarity of the world, the organic philosophy grants that actual entities—as well as eternal objects—are "repeatable" and "present in" the constitution of other actual entities.[18]

Central to Whitehead's vision, then, is the theme of the organic interweaving of elements that render an interconnected universe. He employs the ontological principle and the principle of relativity to create a system that embodies this solidarity. This is not Santayana's chief goal; more important to him is distinguishing the different realms of being so that we do not surreptitiously attribute power to essence or (as we shall see) to spirit. Whitehead also denies power and efficacy to the eternal, but his philosophical vision requires him to show how eternal objects are a formative element in the adventures of the world. The eternal thus represents one pole of an ideal contrast between permanence and flux (cf. PR 337–41), a contrast of opposites whose ultimate harmony is expressive of the organic interconnectedness of the world.

Spirit and the Eternal

The significance of Whitehead and Santayana's disagreement about the status of the eternal becomes even clearer in their different views of the nature and efficacy of spirit or consciousness. Santayana describes spirit as "an awareness natural to animals, revealing the world and themselves in it. Other names for spirit are consciousness, attention, feeling, thought or any word that marks the difference between being awake and being asleep, alive or dead" (RB 572); spirit is properly no *thing* but rather pure light. Though spirit is itself born of the realm of matter and belongs to psyche,[19] Santayana argues that it has a direct relation to essence. Spirit, or consciousness, is the pure light that falls on an essence through the deliverance of intuition (the apprehension or direct possession of what is apparent). For psyche, essences are symbols, weighed and valued not for themselves but rather as signs of things to come. The appearance of a fox indicates danger to psyche. In pure intuition, however, spirit is undistracted by the demands of psyche and contemplates each essence presented to it *qua* essence, stripped of any commitments to its truth, significance, or material existence (RB 646).

Psyche has needs and desires in light of which things are valued and selected; these are not spirit's concern. Spirit's function is not to choose one essence to the exclusion of another; rather, its vocation is "to be sympathetic and warm towards all endeavours" (RB 823), to embrace each essence without judging it good or evil. Spirit *exists* and belongs to the world of selective psyche. Yet when its light falls on an essence in pure intuition, it is united harmoniously with whatever essence appears before it, until psyche or the changing scene of the world shifts spirit's focus to another essence.

In spreading its light over some part of the realm of essence, spirit finds in the eternal respite from the demands of psyche. To properly understand the nature of spiritual life, however, we must avoid two problems. The first results when we think of the spiritual life as an escape from this world and a retreat to a heaven above. Such an interpretation hypostatizes the realm of essence. Santayana argues that "[t]here is only one world, the natural world, and only one truth about it; but this world has a spiritual life possible in it, which looks not to another world but to the beauty and perfection that this world suggests, approaches, and misses" (RB 833). Consequently, spirit does not retreat to another world, nor could it, for spirit is born of and incapable of escaping from animal life. Indeed, Santayana explains that the more integrated psyche is, the more spirit is able to "become aware of the world to any depth, in any degree of complexity" (RB 824). Spirit's liberation consists in finding in pure intuition enjoyment of immediacy presented to it by the world.

The second problem occurs when we misinterpret spirit to be a substance with the power to move us and change the world. Though attainment of spiritual enlightenment marks a highpoint in the development of animal life, spirit is not a force active in better utilizing material means to make the world more hospitable to human needs and desires; that is psyche's vocation. Santayana argues that by means of spirit "we shall not have saved the world; all its titular saviours have left the world much as it was. But we can reconcile ourselves with the world by doing it justice" (RB 824). Spirit is witness to the world, not a power or agent within it. We must not attribute power or efficacy to spirit, for we then conflate realms and misunderstand spirit. In doing so, Santayana argues, we engage in literary psychology, which consists in the propensity to "read actions in terms of spirit and to divine the thought that doubtless accompanied them" (RB 836). Spirit is a flowering of psyche, an awareness that accompanies its activity as a concomitant, and not some competing force that seeks to direct our behavior. Whatever moves us does so through psyche, not spirit. Santayana explains that "I do not, then, deny either the efficacy or the indetermination of human action or Will, but only a miraculous interference of spirit or of visionary objects with the flux of matter" (RB 836).

Here we come face to face with Santayana's epiphenomenalism: just as essence remains inert and incapable of efficacy, so too is spirit powerless. As we noted earlier, one of Santayana's primary goals is to articulate the realms of being without mixing the characteristics of each. Power belongs to the realm of matter, and though spirit is a product of psyche, it is immaterial and therefore without efficacy. Spirit's contemplation of the eternal is liberation from the distractions of animal life, but it is neither a substitute for nor a transforming agent of that life. In so describing spirit, Santayana unveils moments of immersion in immediacy which are possible in animal life. Consistent with much of the philosophic tradition, he gives us a vision of the spiritual life that is inherently contemplative—a communion with the eternal. Santayana, however, does not succumb to the temptation to transform this unique natural product into a supernatural force. It is precisely this sort of superstitious attribution of power to the eternal and spiritual which Santayana consistently averts in his philosophy.

Turning to Whitehead, we see that he, like Santayana, locates the roots of consciousness in material existence; his treatment, however, leads to rather different conclusions. Whitehead describes consciousness as an achievement of certain actual entities whose physical stability allows for the development of a heightened mental pole. It arises in some (albeit few) actual entities where a heightened contrast is felt, especially in the form of negation. For instance, conscious feelings are akin to the proposition "The stone is not grey." Here what is physically felt (the stone, as given) contrasts with a conceptual possibility (grey). Whitehead describes consciousness as the "subjective form involved in feeling the contrast between the 'theory' which may be erroneous and the fact which is 'given'" (PR 161–62). Requisite for consciousness is some eternal object not given in the immediate data of the past actual world (the theory) contrasted with the nexus of actual entities given in that past (the given fact).

As with Santayana, Whitehead roots consciousness in animal life; without the physical feelings of an actual entity there could be no contrast with an eternal object not given in the entity's past actual world. Rather unlike Santayana, however, he attributes to conscious entities an *objective* immortality whereby they have an everlasting influence on the character of the world. Indeed, relevance to the actual world belongs to every actual entity, whether conscious or not. Each entity bears a relation to the eternal insofar as eternal objects are relevant to it through the initial aim (which begins the process whereby that entity becomes what it is) provided by God. Conscious entities also involve the further ingression of eternal objects (through conceptual feelings) which are not actually given in the entity's past actual world. This makes possible the achievement of richer contrasts and so of greater values than those possible in lower grade actual entities. Though each entity achieves its own unique value through the integration of the features of its world, this value (whether in the case of a low-grade actual entity or a high-grade conscious entity) loses all subjective immediacy once the entity becomes the entity that it is.

Once its adventure in becoming is over, then, the entity perishes—at least subjectively; it has no further decisions to make. The entity achieves, however, objective immortality in that God embraces its value in his consequent nature which, interwoven with his primordial nature, makes available to future entities the values achieved in the past actual world.[20] Each entity, once complete, becomes available as an ingredient for all future entities through its objective immortality. It thereby achieves not its own eternity, but rather a form of what Whitehead calls *everlastingness.*[21] Each entity contributes to the consequent nature of God and so to the subsequent attainment of value in the world. Conscious entities, like all entities, contribute to the character of the future. The heightened value achieved by them enriches the possibilities made available to future entities through God's consequent nature. Importantly, consciousness is not a thing, but rather a subjective form, a way an entity feels a contrast. Consequently, Whitehead avoids charges of hypostatizing consciousness. Nevertheless, he integrates consciousness into the constitution of an entity, just as he does eternal objects. The resulting view is a vision of an interconnected world of which the principle of universal relativity is the chief expression.

Their views of spirit or consciousness, then, underscore differences in the way each philosopher believes the eternal relates to the actual. For Santayana, the realm of essence consists of an infinite number of forms, none of which exercise any efficacy on the world. Spirit, born of psyche, can contemplate and find union with essences in pure intuition, but this union does not change the essences. Moreover, just as essences by themselves are incapable of affecting anything, so too is spirit incapable of saving or changing the world in virtue of its commerce with the eternal. Psyche is the seat of agency. By contrast, Whitehead subordinates eternal objects to actuality via God's primordial envisagement in order to secure their relevance as ingredients in the world. Through ingression in actual entities, eternal objects give definiteness to the world, and when contrasted with what is given in the physical feelings of a conscious actual entity, they give rise to enriched value which can be passed on to subsequent entities. Consciousness contributes enhanced value to the ongoing creativity of the world and so conditions its character. In contrast, then, to Santayana's account of spirit's tranquil but impotent union with the eternal, Whitehead treats consciousness as an achievement of value which contributes to the ongoing adventures of the world.

The contrast between Santayana and Whitehead can be further sharpened by relating them to American pragmatists such as William James and John Dewey. Both Whitehead and Santayana root spirit in nature as the pragmatists do. Spirit can never exist apart from its animal base; neither can values be achieved apart from the adventures of actual entities. Santayana's epiphenomenalism, however, is apparent in his doctrine of spirit. Spirit's journey in the realm of essence, whether haphazard or logical, does not thereby represent an improvement in the temporal by means of the eternal. Rather, what Santayana gives us is a quietist acceptance of the way the world is; spirit transcends the transitoriness of the world, though this is never an absolute transcendence. In Whitehead's system, though, the eternal is inextricably interwoven with God's conditioning efficacy. Whitehead's vision is thus close to that of James and Dewey who found it impossible to conceive of the eternal apart from its function in the improvement of the world. Though both James and Dewey would be suspicious that Whitehead hypostatizes the eternal,[22] Whitehead's metaphysics shares the pragmatic spirit of meliorism, tethering the eternal to the actual to explain the achievement of value in the world. Santayana's commitment to a contemplative but nontransformative spiritual life contrasts with this meliorism. He is able to maintain the parity and perfect peace of the eternal, but he does so at the cost (and with the intention) of draining it of any efficacy.

Santayana, however, is not indifferent to meliorism and affords it a place within the sphere of psyche. The activity of transforming the world belongs not to the life of spirit (which is really not a life at all), but rather to the life of reason, which Santayana explores extensively in a work of the same name. Santayana thus acknowledges, indeed deals extensively with, psyche's interaction in the world. What he believes is distinctive of spirit or consciousness, though, is the liberation it gives us from the ongoing trials and travails of material existence. Our spiritual experience is not an escape or an alternate life that replaces that of psyche, yet it is a significant mode of liberation whereby we enjoy immediacy and the eternal, free from the demands and constraints of selectivity and partiality. It is a relation to the world whereby we are reconciled to the world, even as we try to cope with and transform it. Consequently, Santayana's resistance to subordinating the eternal to the actual, to subordinating spirit to the demands of animal life, opens an avenue of spirituality which is an ever-present possibility of human existence.

Whitehead and Santayana alike recognize the distinctive nature and need for the eternal in a systematic account of our experience. Yet although they describe it similarly, they assign it considerably different functions in their overall systems. For Whitehead, eternal objects are required in explaining the processive and interconnected nature of our world and experience. Though we must not conflate the eternal with the actual, the former is nevertheless a constituent of the latter, playing a vital role in both the becoming of an actual entity and its superjective character that conditions the world beyond it. Whitehead offers us an organic account of our experience that decidedly celebrates the solidarity of the world, but this solidarity is impossible without the eternal. Central to Santayana's vision is distinguishing the realms of being, especially to avoid attributing to essence or spirit the sort of power and efficacy that properly belong to the realm of matter. Essences have their proper mode of being, but they do not enjoy the adventures of material existence. Spirit exists and is born of psyche, but it is psyche that moves; spirit only (but significantly) illuminates. Santayana thus captures the spiritual life in its purity and envisions an untainted mode of liberation from the world.

Part of the novelty of Santayana and Whitehead is that they each embrace the eternal during a time when philosophers are inclined to ignore or dismiss it. Neither neglects the centrality of time or change to existence, but neither thinks we must sacrifice the eternal in describing our human experience. My aim here has been to demonstrate that an examination of the role the eternal plays for each offers significant insight into the core of each philosopher's system. It is in their treatment of the eternal that their kinship becomes apparent, as does the unique character of their respective philosophical visions.

Notes

Special thanks to John Lachs, Lisa Bellantoni, and Angus Kerr-Lawson, each of whom made helpful comments on earlier versions of this paper. All three helped me see the broader significance of my topic. Kerr-Lawson also kindly shared with me his unpublished paper, "Whitehead, Santayana, and Abstract Objects." Though this paper differs from mine in emphasis, it shares basic convictions; I am grateful for the additional insights his discussion brought to light.

1. For instance, pragmatists explain the "eternal" as designating those elements of experience that have proven both relatively stable and important in promoting successful interaction with the environment. Such an account, however, differentiates the eternal from the temporal in light of its function, not its designation of a unique kind of reality.

2. George Santayana, *Realms of Being* (New York: Cooper Square Publishers, Inc., 1972), 169. Hereafter referred to as RB.

3. *Process and Reality,* Corrected Edition (New York: The Free Press, 1978), 142. Hereafter referred to as PR. According to Santayana, intuitions cannot be among the data of intuitions, since intuitions themselves are existent ('facts,' in Whitehead's language). In *Scepticism and Animal Faith,* Santayana argues that the only datum given in intuition is an essence. (See, for instance, SAF 34: "existence or fact . . . cannot be a datum at all, because existence involves external relations and actual (not merely specious) flux: whereas [a datum] . . . must be embraced in a single stroke of apperception, and nothing outside it can belong to it at all.") Whitehead's organic philosophy embraces a principle of relativity according to which actual entities (facts) in addition to eternal objects (essences) are given in experience. I explore this point more fully when presenting Whitehead's view of eternal objects.

4. This kinship has been acknowledged and discussed by a number of different authors. See Abner Shimony's "Status and Nature of Essences," *The Review of Metaphysics* 1 (March 1948): 38–79, especially 48–53. The most direct exploration of it, however, comes in John Ashmore's "Essence in Recent Philosophy: Husserl, Whitehead, Santayana," *Philosophy Today* 18 (1974): 198–210. Ashmore catalogues the similarities, but does not delve into their systematic implications.

5. *Scepticism and Animal Faith* (New York: Dover, 1955). Hereafter referred to as SAF.

6. By intuition, Santayana means the "direct and obvious possession of the apparent, without commitments of any sort about its truth, significance, or material existence. The deliverance of intuition is some pure essence" (RB 646).

7. Santayana himself explains that this work is not *metaphysical,* if that word indicates an exploration of the efficacy of nonmaterial entities. Metaphysics in this sense is "an abuse that occurs whenever logical, moral, or psychological figments are turned into substances or powers and placed beneath or behind the material world, to create, govern, or explain it" (RB 828). His critique of this kind of metaphysics lies at the heart of Santayana's vision. He nevertheless acknowledges that his work in *Realms of Being* is metaphysical in the rather generic sense of systematically exploring the nature of reality.

8. Commenting especially on the determinacy of essences, Charles Hartshorne develops what he deems the "Neglected Alternative" to Santayana's position ("Santayana's Doctrine of Essence," in *The Philosophy of George Santayana,* edited by Paul Schilpp [La Salle: Open Court, 1989], 135–82). He takes issue with Santayana's contention that essences are absolutely determinate and independent of existence, offering as his alternative that "[i]n addition to actual existence

there may be potential existence, and potential existence may be the indeterminate but determinable aspect, as actuality is the determined aspect, of existence, the two aspects together making up existent substances" (141). Santayana himself responds that Hartshorne's alternative overlooks the distinction between essence and existence. It presents us with the view that essences only become determinate when exemplified in the material world—a problematic view that he charges with effectively "reducing what we discover to the fact that we have discovered it" (p. 590 of "Apologia Pro Mente Sua" in the same volume; for Santayana's full response, see 589–95).

9. Whitehead explains that "[i]f the term 'eternal objects' is disliked, the term 'potentials' would be suitable. The eternal objects are the pure potentials of the universe; and the actual entities differ from each other in their realization of potentials" (PR 149).

10. Whitehead explains that "I have adopted the term 'prehension,' to express the activity whereby an actual entity effects its own concretion of other things" (PR 52).

11. Alfred North Whitehead, *Science and the Modern World* (New York: The Free Press, 1967), 159. Hereafter referred to as SMW.

12. See John Lachs's discussion of primacy among the realms of being in *George Santayana* (New York: Twayne Publications, 1988), 64–65. Stephen David Ross argues for a similar perspectival approach to categories in *Perspective in Whitehead's Metaphysics* (Albany: State University of New York Press, 1983). Ross is especially critical of Whitehead's ontological principle. For a similar critique, see Justus Buchler's "On a Strain of Arbitrariness in Whitehead's System," *The Journal of Philosophy* 66 (1969): 589–601.

13. Some critics argue that actual entities alone could perform all the functions served by eternal objects. For instance, if actual entities and eternal objects alike are universal and particular—according to the principle of relativity—why are both categories needed? For more on this, see Everett W. Hall's "Of What Use are Whitehead's Eternal Objects?" *The Journal of Philosophy* 27 (1930): 29–44.

14. Whitehead explains that "[t]he notion of a universal is that which can enter into the description of many particulars; whereas the notion of a particular is that it is described by universals, and does not itself enter into the description of any other particular. According to the doctrine of relativity which is the basis of the metaphysical system of the present lectures, both these notions involve a misconception" (PR 48).

15. Whitehead further argues that "[o]ne actual entity has a status among other actual entities, not expressible wholly in terms of contrasts between eternal objects" (PR 229).

16. This doctrine really consists of two principles. According to the first, the subjectivist principle, "the datum in the act of experience can be adequately analysed purely in terms of universals" (PR 157). The second principle is the sensationalist principle, which stipulates that "the primary activity in the act of experience is the bare subjective entertainment of the datum, devoid of any subjective

form of receptivity" (PR 157). Whitehead adopts a revised version of the former principle (that "apart from the experience of subjects, there is nothing, nothing, nothing, bare nothingness" [PR 167]), but is highly critical of the latter.

17. The heart of such superstition is attributing power to appearances. Santayana argues that "[a]ll that is requisite in order to transform such superstition into a critical philosophy is to trace back all power to the continuous transformation of physical forces, in other words, to matter; and at the same time, by the same insight, to recognize all appearances to be mere appearances . . . sensible signs of power manifest in spirit, but having no substance or power in themselves" (RB 834).

18. In addition to accounting for permanence and identity in the world, eternal objects also play a significant role in its solidarity. For instance, Whitehead argues that "[o]ne role of the eternal objects is that they are those elements which express how any one actual entity is constituted by its synthesis of other actual entities" (PR 50). Whitehead's complete explanation of solidarity is, of course, more complex. Moreover, important as eternal objects are to the solidarity of the world, Jorge Luis Nobo argues that solidarity cannot be understood properly without recourse to the extensive continuum. See in particular Nobo's *Whitehead's Metaphysics of Extension and Solidarity* (Albany: State University of New York Press, 1986).

19. "The self-maintaining and reproducing pattern or structure of an organism, conceived as a power, is called a psyche" (RB 569).

20. The entity attains *objective* immortality in that, although its subjective immediacy has ceased, it is nevertheless available through God as an objective datum in the becoming of future entities. It is the *superjective,* and not subjective, nature of the entity which so functions.

21. Whitehead explains that "[t]he property of combining creative advance with the retention of mutual immediacy is what . . . is meant by the term 'everlasting'" (PR 346).

22. Dewey is in fact critical of what he calls a "mathematical" strain in Whitehead's thought. (See for instance, "Whitehead's Philosophy," in *The Philosophy of Alfred North Whitehead,* edited by Paul Schilpp [La Salle: Open Court, 1991], 643–61.) Dewey generally argues against hypostatizing abstractions:

> Objection comes in, and comes in with warranted force, when the results of an abstractive operation are given a standing which belongs only to the total situation from which they have been selected. All specialization breeds a familiarity which tends to create an illusion. Material dealt with by specialized abstractive processes comes to have a psychological independence and completion which is converted—hypostatized—into objective independence and self-sufficiency. (*The Quest for Certainty, John Dewey: The Later Works,* 1925–1953, vol. 4, edited by Jo Ann Boydston [Carbondale: Southern Illinois University Press, 1984], 173–74)

Part Three

Whitehead and Contemporary American Philosophy

CHAPTER 5

Whitehead, Rorty, and the Return of the Exiled Poets

DAVID L. HALL

A Quarrel Revisited

Whitehead's well-worn generalization that "the European philosophical tradition . . . consists of a series of footnotes to Plato" (Whitehead 1978, 39) invites the question just who it might have been that Plato himself footnoted. We must exclude the most obvious candidate since there is no consensus as to how we might finally distinguish the views of Socrates from those of his student. Indeed, as Emerson insisted, Plato and Socrates constitute a "double star which the most powerful of instruments will not entirely separate" (Emerson 1950, 48). Certainly, Pythagoras, Parmenides, Heracleitus, and Protagoras must be mentioned as significant Platonic sources. But there is a figure more important than any of these. The safest characterization of Plato's philosophical speculations is that they are a series of footnotes to Homer. No matter that these notes are so often carping and censorious, Plato's thought is one sustained engagement with Homer and Homeric poetry.

Plato's contest with Homer, truly Oedipal in character, was nothing less than a struggle to see who would finally be "the educator of Greece"—and, ultimately, of the civilization nurtured by it. This contest has not only influenced the thematics of Western philosophical discourse in a singularly important manner, it has set the tone within which that discourse has proceeded. Consequently, a substantial number of those footnotes to Plato said to comprise the tradition of European philosophical speculation are a continuation of Plato's *agon* with the poets.

Plato's quarrel with the poets receives its most elaborate expression in *The Republic*. In the early books, Homeric poetry is critiqued and expurgated. Only that part of poetry that is praise to the gods or the celebration of truly moral men is to be allowed. Poets themselves are politely exiled from the ideal *polis*-in-the-making. There follows throughout the later books a gradual development of a social context within which philosophical meditation and speculation may be nurtured. This development culminates in the substitution of Plato's hero for Homer's—Socrates for Achilles.

Plato's Oedipal struggle with Homer is climaxed in the final book of the *Republic*. Homeric poetry is vanquished. Socrates is presented as an exemplar of the redefined poet of the sort who could be welcomed in the new society. Socratic poets will function in the service of argument. That is, one can—as is the case in the *Republic*—set up an argument for which poetic images, mythical narratives (as "likely stories") can extend the sense of philosophical terms and clothe doctrines with positive emotions that serve to intensify the desire for knowledge.

In the substitution of Socratic for Homeric poets, something else is to be recognized: the transvaluation of the sense of immortality. The immortality of Homer, like that of his heroes Achilles and Hector, is that accorded to the famous. The philosopher envisions a different immortality. It is the immortality of rational harmony expressed through a sense of the persistence of achieved value. Thus, from Plato's perspective, the principal issue dividing poets and philosophers is whether human beings and societies are to be primarily shaped by the desire for fame or by an intuition of the persistence of realized value.

More than twenty-three centuries have passed since Plato rose up to slay Father Homer. Philosophers are now met on a great battlefield, testing whether the tradition they have so valiantly served is any longer worth defending. Continued loyalty to Plato's vision, celebrated in countless footnotes down the centuries, is now very much in doubt. Indeed, it is no exaggeration to say that a significant part of contemporary philosophy may be read as a series of epitaphs to Plato. In Europe Jacques Derrida is wreaking the Revenge of the Sophists and in America Richard Rorty has arisen to sponsor a rather anti-Platonic version of the Return of the Exiled Poets. In seems that only the process school of speculative philosophy remains to defend the Platonic sensibility.

I wish to argue that the most productive manner of engaging the thought of Alfred North Whitehead and Richard Rorty is by assessing their respective positions in the recently reenergized quarrel over the relations of philosophy and poetry. It is, of course, no stretch to employ Whitehead as a contemporary representative of Plato. After all, Whitehead's project was nothing less than "to render Plato's general point of view with the least changes made necessary by the intervening two thousand years of human experience in social organization, in aesthetic attainment, in science, and in religion" (Whitehead 1978, 39).

Having said that, several of the changes we must take into account if we are to render Plato *de modo* are rather dramatic. Alterations in social organization principally include the development of liberal democracies that render the functional hierarchy of Plato's model society untenable. In science, we have traded our belief in universal forms and natural kinds for the celebration of a complex interplay of discreteness and continuity in a universe punctuated at all levels by process and evolutionary change. In aesthetic attainment, there has been an increasing liberation of creativity from the rational impulse. In religion, we are now able to appeal to a Fellow-Sufferer Who Understands in place of Plato's *Demiurgos* and Form of the Good, later transformed by Judeo-Christianity into an all-powerful and all-knowing God.

I shall be primarily concerned with Whitehead's Platonic reconstruction of the aesthetic and religious sensibilities. That reconstruction conditions his construal of the contribution of poetic activity to the intuition of immortality. As we shall see, Whitehead's processive sense of immortality as the persistence of achieved value precludes any possibility of holding to a narrow instrumental interpretation of immortality as the continuance of the individual person—a belief that certainly belongs more to the Christianized Plato than to Plato himself.

What changes are necessary to permit Rorty to play the role of the champion of Homer? In the first place, the alterations concern the rather highly refined self-consciousness with which philosophy is now practiced. This self-consciousness significantly affects the understanding of poetic language and linguistic activity by raising the issue to the meta-level of competing "vocabularies." Secondly, Rorty's essentially Homeric gestures that make self-identity contingent upon the act of poetic creation are contextualized within a liberal democratic society. Thus, not only the famous few are self-made—each of us is called upon to create him- or herself.

In sum, Whitehead removes any hint of the merely instrumental and self-serving narrowness from the intuition of immortality and renders poetry in service to intimations of the persistence of achieved value. In his turn, Rorty takes the edge off "the last infirmity of noble mind" by allowing for a democratization of the poetic function. This leads him to enjoin poets to create the richest and most varied of linguistic resources as media of self-creation. The conflict is still between "immortality" and "fame" as final ends, but we shall see that the contemporary shades of Plato and of Homer ring some interesting variations on the old conflict.

Poetic Twists in the Linguistic Turn

As all good Whiteheadians know, Rorty has declared Whitehead's speculative system, and all such metaphysical efforts, to have been effectively circumvented by the substitution of "language" for "experience" as the medium of philosophic expression. In some form or other, this "linguistic turn" has characterized the dominant strains of Anglo-American philosophy since the emergence of logical positivism. However, we shall see that Rorty's idiosyncratic interpretation of this linguistic strain in contemporary philosophy has increasingly led him away from the concerns of mainstream language philosophers and closer to the interests of speculative thinkers such as Whitehead.

In his essay, "The Subjectivist Principle and the Linguistic Turn" (Kline 1963, 134–57), Rorty claimed that Whitehead shares with a number of the analytic philosophers the desire to reconcile "the fact that all knowledge is perspectival with the fact that such knowledge is about objects distinct from and independent of the experiencing subject" (Kline 1963, 153). In this essay, Rorty insists that language philosophers have discovered new and better methods for achieving this reconciliation. These methods permit a movement away from the speculative, systematic use of language of "experiencing subjects" toward the employment of "the language of language."

In his attempt to demonstrate that Whitehead's strategy could be better achieved through the analysis of language than by appeal to ontological constructions, Rorty invoked a distinction between "semantic" and "empirical" statements. Empirical statements purport to be about objects. Semantic statements are about facts. Semantic statements are token-reflexive in the sense that they "always involve explicit reference to the language we speak now" (Kline 1963, 153). Unlike empirical statements, however, semantic statements are not either direct or indirect experiential reports. That is, the empirical statement "George is thinking *X*" may be semantically expressed as "Under certain conditions George is disposed to utter *X*, and *X* means that. . . ." The ability to translate empirical into semantic statements precludes the necessity for any direct experiential appeals requiring ontological constructions for their articulation and/or defense.

Now, we must accept Rorty at his word when, more than thirty years after writing his essay on Whitehead, he stated that he still "agree(s) with most of it" (Saatkamp 1995, 211, Note 5). Nonetheless, it seems clear that Rorty's subsequent philosophical development manifests a rather dramatic redirection of interests. This has led him to offer a distinctly poetic twist to the linguistic turn he still purports to champion. Rorty has begun to emphasize the creative power of poets to introduce new metaphorical extensions of language. This emphasis derives, in part, from his appropriation and extension of several of Donald Davidson's speculations.

Among the Davidsonian elements in Rorty's thought is the denial of any "scheme-content" distinction. This denial entails a refusal to entertain questions of the relations of language (scheme) and the world (content). The collapse of the language/world distinction entails the view that language neither characterizes an objective, extra-experiential world nor does it express our experience of such a world. With this new understanding, language is to be assessed as "strings of marks and noises used in the development and pursuit of social practices—practices which enabled people to achieve their ends, ends which do not include 'representing reality as it is in itself'" (Rorty 1992, 373).

Rorty's new twist carries the nonrepresentationalist, nonexpressionist understanding of language to its behavioral extremes. Language is to be assessed almost exclusively in terms of social practices—that is, in terms of beliefs and desires of individuals with whom we are likely to have some real or imagined interactions. "Decisions about truth or falsity are always ways of rendering practices more coherent or of developing new practices. . . . [A]nd the search for truth . . . can only be a matter of searching for a discourse that works better than previous discourses" (Rorty 1998, 129).

If the search for truth is the search for a more adequate discourse, the question arises as to how such discourses are developed and promulgated. It is here that the topic of poets and philosophers becomes germane. Interpreting Davidson's arguments against representationalism and the correspondence theory of truth by appeal to Thomas Kuhn's claims about theoretical incommensurability leads to a position in which changes in discourse or vocabularies are effectively nonrational. The agency of the change is *metaphor.*

Rorty shares with Davidson a causal theory in which metaphors are held to be unfamiliar noises or marks employed in manners that sometimes cause individuals to understand in new ways. The effects of such metaphors are most cogently assessed in terms of changes in attitude, beliefs, or desires. Changes resulting from the impulsion of metaphor may be construed after the fashion of evolutionary changes resulting from the mechanism of linguistic mutation.

Metaphors are new ways of speaking that produce an effect without in the strict sense having a meaning. If accepted, these new ways of speaking can become candidates for literal terms. Dead metaphors are drafted to serve in truth-functional sentences. The creation of metaphors may be said to be a distinctly "poetic" activity provided only that poets are construed broadly enough to include all linguistic revolutionaries.

In spite of Rorty's claim that he still is in essential agreement with his early essay on Whitehead, I believe it would be a mistake to assess the relations of these two thinkers by appeal to those early arguments. In the following paragraphs I will argue that Rorty's recent poetic twist has brought him much closer to Whitehead than before. Anticipating one of my principal conclusions, I would have to say that it is a toss-up as to which of these thinkers holds poets and poetry in higher esteem.

Language, Experience, and Poetry

Whitehead is certainly no exception to the late-modern focus upon language. In *Principia Mathematica,* he and Bertrand Russell celebrated the power of language in its highest degree of formal abstraction. In his later philosophical work, he increasingly noted the inadequacies of language to capture and convey the most concrete and particular of experiences. Having said this, Rorty's characterization of his principal difference with Whitehead in terms of the latter's appeal to experience and his appeal to language is essentially on target. What Rorty has not sufficiently noted is that the experience/language contrast concerns not only the medium of philosophical expression, *but how the world is initially entertained.*

Whitehead begins with the intuition, the *experience,* of creative advance. Rorty begins with the self-creative actions of strong poets as advertised through language. Thus, Whitehead's fundamental problematic was not the same as Rorty's. He was not, first and foremost, interested in solving an epistemological problem created by the putative inadequacies of alternative philosophical vocabularies. Whitehead's problematic was how to characterize an intuition that, for a variety of reasons, had been marginalized in traditional philosophical discussions—namely, the intuition of flux and change.

> That "all things flow" is the first vague generalization which the unsystematized, barely analyzed, intuition of men has produced. . . . If we are to go back to that ultimate, integral experience, unwarped by the sophistications of theory, that experience whose elucidation is the sole aim of philosophy, the flux of things is the one ultimate generalization around which we must weave our philosophic theory. (Whitehead 1978, 208)

The intuition of the spontaneous production of novelty expressed in Whitehead's Category of the Ultimate was not generated by meditation upon philosophical dead ends, or upon the inadequacies of previous vocabularies. Further, Whitehead believes that this experience swings free of any systematic specifications of it.

Rorty's claim that the appeal to the resources of linguistic philosophy provides a more efficient solution to certain epistemological problems at the distinctly meta-philosophical level would be relevant to Whitehead's thinking only if the two shared a common problematic. Since they do not, however, Rorty's belief in the superiority of "language" over "experience" as the medium of philosophical discussions begs the question.

The meta-philosophical Rorty has construed Whitehead's apologetic considerations as fundamental to his philosophical speculations. In so doing, he has effectively sidestepped the issue of how Whitehead's philosophy was generated out of the resources of his own private psychological field. That sidestepping has allowed him to focus upon language—the analytic language of the linguistic philosopher and the constructive language of the speculative thinker—at the expense of quite legitimate appeals to *experience.*

Rorty is certainly not the only one who misconstrues the principal focus of Whitehead's thinking. Indeed, the vast majority of his interpreters have been so enamored by the systematic apparatus of *Process and Reality* that they have forgotten the motivation for its construction. We can redress this mistaken emphasis upon "the system" only if we distinguish Whitehead's broadly *poetic* from his more narrowly *philosophical* concerns.

The constructive task of Whitehead's philosophy is to appeal to the immediate self-evidence of intuitive experience. "Philosophy," he says, "is either self-evident or it is not philosophy. . . . The aim of philosophy is sheer disclosure" (Whitehead 1938, 49). This is Whitehead functioning as a "poet." In his strictly philosophical endeavors, Whitehead attempts "to find a conventional phraseology for the vivid suggestiveness of the poet . . . and thereby to produce a verbal symbolism manageable in other connections of thought" (Whitehead 1938, 50).

The implication is that Whitehead uses language in two manners: The first use is as a means of creating conditions leading to immediate experience—that is, *self-evidence.* Secondly, language is employed *apologetically* to articulate the applicability of the expressions of poetic suggestiveness with other areas of cultural interest. Though the speculative philosopher definitely spends the greater part of his energies in the latter task, it is the former appeal that grounds the philosophic enterprise. What this means is that the philosopher, when he is not himself functioning as a poet, is still in the service of poetry.

> Philosophy is akin to poetry. . . . In each case there is reference to form beyond the direct meanings of words. Poetry allies itself to metre, philosophy to mathematical pattern. (Whitehead 1938, 174)

This is, perhaps, Whitehead's most telling statement about the relations between poetry and philosophy. The poet functions in the service of meter; the philosopher is disciplined by the claims of mathematical pattern. Moreover, this distinction is not a disciplinary but a functional one. No one who has read Whitehead can avoid the conclusion that, by his own definition, he often plays the role of a poet.

Whitehead's characterizations of poetry and philosophy depend upon his contrast of meter and mathematical pattern. The key to this contrast is found in his functional analysis of "understanding." The poet and the philosopher understand in different manners. The differences in their modes of understanding are functions of the difference between meter and mathematical pattern as termini of acts of understanding—each terminus lying beyond the final reach of language.

As Whitehead notes in his *Modes of Thought,* the act of understanding is really two acts—not easily combined. To understand is to grasp meaning, which is to grasp patterns as types of order. A pattern is comprised both of particulars and of the manner of their relatedness. Foregrounding the formal relations in a given pattern involves a different type of understanding than that involved in the foregrounding of its particular elements.

Foregrounding relations requires the gathering of details under an assigned pattern. This is rational or logical understanding. It involves the use of a principle or principles as an antecedent pattern in terms of which to articulate instances or applications. Mathematical patterns are the termini of such acts of understanding. The *telos* of rational understanding is the discovery of the most general of such patterns—the Form of Forms—that would express an indefinitely repeatable mode of relatedness adequate to the interpretation of all possible connections of any and all entities. The final indirectness of logical understanding lies in the fact that patterns of such generality may only be *suggested.*

In the second instance, to understand means to discover novel patterns that elicit interest in novel details. These novel patterns are themselves entertained as particulars, as are the constituents of the patterns. Here we are concerned with the aesthetic understanding of the unrepeatable items of the world. The presentation of these items is abetted by the aesthetic analogue of logical pattern—namely, *meter* in the senses of cadence, pulse, beat, rhythm. Meter and logical pattern, though analogous, are recognizably distinct modes of presentation. The former abets the presentation of insistent particulars; the latter presents formal relationships indifferent to any particulars so related.

The greatest problem in understanding the different functions of poets and philosophers lies in the logical bias leading one to construe meter in terms of mathematical pattern. The emphasis of meter, beat, cadence, rhythm is upon the particulars not upon their relations. As Whitehead has noted, "[I]n the history of European thought the discussion of aesthetics has been almost ruined by the emphasis upon the harmony of the details" (Whitehead 1938, 62). The principal cause of this near-ruin has been an inability to note the distinctive functions of meter and of mathematical pattern in the act of understanding.

Discerning "the harmony of details" is accomplished by appeal to formal or mathematical patterns. The appeal to meter, on the other hand, is meant to facilitate awareness of what, *in particular,* is metered. Meter is not a relation among beats—it is the beats, the pulses, the insistently particular items. The decidedly rational motivations of most philosophers and critics precludes the broad appreciation of the particularities, the unharmonized details, upon which all true art and aesthetic appreciation depends.

In his most constructive acts of philosophizing, Whitehead privileges the aesthetic over the rational mode of expression. In seeking a reference beyond the direct meanings of words, both philosophers *qua* poets and poets per se seek the "sheer disclosure" of the immediate, the self-evident. In his apologetic function, as a philosopher of culture articulating systematic connections with and among other areas of experience, Whitehead returns to the logical or rational mode of understanding in order to seek a more "conventional phraseology."

The rather naïve interpretation of Whitehead as a representational realist, armed with a "correspondence" theory of truth is highly misleading. Fundamentally, Whitehead's theory involves a causal or conformal perspective since, with respect to "blunt truth," the subjective form of reception is conformal to the objective sensa.

> We enjoy the green foliage of the spring greenly; we enjoy the sunset with an emotional pattern including among its elements the colours and contrasts of the vision. . . . It is this that makes Art possible. (Whitehead 1933, 321)

Conformal feelings are the basis of aesthetic experience. Language allied with meter is not representational, but *causal: That dolphin-torn / That gong-tormented sea* makes something happen. No one—certainly not

Whitehead—really believes that Yeats's line is a description or representation of anything. Though there is no way to get behind these words to see what is taking place, the principal function of poetry, as of all art, is to provoke conformal feelings.

From the perspective of Whitehead *qua* philosopher, a world characterized by processes (happenings) and events (happenings that have reached some culmination) is a world open only to immediate experiencing. It is a world of insistent particulars. Attempts to allude to such a world do not move one from the particular to the general, or from the concrete to the (formally) abstract, or from the causally efficacious to the presentationally immediate, or from this unmediated experience to experiences of this type, or the categoreal conditions shared by experience as such. Instead, one is interested in doing what our poets are best at doing—namely, using language in order to promote the causal conditions for a shared (conformal) experience.

Even the more systematic uses of philosophic explanation are disciplined by the poetic motive. When Whitehead claims that speculative philosophy "appeals to direct insight and endeavors to indicate its meanings by appeal to further situations which promote such specific insights" (Whitehead 1938, 173), it is clear that he is not siding with those who are trying to get something right, but with those who are trying to create the conditions for the experience of specific intuitions. Anyone who uses language with this intent knows full well the potential futility of the enterprise. There are never any guarantees. Just as most acorns do not give rise to mighty oaks, but sustain the population of squirrels, so poetic language all too often serves as tenure-fodder for some college professor, or grist for some disciple's scholastic mill.

It may initially seem outrageous to claim that Whitehead was principally concerned with the aesthetic uses of language. What about all that front-matter in *Process and Reality* that assays a "Categoreal Scheme"? And what of that legendary House of Pain, Part IV (with its "flat loci" and "extensive connection")? The incontrovertible reply is simply that making the intuition of "creativity" central to one's philosophical speculations and then proceeding to frustrate that intuition through systematic recourse to "bloodless abstractions" and "gray theory" would constitute philosophical immolation. Contrary to the unfortunate interpretations by Whiteheadian scholastics, we must begin to insist that Whitehead's Category of the Ultimate is, in fact, *ultimate.* Only then will we be able to accept the priority of that language which attempts to promote the experience of creativity.

This does not mean that philosophers are simply poets *manqué.* In addition to creating the conditions for immediate experience, one has to be concerned with what one does with that experience. Just as "religion is what the individual does with his own solitariness" (Whitehead 1960, 16), so science is what a particular community contrives to do with nature construed as the terminus of sense perception, and art involves trafficking in *objets d'art* as a means of promoting aesthetic experience.

The apologetic context in the modern West is one that requires a development of formal abstractions in philosophy useful in other formal enterprises—art, science, historiography, etc. There should be no difficulty in considering the systematic phase of speculative philosophy as primarily an exercise in the philosophy of culture—namely, an effort to discover a conventional phraseology rendering the poet's suggestive language applicable to every area of cultural interest.

It must be said that Whitehead goes a long way toward recognizing the value of the poetic function—a long enough way to strain his relationship with Plato on this point. The substitution of the intuition of process for that of permanence leads to an increased sense of the importance of the aesthetic language of particularity—the language of poetry.

Whitehead's offer of amnesty to the exiled poets is a fundamental element of his philosophical project. Moreover, the terms he offers are far less stringent than those Plato had suggested. Far from subordinating poetry to philosophical argument, Whitehead holds poetry to be fundamental: both the entertainment of form beyond the direct meanings of words and the immediate grasp of unrepeatable particulars are acts of aesthetic understanding. Whitehead's philosophy is first and foremost an exercise in aesthetic thinking. His distinctly rational discourses are related to the apologetic functions of his thought that seek to articulate his constructive insights with respect to broader areas of cultural interest.

The speculative constructions Rorty finds offensive in Whitehead's thought are less concerned with getting something right than with either creating the conditions that provoke the immediate experience of flux and change, or with noting the consequences within alternative areas of cultural sensibility of holding that intuition primary. Moreover, as distinct in temperament and in styles of expression as are Rorty and Whitehead, we shall see that they share the belief that "all things flow." It is this commonality in their thinking that leads each of them, by interestingly different routes, to seek a return of the exiled poets.

Language, Poets, and Philosophers

Rorty has recently said that he would like to "free Whitehead's Category of the Ultimate (i.e., 'Creativity'), not just from the theory of eternal objects, but from the fetters of a correspondence theory of truth, and from the idea that we need a super-science called metaphysics" (Saatkamp 1995, 34–35). I believe that this is more than just a throwaway line. Rorty's thought is definitely an attempt to free *a certain type of* creativity from any sort of theoretical accouterments. There is, however, a real difference between Rorty and Whitehead with respect to the construal of the term *creativity*.

Whitehead understands creativity as the spontaneous emergence of novelty associated with the process of creative becoming. Rorty has a more human-centered perspective. As he has indicated: "I do not believe it matters whether we accept 'the essentially creative aspect of becoming' as long as we keep trying to create ever more open space for the play of the human imagination" (Saatkamp 1995, 35).

Accepting the human imagination as the fundamental locus of creativity precludes the necessity to account for creative becoming in any more generic sense. It is precisely this necessity that burdens Whitehead with the need to construct a metaphysical system that offers interpretations of the intuition of creativity relevant to the broadest areas of natural and cultural circumstance. Rorty's understanding of creativity requires only the articulation of the individual and cultural contexts associated with distinctly human activity. As he says, "I see cultural politics rather than metaphysics, as the place in which to place everything else" (Saatkamp 1995, 35).

By "cultural politics" Rorty is presumably referring to the arbitrary play of forces within a society that determines the success or failure of a particular human enterprise. Further, since Rorty's utopia is "a place where poets and not scientists or priests or religious prophets are thought of as the cutting edge of civilization" (Saatkamp 1995, 32), we are concerned with the politics of an essentially *poetized* culture. Such a culture is one in which "we substitute the hope that chances for the fulfillment of idiosyncratic fantasies will be equalized for the hope that everyone will replace 'passion' or fantasy with 'reason'" (Rorty 1989, 53).

Though he denies that metaphysics is the place in which to place everything else, the implication is clear that the most felicitous sort of cultural politics would definitely find a place for at least some so-called metaphysical expressions since, as Rorty maintains, poets must be understood in a sense "wide enough to include the much footnoted Plato" (Saatkamp 1995, 211).

The poet offers metaphorical allusions motivated by the desire to create herself as something other than a mere replica of other selves. "The accidental coincidence of a private obsession with a public need" (Rorty 1989, 37) then determines who will in fact emerge as the principal shapers of a culture. The result of this process is "a society that recognizes that it is what it is . . . because certain poets and revolutionaries of the past spoke as they did" (Rorty 1989, 61).

This provides us some understanding of Rorty's views on the function of poets and poetry. But how are philosophers to be seen? First, we should note that Rorty claims that he has "never seen the point of Heidegger's distinction between *Dichter* and *Denker*" (Saatkamp 1995, 211). This should alert us to the fact that, like Whitehead, Rorty will discuss philosophy and poetry in broadly functional terms.

Poets create new language that serves as means of self-creation and can, in addition, serve other individuals and society as a whole in attempts to develop personal identity and self-awareness. On the other hand, philosophers function as mediators in situations in which "the language of the past is in conflict with the needs of the future" (Saatkamp 1995, 199). In assisting efforts to mediate between the old and the new, philosophers serve to "reduce metaphors to the status of tools for social progress" (Rorty 1991, 93).

In sum, the products of philosophical activity can serve three functions—only two of which are acceptable. The search for secure dogmas in the form of "necessary truths," or any other attempt to close philosophical conversation, is to be rejected out of hand. The primary function of philosophers is to serve as mediators between the old and new vocabularies—that is, "to mediate between historical epochs, to reconcile old and new truth" (Saatkamp 1995, 200). Finally, philosophical products may function poetically to the extent that they serve a more qualified role as interesting sources of novel vocabularies that occasion shifts in meaning. This is but to say that, though we may expect the new metaphors and vocabularies to come primarily from poets per se, vocabularies such as those produced by Plato and Whitehead may themselves introduce novel resources for self-creation.

Poets per se are on the cutting age because they generate new uses of language. The philosopher, on the other hand, is the mediator between the old and the new. But, ultimately, they both may contribute to "human history as a long swelling, increasingly polyphonic poem that leads up to nothing save itself" (Saatkamp 1995, 33).

Rorty sometimes distinguishes the role of prophet from that of poet and philosopher. Prophets are those who attempt to rid the world of obstacles that stand in the way of transformation. New vocabularies arise from poetic acts of creative genius. Prophets and philosophers then assist in the substitution of the new for the old. Prophets, in the tradition of the French revolutionaries, endorse a wholesale clearing away of the past to make way for a utopian future. Philosophers work at the retail level, serving "as honest brokers between generations, between areas of cultural activity, and between traditions" (Saatkamp 1995, 203).

Rorty's laissez-faire nominalism—his attempt to leave everything (except language) as it is—means that he is forced to remain at the "meta" level. His subject matter is not experience, but *vocabularies.* These vocabularies serve as the semantic contexts expressing an individual's (and possibly a community's) form of self-identification. Working at this level requires that one be concerned with the creation of new vocabularies and the subsequent influence of these vocabularies in broader areas of culture. For Rorty, both the prophetic and philosophical functions depend upon poetic activity.

We are now in a position to draw the rather surprising conclusion that, not only do Whitehead and Rorty agree upon the priority of the poetic activity, they are in fundamental agreement in claiming that the philosopher serves the poet by attempting to find, in the words of Whitehead cited earlier, "a conventional phraseology for the vivid suggestiveness of the poet."

There is a more fundamental ground of difference, however—one that advertises a real contrast between these two. The contrast is not with respect to the centrality of poetic activity, but with the specific character of the utopian societies that poets are called upon to create. Rorty's Homeric utopia is motored by a democratized desire for self-creation. Whitehead's Platonic utopia, on the other hand, is sustained by the intuition of the everlasting persistence of achieved value.

Fame, Peace, and Immortality

Both Whitehead and Rorty have welcomed the poets home—and on surprisingly similar terms. Whitehead believes that the suggestive language of the poet is the fundamental resource from which the philosopher promotes a progressive articulation of values essential to a civilized society. Rorty agrees to the priority and centrality of poetic activity and, though his interests are more piecemeal and unsystematic, he accepts as well the philosopher's role in the subsequent articulation of poetic language as means of mediating between the old and the new.

However, Rorty and Whitehead have different understandings of the primary message of the poets. For Rorty, poets are not only messengers—they are the message as well. Rorty does not see poetry as providing us intimations of anything beyond itself. Thus, Rorty claims that he does not use Wordsworth to give himself "a sense of participation in the 'life of things' . . . (but) a sense of participation in the life of Wordsworth" (Saatkamp 1995, 31).

Rorty wishes to promote both a poetized and a *democratized* culture. In fact, he presumes the priority of democracy to both poetry and philosophy (see Rorty 1991, 175–96). It is this priority that is primarily responsible for his particular vision of both the *creation* and the *enjoyment* of poetry.

The Homeric ideal of the celebration of heroes is maintained: "We can't get along without heroes . . . we need to tell ourselves stories of the mighty dead in order to make our hopes of surpassing them concrete" (Rorty 1991, 73). Though the democratic hope is that each individual will be offered the opportunity to create himself, the forces of "cultural politics" will ensure that only a few will be lucky enough to become one of the notables by having their private obsession intersect with a public need. Most of us will be left with acts of private self-creation in which we use the language of the poets to "tailor a coherent image of ourselves and then use it to tinker with our behavior" (Rorty 1991b, 162). Beyond that, we can attempt to embed the unheroic stories of our own lives within a larger heroic narrative—that of the Enlightenment, or of the rise of democratic societies. Rorty's democratic ideal reshapes the *enjoyment* of poetry as well. In addition to their heroic functions, poets in the largest sense (Rorty often instances Dickens and Orwell) may sensitize us to the pain and suffering of others, and so further humanize our actions.

There is a sense in which Whitehead agrees with Rorty that, with respect to poetry, the medium is the message. The difference that makes all the difference is that he sees the poetic medium as the process of creativity itself rather than as the poet created through that process. That is, Whitehead clearly believed that the primary message of the poet was a fundamental intuition central to the experience of each of us—namely, the sense that "the creative advance of the world is the becoming, the perishing, and the objective immortalities of those things which jointly constitute *stubborn fact*" (Whitehead 1978, xiv). For Whitehead, poetry provides us intimations of immortality as the persistence of achieved value and thereby promotes the message that "the creature perishes *and* is immortal" (Whitehead 1978, 82).

In *Adventures of Ideas,* Whitehead discusses this intuition in terms of a sense of "Peace," which he construes as a value essential to the realization of a civilized society. Peace as a trust in the persistence of value beyond itself involves "the harmony of the soul's activities with ideal aims that lie beyond any personal satisfaction" (Whitehead 1933, 371). Elsewhere,

Whitehead identifies this sense of Peace as the intuition of *holiness*—"a sense of the value of the details for the totality" (MT 1938, 120).

Peace requires balancing the tension between individual absoluteness and individual relativity. "'Absoluteness' means a release of essential dependence on other members of the community in respect to modes of activity, while 'relativity' means the converse fact of essential relatedness" (Whitehead 1933, 54). The extreme sense of relativity is expressed in the total self-absorption in an ideal; the extreme of absoluteness is to be found in an overweening desire for fame—the unqualified demand for the recognition and celebration of one's individual actions.

The desire for fame is "an inversion of the social impulse, and yet presupposes it" (Whitehead 1933, 371). The sense of Peace inverts the individualistic impulse, while presupposing it. With respect to both the sense of Peace and the desire for fame, however, "the zest of human adventure presupposes for its material a scheme of things with a worth beyond any single occasion" (Whitehead 1933, 372). With appropriate qualifications, this contrast can assist us in summarizing the principal differences between Whitehead's vision and that of Rorty.

By placing the desire for fame within the context of an interest in promoting equal opportunity for self-creation, Rorty invites the poets to serve more than their own creative ends. The hope is that they might see themselves as did Emerson and Whitman, as poets who would enlarge our democratic vistas. In their provision of resources for self-creation, poets are to serve a distinctly moral purpose. On the other hand, Whitehead's understanding of the poetic message as a celebration of immortality, as the persistence of achieved value, moves us beyond the strictly moral context.

Goodness emerges from finite situations concerning obligations and responsibilities toward another individual or individuals, or one's family, society, country—or Mankind as such. It is primarily human-centered. The sense of Peace, or holiness, requires an indefinitely broad context: it concerns the value of the finite detail for the totality of things. Morality can be referenced to both short- and long-term contexts, but it makes little sense to ask after the ethical value of a decision or an action in the interminably long run. Holiness and goodness are distinctive values, and the latter doesn't ground the former. Simply put: You don't have to be good to be holy.

Nor is it normally thought that one must be holy to be good. Most of us presume that there are lots of morally strait individuals who lay no claim to spiritual allegiances. In fact, it would be destructive of the very idea of secular society in general, and of liberal democracies in particular, to believe that holiness must be sought if goodness is to be achieved. This is one of the grounds for Rorty's oft-expressed (Jeffersonian) arguments against the promotion of religious values in public life.

Nonetheless, there is a persistent intuition within Western civilization suggesting that without a sense of Peace, or holiness, there can be no lasting goodness. The problem comes when that sense of holiness is used to support the assurance of an instrumental reward for a life of goodness. This intuition underwrites the meanest forms of fundamentalism expressed in America today by the Religious Right. And the suspicion with which many individuals greet all forms of spiritual expression is a consequence of seeing the bigoted and intolerant shapes that may be taken by the spiritual impulse which, in its finer forms, moves us beyond mere civility to civilized conduct.

Socrates first advertised for our tradition that virtue is its own reward. The intrinsic goodness of an act, not any extraneous rewards it might purchase, provides assurance that no evil can befall a good person. But what if, as in the case of Socrates, one who believes that virtue is its own reward also has intimations of immortality? There's the problem. These two primary beliefs are in real tension since any easement provided by the latter can too easily vitiate the motivations for performing in accordance with the former.

One of the fundamental moral problematics of Western culture is wrapped up in the question: "How are we to live in the recognition that virtue is its own reward if we are burdened by intimations of immortality?" It might seem that a heuristic skepticism toward the doctrine of immortal bliss, or any other guarantee of extraneous benefits for that matter, far better promotes virtuous actions than does the certainty of an eternal reward. And yet . . . there is reason to believe that a *civilized,* as opposed to a merely *civil,* society is nurtured by a faith in the persistence of achieved value.

The irony of our situation as basically decent folks attempting to promote refinements in our present forms of civility is that we must find a means of accommodating the irresolvable intrinsic/instrumental dilemma that qualifies all productive human action. I insist that this is more than a narrowly moral or religious issue. It touches every aspect of the intellectual life construed in its broadest sense. It is not only that so many True Believers, squinting through a dark glass, are able to discern their own comfortable vision of paradise backlighted by the White Radiance of Eternity. There are more than enough metaphysicians who see that final list of Necessary Truths arrayed in orderly fashion before them. How many prophets, confused and marginalized by their living present, have mapped in excruciating detail worlds that must inevitably come to pass? And how many ordinary folk find that the commonsense validity of their own parochial customs provides the only sensible means of living a life?

John Dewey argued that the quest for certainty is for the *comforts* of certitude, for the assurance of an escape from the perils of uncontrollable circumstance. That quest has, in the past, compelled us to search for final securing dogmas in religion, science, and philosophy alike. Rorty believes that he sides with Dewey in rejecting all forms of metaphysical comfort. In fact, Dewey stands closer to Whitehead on this issue. Consider these words from Dewey's *Human Nature and Conduct:*

> The religious experience is a reality in so far as in the midst of the effort to foresee and regulate future objects we are sustained and expanded in feebleness and failure by a sense of an enveloping whole. Peace in action not after it is the contribution of the ideal to conduct. (Dewey 1957, 264)

Dewey welcomes the comfort of enveloping wholes as something other than a more or less desperate desire for securing ourselves amidst the perils of existence.

There are intuitions (beliefs, habits, biases) so fundamental that they may not be expunged, but for which no proof is possible, and for which undue efforts at justification may be both unproductive and unrewarding. The belief in immortality generally construed, the belief in the everlasting persistence of value, is just such an intuition—for *me.* But it is definitely not such a belief for everyone. Thus, while I do find myself believing with Whitehead in "the ever-present, unfading importance of our immediate actions, which perish and yet live forevermore" (Whitehead 1978, 351), I find myself also sympathetic with those who might claim that, if all we have is us, we can nonetheless muddle through. I insist that any other attitude would render me less able to distinguish between the bad faith associated with the fervent quest for certainty and the good faith that sustains one's sense of unique relatedness to an ever-opening totality. Furthermore, I would suggest that those whose leanings are in the other direction can maintain best their good faith by allowing for the alternative possibility. To his credit, Rorty does make this allowance: "If there really is an eternal fellow-sufferer who understands . . . so much the better, (but) . . . we can carry on perfectly well even if we suspect that there is not" (Saatkamp 1995, 34).

Whitehead wishes the poets to celebrate that form of immortality beyond mere personal continuation—an immortality of achieved value. Rorty's desire to have the poets as models and resources for individual self-creation has as its final aim the creation of a "grand democracy of Forest Trees."

The juxtaposition of the reflections of Rorty and Whitehead on the role of the poets and poetry has presented an opportunity to reflect upon one of the more intransigent of the dilemmas that has shaped the moral problematics of our Western cultural tradition. There really is no issue here of who got it right and who missed the point. By advertising the distinctive dangers associated with the alternative horns of this dilemma, each of these thinkers has performed a valuable service. We are, therefore, no more required to make a final choice between Rorty and Whitehead than we are between Homer and Plato as authentic founding fathers of Western civilization.

Works Cited

Dewey, John. 1957. *Human Nature and Conduct.* New York: Random House.

Emerson, Ralph Waldo. 1950. "Plato, or the Philosopher." In *Complete Essays of Ralph Waldo Emerson.* New York: Modern Library.

Kline, George. ed. 1963. *Alfred North Whitehead—Essays on His Philosophy.* Englewood Cliffs, N.J.: Prentice-Hall.

Rorty, Richard. 1989. *Contingency, Irony, Solidarity.* Cambridge: Cambridge University Press.

———. 1990. "The Philosopher and the Prophet," *Transition* No. 52.

———. 1991. *Objectivity, Relativism, and Truth—Philosophical Papers, Volume 1.* Cambridge: Cambridge University Press.

———. 1991b. *Essays on Heidegger and Others—Philosophical Papers, Volume 2.* Cambridge: Cambridge University Press.

———. ed. 1992. "Twenty-Five Years After." In *The Linguistic Turn.* Chicago: The University of Chicago Press.

———. 1998. *Truth and Progress—Philosophical Papers, Volume 3.* Cambridge: Cambridge University Press.

———. 1999. *Philosophy and Social Hope.* New York: Penguin Books.

Saatkamp, Herman, ed. 1995. *Rorty and Pragmatism—The Philosopher Responds to His Critics.* Nashville: Vanderbilt University Press.

Whitehead, A. N. 1933. *Adventures of Ideas.* New York: Macmillan.

———. 1938. *Modes of Thought.* New York: Macmillan.

———. 1960. *Religion in the Making.* New York: Meridian Books.

———. 1978. *Process and Reality—an Essay in Cosmology.* Corrected edition. Edited by David Ray Griffin and Donald W. Sherburne. New York: The Free Press.

CHAPTER 6

Future Ethics: MacIntyre and Whitehead on Moral Progress

LISA BELLANTONI

In his widely influential work *After Virtue,* Alasdair MacIntyre argues that a "moral crisis" saturates our culture. We continue, he maintains, to use familiar moral terms such as justice and virtue, yet now lack the shared understandings that once—but no longer—lent those terms unequivocal moral force. Premodern ethical traditions, those of Aristotle and Aquinas for instance, offer us teleological systems within which we could agree upon the ends most appropriate to the good life, and the means by which we might pursue that life. Yet modern ethicists have rejected these shared conceptions of the good life as rooted in perfectionistic and theological systems, in first principles and final causes. Thereby they have dissolved our once common standards of moral discourse and practice. As a result, we find ourselves adrift in a sea of incommensurable moral claims, whose animating terms offer no shared meanings, and no bases for rationally resolving our practical disputes. Worse still, now lacking any common standards by which to secure practical consensus, we all too readily conclude that such disagreements reduce to matters of individual taste, or interest, or preference. The "interminable" moral disagreements that now plague us, MacIntyre suggests, thus augur the ascent of emotivism, the currently popular insistence that all evaluative claims "are nothing but expressions of preference, expressions of attitude or feeling . . ." (AV, 11).[1] Emotivism, he argues, is "catastrophic," because it undercuts the very possibility of ethical discourse and practice: "I am not merely contending that morality is not what it once was, but also and more importantly that what once was morality has to some large degree disappeared—and that this marks a degeneration, a grave cultural loss" (AV, 3, 21).

To contest that loss, MacIntyre proposes a restorative moral project aimed at reanimating a traditional theological perfectionism, and so at restoring what he terms "the rationality of traditions." In this endeavor, MacIntyre's effort finds an unanticipated ally in Alfred North Whitehead's metaphysical cosmology, which likewise advances a teleological account of practical enquiry. Whitehead's account, I will argue, shares MacIntyre's resistance both to emotivism and to modern ethicists' efforts to establish the strict "warranted assertability" of our practical claims sans any teleological references. Indeed, Whitehead would applaud MacIntyre's claim that practical enquiry entails a complex, historically extended view of how we vindicate our practical claims. While, however, Whitehead would share MacIntyre's perfectionism and his depiction of practical enquiry as a historically extended social practice, Whitehead's account differs in highlighting the creative, futural orientation of such enquiries. Whitehead's account thereby effectively thematizes a central challenge facing contemporary ethicists: the need to integrate into our current moral deliberations, systematically, a concern for future generations. To that end, I will argue, Whitehead's approach identifies not emotivism but the amoralism it portends as the main current challenge our practical enquiries face. Conversely, his account suggests a novel means of response to our "interminable" moral disputes. In Whitehead's view, our irreducible disagreements perpetuate rather than imperil our moral enquiries, as they drive the practical progress such enquiries properly aim to secure. Whitehead's perfectionism would agree with MacIntyre's, then, that our practical enquiries endeavor to allow us to live well. Nevertheless, Whitehead suggests, our enquiries allow us to live well, finally, only if they also embody and advance our aspirations to live better.

The Progress of Practical Enquiries

According to MacIntyre, the irresolvable practical conflicts we face undercut our ability to exercise rational moral agency. To be rational, he maintains, our deliberations must enact a social practice of practical rationality that allows us to order and select among those ends and means most appropriate to the good life. Our choices thereby presuppose a polis "whose shared mode of life" already expresses the collective answer of its citizens to the question "What is the best mode of life for human beings?" (WJ, 133).[2] Only moral traditions so ordered can embody "standards of rational action directed toward the good and the best" (WJ, 141). Among these standards MacIntyre includes virtues of character, those ideals through which the adherents of such traditions learn how to pursue the best life. Taking Aquinas's enquiries as an exemplar, MacIntyre traces out those practices of apprenticeship to a moral tradition through which agents come to discover how the objective standards marking that tradition accrue their authority over time. Such enquiries, MacIntyre maintains, share three features. First, they are essentially teleological, and aim to secure a "perfected science" through which we can identify our appropriate ends, "an understanding completed by an apprehension of first principles" (FP, 5).[3] Second, they include an "ineliminable theological dimension," for "enquiry aspires to and is intelligible only in terms of its aspiration to finality, comprehensiveness and unity of explanation and understanding" (FP, 29). Third, these enquiries advance social practices which establish complex networks of justification for our claims, and which thereby support our enquiries' progressive adequation to practical truths at once tradition-constituted and tradition-independent (FP, 59–60).

On these three counts, MacIntyre's project finds a ready ally in Whitehead's metaphysical cosmology. Like MacIntyre, Whitehead roots rational enquiry within a teleology that sets forth first principles and final ends (FR, 24–25).[4] Also like MacIntyre's, Whitehead's teleology bears essential theological reference. Indeed, God plays three essential roles in Whitehead's system. First, He harbors the eternal objects or enduring ideal possibilities that actual entities come to embody during their self-creating processes. Second, He supplies actual entities with their initial subjective aims, that is, with the inchoate appetitions by which He induces them to serve His aims, which are novelty, intensity, and harmony of valuation. Third, He sustains in his consequent nature the valuations that each actual entity produces in and through its concrescence. Moreover, Whitehead grounds our enquiries in a theological teleology according to perfections God envisions, and also describes rationality as immanent within that framework and as approximating to its ends: "The religious insight is the grasp of this truth: . . . that the universe exhibits a creativity with infinite freedom, and a realm of forms with infinite possibilities, but that this creativity and these forms are together impotent to achieve actuality apart from the completed ideal harmony, which is God" (RM, 119–20).[5] At the same time, however, Whitehead's account of the creativity of the universe proposes an aesthetic teleology wherein God and actual entities are co-creators. This open-ended teleology leads Whitehead to describe the progress of rational enquiry into that teleology, and the complex truth it reveals, much differently than does MacIntyre.

For MacIntyre, rational enquiries unfold in response to "epistemic crises." His ethical particularism famously maintains that "[t]here is no standing ground, no place for enquiry, no way to engage in the practices of advancing, evaluating, accepting, and rejecting reasoned argument apart from that which is provided by some particular tradition or other" (WJ, 350). Moreover, he argues: "Every such form of enquiry begins in and from some condition of pure historical contingency, from the beliefs, institutions, and practices of some particular community which constitute a given" (WJ, 354). These social practices institutionalize background beliefs and regulate agents' methods of enquiry, forms of argument, and means of justifying practical claims. Such enquiries unfold historically and dialectically: "At every stage beliefs and judgments will be justified by reference to the beliefs and judgments of the previous stage, and insofar as a tradition has constituted itself as a successful form of enquiry, the claims to truth made within that tradition will always be in some specifiable way less vulnerable to dialectical questioning and objection than were their predecessors" (WJ, 359). While authoritative for a time, however, truths thus founded face "epistemic crises" when "[b]etween those older beliefs and the world as they [the tradition's adherents] now understand it there is a radical discrepancy to be perceived" (WJ, 356). Enquirers must then restore the epistemic equilibrium, the coherence among foundational beliefs, which their tradition had previously enjoyed. To unfold rationally, however, agents' reformulations must be systematically theorized, must show substantive continuity with their prior formulations, and must aim to secure unequivocal truth: "To claim truth for one's present mindset and the judgments which are its expression is to claim that this kind of inadequacy, this kind of discrepancy, will never appear in any possible future situation, no matter how searching the enquiry, no matter how much evidence is provided, no matter what developments in rational enquiry may occur" (WJ, 358).

In responding to epistemic crises, then, traditions unfold rationally only when they espouse a view of truth at once tradition-constituted and tradition-independent. Insofar as these modes of enquiry are historical and dialectical, and begin from the contingency of established belief, MacIntyre depicts their rationality as "inescapably anti-Cartesian." Modern accounts of truth or "warranted assertability," as premised either upon the coherence among propositions within a logical system, or upon their correspondence with objective facts, undercut our only means of defending practical claims: "Abstract these conceptions of truth and reality from the teleological framework, and you will thereby deprive them of the only context by reference to which they can be made fully intelligible and rationally defensible" (FP, 61). Instead, he argues, practical claims secure several species of truth, and their modes of justification are rooted in the complex teleology they uncover. Practical propositions, he says, are constituted within a particular tradition, and "are justified insofar as in the history of this tradition they have, by surviving the process of dialectical questioning, vindicated themselves as superior to their historical predecessors" (WJ, 360). At the same time, however, our enquiries are also "anti-Hegelian," as they preclude perfect adequation between our judgments and their objects: "No one at any stage can ever rule out the future possibility of their present beliefs and judgments being shown to be inadequate" (WJ, 361). Nevertheless, he argues, "[i]t is in respect of their adequacy or inadequacy in their responses to epistemological crises that traditions are vindicated or fail to be vindicated" (WJ, 366). Such vindication requires not only that our practical truths be justified at some time and place, interior to and coherent with some tradition, but also that they secure a timeless truth adequate to the realities thus uncovered: "To claim that some thesis is true is not only to claim for all possible times and places that it cannot be shown to fail to correspond to reality . . . but also that the mind which expresses its thought in that thesis is in fact adequate to its object" (WJ, 363).

Such, MacIntyre argues, was Aquinas's great achievement. Practical traditions face epistemic crises either when incoherencies arise among their constituent beliefs, or when those beliefs no longer adequately encompass the experiences available to that tradition's adherents. Then: "Imaginative conceptual innovation will have had to occur" (WJ, 362). Such innovations, MacIntyre maintains, require enquirers to develop "enriched schemes" that (1) exhibit substantive continuity with the prior beliefs of their tradition, (2) explain why that tradition's original conceptual resources proved inadequate, and (3) better adequate the tradition's beliefs to those evidences currently available to the tradition's adherents (WJ, 362). Aquinas's distinctive challenge, he notes, was to render coherent two discordant inheritances: Aristotle's naturalistic teleology, which affirmed reason's self-sufficiency in practical enquiry, and Augustine's intensely theistic moral psychology, which affirmed human reason's dependence on God's grace to identify our appropriate ends. To resolve the tension between these positions, Aquinas referred them mutually to the metaphysical ground he believed they shared, viz., God, the theological referent even Aristotle's naturalist cosmology evoked as its underlying principle of unity (TR, 123–26).[6] Aquinas's approach, MacIntyre says, exemplifies how practical enquiries retain historical continuity with their inheritances, and how they thereby progress asymptotically toward the fixed, univocal truths, the first principles and final causes, they aim properly to reveal. To this end, our enquiries inhabit a closed-ended teleology, and progress as they approximate ever closer to the "perfected sciences" which univocally characterize that teleology and our place within it.

In contrast, while Whitehead, like MacIntyre, espouses a theistic teleology, Whitehead's teleology is open-ended and evolving, a texture that he suggests properly guides our enquiries. Whitehead's account affirms, as would MacIntyre's, that God proposes to us a range of initial valuations, a given order of means and ends. Yet for Whitehead that order is animated by and serves God's aesthetic aim at novelty, intensity, and harmony of experience. All actual entities, Whitehead maintains, creatively appropriate the elements that contribute to their concrescence: other actualities, eternal objects, and God. During its process of self-constitution, each actual entity moves from the stage of appropriating its inheritances to the stage of enjoying the results of that valuative activity. Such satisfactions, Whitehead insists, presuppose God's initial creative act, that is, His primordial valuing of those initial possibilities. Similarly, those satisfactions also presuppose His perpetuation of the achievements of past actual entities, which His consequent nature sustains as themselves potential contributors to the satisfactions of subsequent actual entities. Moreover, Whitehead also affirms that actual entities inherit their initial subjective aims from God. Even given this intensity of inheritance, however, essential novelty attaches to how these actual entities appropriate their data: "These subjective ways of feeling are not merely receptive of the data as alien facts; they clothe the dry bones with the flesh of a real being, emotional, purposive, appreciative (PR, 85).[7] God's ends thus enjoin actual entities not to recapitulate but to recreate their inheritances, and so to create novel perfections: "In its self-creation the actual entity is guided by its ideal of itself as individual satisfaction and as transcendent creator" (PR, 85). In such passages Whitehead is describing God not as commanding but as persuading. While God proposes an ideal order, that vision is neither eternally fixed nor unilaterally enacted. Rather, individuals are called to recreate God's vision in light of their inheritances, their present prospects, and their future aspirations.

For Whitehead, moreover, our enquiries into this teleology must reflect its creativity. In MacIntyre's view, practical enquiry aims to uncover that fixed, univocal set of ends, principles, and ideals by which agents may learn how to pursue the good life. To that end, such enquiry measures its progress insofar as it approximates to the perfected sciences that are its ideal issue. For Whitehead, in contrast, our practical enquiries must not only teach us how to live well, but must also hold out the prospect that we might live better (FR, 5). To that end, traditions of enquiry unfurl their constituent ideals in three stages: (1) the stage of romance, wherein those ideals elicit the excitement of novel valuative possibilities, of novel appetitions, (2) the stage of precision, wherein those ideals discipline the action of agents in order to realize sustained value of a particular type, and (3) the stage of generalization, wherein those ideals suggest potentially enduring perfections. Whitehead, like MacIntyre, would maintain that such enquiries lead us to identify those ends, principles, and ideals that would allow us to coordinate our individual and social pursuits, and thereby to pursue a wide range of enjoyments. Of any such tradition of enquiry, however, Whitehead notes: "In its prime it satisfies the immediate conditions for the good life. But the good life is unstable: the law of fatigue is inexorable. When any methodology of life has exhausted the novelties within its scope . . . one final decision determines the fate of a species. It can stabilize itself, and relapse so as to live; or it can shake itself free, and enter upon the adventure of living better" (FR, 14).

According to Whitehead, "The prolongation of outworn forms of life means a slow decadence in which there is repetition without any fruit in the reaping of value. There may be high survival power. . . . But the values of life are slowly ebbing. There remains the show of civilization, without any of its realities" (AI, 278).[8] Such, MacIntyre avers, was the fate of the Thomist synthesis: "They [medieval theorists] were salvaging the old virtues which had made the race the great race that it had been . . . and were not straining forward towards the new virtues to make the common life the City of God that it should be" (RM, 39). Such conservatism, Whitehead acknowledges, serves us well when it perpetuates those "living ideals" which current and future enquirers take over as their practical inheritances. Yet that same conservatism threatens the moral enterprise when it enjoins us to recapitulate, rather than to recreate those inheritances: "The effect of the present on the future is the business of morals. . . . Thus stagnation is the deadly foe of morality. Yet in human society the champions of morality are on the whole the fierce opponents of new ideals" (AI, 269). Indeed, Whitehead suggests, the business of morals is not only to recreate the perfections we inherit, but also—and more importantly—to propose novel perfections, and to hand them over as live options to our successors. Such, he hints, is both the essential mandate and the essential measure of our moral endeavors, whose business "is to make thought creative of the future" (FR, 65).

Practical Propositions and Civilizing Ideals

For Whitehead, MacIntyre's insistence on the fixed truth of practical claims and on the univocal truth accruing to one tradition alone, to one set of perfections, would mischaracterize both the discordance among practical propositions and the temporal constraints practical truths admit. In MacIntyre's view, practical propositions secure truth only within the specific traditions that spawn them, and wherein alone those truths prove justified, and thus intelligible and motivating to their adherents. Here, Whitehead would agree with MacIntyre that practical propositions arise in specific traditions and are justified with respect to those traditions' particular truth conditions. He would also agree with MacIntyre's view that while practical traditions share certain logical commitments, they do not share all elements of their substantive rationalities. He would disagree, however, with MacIntyre's claim that these propositions and the traditions that house them can be only rivals and competitors. According to MacIntyre: "The multiplicity of traditions does not afford a multiplicity of perspectives among which we can move, but a multiplicity of antagonistic commitments, between which only conflict, rational or non-rational, is possible" (WJ, 368). Moreover, he maintains, "genuinely to adopt the standpoint of a tradition thereby commits one to its view of what is true and false and, in so committing one, prohibits one from adopting any rival standpoint" (WJ, 367). Indeed, the truth conditions of rival practical traditions must be mutually exclusive: "For if there is a multiplicity of rival traditions"—each offering a viable set of truth conditions—"that very fact entails that no one tradition can offer those outside it good reasons for excluding the theses of its rivals" (WJ, 352). Additionally, he notes, traditions must exclude the competing theses of their rivals, because any given tradition must resolve its internal incoherencies if it is to progress rationally toward its telos as a perfected science (FP, 38–40).

In contrast, while Whitehead grants that such closed or "dogmatic" traditions can distill partial truths, he also argues that those same traditions issue in falsehoods if we press them beyond their conceptual limits: "But if the same dogma be used intolerantly so as to check the employment of other modes of analyzing the subject matter, then, for all its truth, it will be doing the work of falsehood" (RM, 131). For MacIntyre, practical propositions secure justification when they cohere with their host tradition's inheritances, adequately correspond to tradition-independent realities, and so establish for themselves a warranted assertability which at least approximates toward eternal truth. To so vindicate their constitutive propositions, however, traditions must defeat or otherwise exclude competing propositions, perpetually restoring their own conceptual equilibrium. Yet while MacIntyre would regard such restoration as marking a tradition's rational progress, Whitehead would regard the claim that rational traditions must achieve such equilibria—as a measure of their progress—as exemplifying "the dogmatic fallacy." About discordant practical propositions, Whitehead maintains that "[s]o long as the dogmatic fallacy infests the world, this discordance will continue to be misinterpreted. . . . But as soon as the true function of rationalism is understood, that it is a gradual approach to ideas of clarity and generality, the discord is what may be expected" (FR, 70–71). Moreover, he suggests, the dogmatic fallacy mischaracterizes not only the discordance of practical propositions, but also how propositions function in practical enquiry: "The conception of propositions as merely material for [logical] judgments is fatal to any understanding of their role in the universe. In that purely logical aspect, non-conformal propositions are merely wrong, and therefore worse than useless. But in their primary role, they pave the way along which the world advances into novelty" (PR, 187).

Like MacIntyre, Whitehead grants that truth relations signal the conformity of our judgments to our objective inheritances. Also like MacIntyre, he resists modern efforts to characterize those truth relations in narrow correspondence, coherence, or warranted assertability modes. Indeed, like MacIntyre, he stresses the social practices—replete with their ingrained background beliefs—through which we undertake to justify our moral claims. MacIntyre, however, maintains that our practical enquiries thematize a fixed, univocal telos to which our judgments progressively approximate. For Whitehead, in contrast, our enquiries track an open-ended, creative teleology, and so reveal our mandate not only to recreate the practical propositions and perfections we inherit, but also to create novel propositions and perfections. True, for Whitehead, as for MacIntyre, the progress of our practical enquiries is underwritten by God's ordered provision of ideals. Whitehead also grants that each actuality inherits from God an initial subjective aim, a conceptual appetition, in the form of a proposition oriented toward God's ends: novelty, intensity, and harmony of experience. Every such proposition, however, depends on the decisions of actual entities for its realization. Those propositions, Whitehead says, act as "lures for feeling" which must induce actual entities to realize them, as only the decisions of individuals convert ideal possibilities into facts, into realized ends and perfections. Actual entities thereby serve as co-creators of the world they and God mutually constitute.

The concrescences of these actual entities, then, exemplify how, on Whitehead's view, standards of truth and goodness serve God's aesthetic ends, since the truth conditions that God proposes generate the creative activity of actual entities. God's initial propositions lure actual entities toward objective conformity with His ideals. Yet each normative aspect of that conformity depends upon the novel pattern of emotional integration within some concrete actual entity: "Thus propositions grow with the creative advance of the world" (PR, 188). As these actualities admit or exclude the propositions God proposes, as they render their decisions upon God's proposals, they thereby decant novel propositions irreducible to the original propositions: "Evidently new propositions come into being with the creative advance of the world. For . . . it cannot be the proposition which it is, unless those logical subjects are the actual entities which they are" (PR, 259). In turn, as those propositions and the norms they come to embody accord to God's aesthetic ends, the truth conditions thus specified are also exemplified in the creative order: "The teleology of the universe is directed to the production of Beauty" (AI, 265). Accordingly, while norms of truth and goodness do lure the valuations made by actualities, these norms owe their valuative potential to the aesthetic ends they serve—novelty, intensity, and harmony of experience—and so serve ends above their own: "In other words, a truth relation is not necessarily beautiful. It may not even be neutral. It may be evil. Thus Beauty is left as the one aim which by its nature is self-justifying" (AI, 266).

To serve the end of beauty, moreover, truth relations narrowly construed (as in logical procedures permitting us but two options for decisions on a proposition—true or false, admit or exclude) are of limited use, as they preclude propositions, false from some limited perspective, that might prove productive of value. "It is more important that a proposition be interesting than that it be true," Whitehead maintains, "interesting" in that it can incite novel conceptual responses in its primary function—as a lure for feeling (AI, 244). Again, like MacIntyre, Whitehead rejects the modern tendency to void practical truth of all but its correspondence and coherentist modes: "Nothing illustrates better the danger of specialist sciences than the confusion due to handing over propositions for theoretical consideration by logicians, exclusively" (AI, 244). The correspondence and coherence truth modes, Whitehead grants, advance our enquiries by allowing us to systematically order, test, contest, and thereby manage our practical inheritances. Moreover, he suggests, our enquiries invariably seek such "blunt truths," as those truths allow us to sustain our inherited moral orders, and the individual and social enjoyments their norms permit. Still, he argues, these "blunt" truth modes are transcended by relatively less determinate adaptations between subjects and their objects, adaptations that approximate more closely to those orderings between parts and wholes indicative of aesthetic orders.

Accordingly, he suggests, the conformities between subjects and objects that the correspondence and coherence truth modes support admit two crucial limits: they are not explicable by the bare relation of identity between subject and object alone, and they form two of several possible truth relations. The correspondence truth mode, he says, presupposes a functional truth relation of perceiver to perceived that is "wider, vaguer, and more diffuse in its reference" than the more determinate correspondence mode and that is exemplified by the proper functioning of the perceiver's body, that is, its accurate appropriation of its objective environs (AI, 247). Conversely, propositions that our enquiries make conceptually determinate and coherent within traditions lurk initially, and indefinitely, in the emotive "penumbra" of those traditions' behavioral habits and patterns. These habits seed the intellectual constructions by which traditions thematize and make precise and generalize their animating ideals. To that extent, those propositions also embody their host traditions' manners, morals, and mores, their dances, rituals, music, and ceremonies. Such "communities of subjective form," Whitehead says, cultivate the enduring habits of interpretation and behavior exhibited by a tradition and thereby secure a mode of truth he describes as "symbolic reference": "This complex fusion of truth-relations, with their falsehoods intermixed, constitutes the indirect interpretative power of Art to express the truth about the nature of things" (AI, 249).

Such artifices, Whitehead suggests, underlie the practical enquiries through which we recreate our practical inheritances. Yet insofar as our practical propositions inhabit an aesthetic teleology, they must also secure pragmatic or timely truth, must respond not only to our present challenges but also to our future aspirations. For Whitehead, beauty signifies the aesthetic adaptation of parts to wholes, and artifice the "purposeful adaptation" of subjects to their world, as for instance in our construction of distinct hierarchies of ends, ideals, and principles (AI, 267). On the basis of such constructions, however, practical traditions secure either "minor" or "major" modes of beauty. In the minor mode, such systems of ends aim to minimize the internal discord of their constitutive elements, and so to afford a mode of determinate harmony, a distinctive tradition, a perfection. At the same time, however, Whitehead grades such traditions according to their "massiveness," the variety of "detail with effective contrast" they encompass, and thereby, the potential intensity and novelty of the valuations they permit. Minor perfections he regards as inferior to major ones, which encompass stark contrasts among their objective contents. While the harmonies offered by minor perfections are valuable, "[p]rogress is founded upon the experience of discordant feelings. The social value of liberty lies in its production of discords. There are perfections beyond perfections. All realization is finite, and there is no perfection that is the infinitude of all perfections. Perfections of diverse types are among themselves discordant" (AI, 257). Moreover, he maintains: "In Discord there is always a frustration. But even Discord may be preferable to a feeling of slow relapse into general anesthesia, or into tameness that is its prelude. Perfection at a low level ranks below Imperfection with higher aim" (AI, 263–64).

Whitehead grants that "in every civilization at its culmination we should find a large measure of realization of a certain type of perfection" (AI, 277). Nevertheless, he maintains, "[a] race preserves its vigour [only] so long as it harbours a real contrast between what has been and what may be; and so long as it is nerved by the vigour to adventure beyond the safeties of the past " (AI, 279). The Greeks, for instance, perfected one form of civilization. But their achievements stagnated at the hands of their successors: "With repetition in successive generations, freshness gradually vanished. Learning and learned taste replaced the ardour of adventure" (AI, 257). Whitehead heartily acknowledges the value of such perfections, and of the practical resources they offer us: "But even perfection will not bear the tedium of indefinite repetition. To sustain a civilization with the intensity of its first ardour requires more than learning. Adventure is essential, namely, the search for new perfections" (AI, 258). While we rightly value these inheritances, then, we cannot look exclusively to them to address our current practical challenges: "For otherwise actuality would consist in a cycle of repetition, realizing only a finite group of possibilities" (AI, 259). That point should teach us that "[i]t really is not sufficient to direct attention to the best that has been said and done in the ancient world. The result is static, repressive, and promotes a decadent habit of mind" (AI, 273). That recourse is unsound because "[t]he foundation of all understanding of sociological theory—that is to say, of all understanding of human life—is that no static maintenance of perfection is possible. This axiom is rooted in the nature of things. Advance or Decadence are the only choices offered to mankind. The pure conservative is fighting against the essence of the universe" (AI, 274).

To advance our enquiries, Whitehead's account, like MacIntyre's, would draw heavily upon our practical inheritances, as these resources seed the "massiveness" and thereby the potentially intense, novel, and harmonious valuations those enquiries might permit. For MacIntyre, however, practical enquiry's main aim is to diminish contrasts within and among the propositions of a tradition and so to secure social consensus. To this end, Whitehead grants that our enquiries properly aim to cultivate such consensus insofar as those social coordinations allow us to pursue a "wide and deep" range of ends and ideals. Indeed, he suggests, some provisional consensus may well prove one condition of a good life: "Morals consists in the aim at the ideal and at its lowest it concerns the prevention of relapse to lower levels" (AI, 269). Our concern with relapse to lower levels, however, should lead us neither to insist on the fixity of our currently operative practical precepts, nor to discourage us from proposing new ideals. Quite the contrary, "civilizing" traditions must offer not only harmony among the individual and shared enjoyments of agents, but also the valuative "massiveness"—the enduring contrast among ends and ideals and perfections—that evokes intense, novel enjoyments: "For civilization is nothing other than the unremitting aim at the major perfections of harmony" (AI, 271). To this end, Whitehead would grant that our enquiries properly offer us bases for provisional social consensus, for those social coordinations of ends and ideals that exemplify one vision of the good life. Nevertheless, he would maintain, these enquiries progress only when they also expand the range of good lives available to us.

Traditions progress, then, insofar as they become more inclusive of irreducibly discordant elements, and aim thereby at more complex harmonies. To that end, however, traditions must also spawn novel goods—new practical propositions and new perfections—if they are to endure as living, civilizing traditions: "I put forward as a general definition of civilization, that a civilized society is exhibiting the five qualities of Truth, Beauty, Adventure, Art, Peace" (AI, 274). In allowing their adherents to live well, his account suggests, traditions must induce some provisional Peace: "I mean a quality of mind steady in its reliance that fine action is treasured in the nature of things" (AI, 274). That Peace must also offer both Truth, the broad adaptations among agents' means and ends that permit stable, massive enjoyments, and Beauty, a wide enough variety of ends to permit intense, novel, and harmonious valuations. On these counts, our enquiries must cultivate the "habit of art," the habit of enjoying an "infinite variety of vivid values" (SMW, 200).[9] At the same time, however Truthful, Beautiful, and Peaceful a tradition proves, however well its adherents live, it must also hold out options for living better. Accordingly, it must also encompass those vivid contrasts among ends and ideals which both induce agents to Adventurously reconsider their valuative options, and permit those agents to Artfully create new practical resources. These five virtues must guide practical enquiry if it is to effectively manage our plural inheritances, as such an endeavor enjoins us not only to recreate our inheritances, but also to spawn the novel ideals that will—finally—succeed them.

Pluralism, Progress, and Practical Faith

In cultivating such progress, a Whiteheadian account would both reconceive the contemporary moral crisis MacIntyre identifies and propose a contrary solution. Recall that for MacIntyre our plural inheritances leave us with irreducible disputes both about what ends we should pursue and how we should pursue them. Our variegated practical inheritances combined with the particularism of moral traditions thus conspire to bequeath us the "problem of diversity," that is, the view that absent social consensus, we cannot exercise rational moral agency because we can neither justify the ends we pursue, nor even identify our true ends. To secure consensus, MacIntyre espouses a moral monism that aims to identify that univocal set of ideals which uniquely embodies those ends most appropriate to the good life, to that one mode of life most appropriate to us. Accordingly, he maintains: "From the standpoint of traditions of rational enquiry the problem of diversity is not abolished, but it is transformed in a way that renders it amenable of solution" (WJ, 10). His restorative solution trumps modern alternatives, he argues, because it best characterizes the problem our irreducible moral disputes indicate, best explains that problem's source in modern ethicists' rejection of tradition-constituted and teleological practical claims, and so best addresses our contemporary challenges. Yet Whitehead's account, I'll suggest, while retaining MacIntyre's teleological and tradition-referent approaches, proposes an alternative view of practical enquiry, which better explains the challenges we now face, and which offers better prospects for addressing those challenges.

On Whitehead's account of practical enquiry, our diverse moral inheritances properly reflect the pluralistic teleology we inhabit, a teleology that enjoins us also to cultivate that diversity. Whitehead's account of such enquiries, however, espouses several positions that would generate broad-based contemporary criticism. For MacIntyre and other contemporary cognitivists, of course, Whitehead's approach would exemplify emotivism, since it roots the truths of practical propositions first in their ability to incite agents' interests and feelings, and only subsequently upon the social practices of rationality through which agents render precise, and generalize, those propositions' initial appeals. For Whitehead, however, the emotivism that MacIntyre laments would reflect a misunderstanding of how practical claims secure their justification over time. Recall that Whitehead describes practical propositions as "lures for feeling." Only through their efficacy as such lures, their capacity to "romance" their potential adherents, do they evoke enquirers' subsequent efforts to make precise, and to generalize, those propositions. Accordingly, whereas contemporary ethical cognitivists depict practical claims as securing first their justification, and thereby their intelligibility and motive force, Whitehead's view precisely reverses that analysis. At the same time, emotivists would join cognitivists of all stripes in rejecting Whitehead's insistence that practical enquiries need not secure consensus. Indeed, as MacIntyre indicates, our inability to secure such consensus stokes our recourse to emotivism in the first place. Strikingly, though, Whitehead's noncognitivism rejects also the widespread insistence among contemporary ethicists that practical disputes must admit full rational resolvability as a condition of their rationality. Here, Whitehead's account would not deny that practical pluralism and the irresolvable moral disputes that attend it come at a price. Still, he suggests, the demand that practical claims either secure foundational rational vindication, or reduce to emotive insistences, exacts an even greater—and far less appreciated—price.

As we have seen, MacIntyre views our "interminable" moral disputes as an unmistakable signal of our decisive failure to secure practical consensus. That demand for consensus, however, on Whitehead's view, would purchase Peace and Truth at the cost of Art, Adventure, and Beauty. It would contravene Art by undercutting our ability to fashion new harmonies and novel traditions, would contravene Adventure by closing up our enquiries within a finite scheme of ideals, and contravene Beauty by truncating the ability of our enquiries to spawn novel perfections. According to Whitehead, "Moral codes have suffered from the exaggerated claims made for them. The dogmatic fallacy has here done its worst. . . . [E]ach code is incapable of improvement; and unfortunately in details they fail to agree either with each other or with our existing moral intuitions" (AI, 290). Yet moral codes, he maintains, are neither perfectible, nor endure indefinitely: "Conduct which in one environment and at one stage produces its measure of harmonious satisfaction, in other surroundings at another stage is destructively degrading" (AI, 290–91). That last point stresses both the particularist and the progressive orientations practical enquiries include. For Whitehead, ethical enquiries must be creative as well as recreative because the truths they yield bubble up from a processive teleology, and invariably reflect that texture. Moreover, the ideals that particular traditions mint embody finite selections from broader valuative possibilities: "Thus the notion that there are certain regulative notions, sufficiently precise to prescribe details of conduct, for all reasonable beings on earth, in every planet, and in every star-system, is at once to be put aside. That is the notion of the one type of perfection at which the Universe aims. All realization of the Good is finite and necessarily excludes certain other types" (AI, 291).

To that extent, Whitehead's account suggests, the price of practical consensus is as extraordinary as it is underappreciated, because it requires us to sacrifice every other competing good, every other potential harmony of ends, every other perfection. Worse still, that demand contravenes the essential mandate of the aesthetic teleology we inhabit, the demand that we not only recreate our inheritances, but also propose the potential successors of those perfections. Whitehead's pluralism would acknowledge that we must sustain our predecessors' practical achievements insofar as they propose live options to present and future enquirers. Recall, though, his belief that the "business of morals" is to create the future, an imperative practical enquiries hamper when they wrongly perpetuate ideals "out of season," and thereby crowd out those ideals waiting to be born. Indeed, he argues, such reiterative efforts are destructive, as they contravene the forward-looking trajectory of the aesthetic teleology and its prime mandate: to spawn novel perfections. To this end, his account suggests, we bear a positive obligation to the future, because we are charged with shepherding into being new ideals, new perfections, for our successors. In both positing and potentially systematizing such an obligation to future generations, Whitehead offers perhaps his most valuable insight into the nature and purpose of ethical enquiry. Many contemporary ethicists, of course, already hold that our current decisions should reflect some recognition of our obligations to our successors. These claims, however, have neither enjoyed a systematic basis, nor, as yet, progressed much farther beyond ethicists' theoretical concerns over how to quantify "future persons'" interests. Whitehead's account, in contrast, suggests that to understand the future's obliging hold upon us, we must first attend to the emotivist crisis that MacIntyre identifies, with its rightful concern that our moral confusions may well imperil practical enquiry itself. At the same time, though, Whitehead's account hints also that if we are to discharge these obligations, we must envision practical enquiry more broadly than does MacIntyre.

For Whitehead, the emotivist crisis MacIntyre identifies would issue not from the interminable moral disputes our plural inheritances offer us, but from the ill-founded assumption that practical disputes must admit wholesale resolvability as a condition of their rationality. For MacIntyre, progress in rational enquiry occurs only within a single tradition, and only when adherents to that tradition succeed in elaborating "ever more comprehensive and adequate statements of their positions through the dialectical procedure of advancing [and answering] objections" (WJ, 144). But this task aims finally at falsifying the claims of competing traditions. MacIntyre notes, for instance, that "Aristotle's accounts of justice and of practical reasoning require it to be the case, if they are true, that those [competing] accounts shall be found erroneous and defective" (WJ, 145). Here, Whitehead would agree that such exclusions permit the widespread harmonies of thought and action that particular traditions enact, and so allow those traditions to distill their distinctive, potentially enduring perfections. Nevertheless, he maintains, the aim at a comprehensive, metaphysically adequate account of how practical enquiries unfold precludes such an exclusionary conception of practical truth: "The chief danger to philosophy is narrowness in the selection of evidence. This narrowness arises from the idiosyncrasies and timidities of particular authors, of particular social groups, of particular schools of thought, of particular epochs in the history of civilization. The evidence relied upon is arbitrarily biased by the temperaments of individuals, by the provincialities of groups, and by the limitations of schemes of thought. The evil, resulting from this distortion of evidence, is at its worst in the consideration of . . . ultimate ideals" (PR, 337).

On MacIntyre's view, rational enquiry entails such an exclusionary account of truth. Yet MacIntyre's moral particularism restricts the ability of even our favored practical resources to offer living ideals to our successors. MacIntyre claims, for instance, that recent efforts to develop a Thomist conception of natural rights have produced only "alien" modern additions to Aquinas's synthesis rather than natural outgrowths (TR, 76–77). But that conclusion overlooks how deeply rooted the central concepts of the natural rights tradition are in theological and teleological concepts that Aquinas helped to develop. Indeed, MacIntyre's particularism precludes such productive collusion among adherents of distinct practical traditions. As he notes, when we refer to our fellow enquirers using the word *we*, "The assumption underlying its use is that there is one and only one overall community of enquiry, sharing substantially one and the same set of concepts and beliefs" (WJ, 169). Such moral tribalism, however, Whitehead's account suggests, unduly restricts our ability to draw upon a broader inheritance of ends and ideals which, despite their admittedly stark contrasts, alike in their creation and in their continuance, face some common social constraints, address some common practical challenges, and adumbrate some shared aspirations. Worse still, though, Whitehead's account suggests, MacIntyre's moral monism imperils not only our ability to draw upon the entire range of practical resources we inherit, it imperils also the social practice of practical rationality.

Such a monism imperils practical enquiry because our inheritances extend not only trans-traditionally, not only across tribes, but also trans-historically. For MacIntyre, moral progress arises interior to one tradition, as that tradition's claims advance toward the univocal, fixed truth to which they approximate. For Whitehead, in contrast, moral progress entails a dual imperative: to recreate that tradition's inheritances, and thereby also to expand the range of ends and ideals, the range of perfections, that that tradition may make available to its successors—near and far, present and future. Like MacIntyre, Whitehead shares a reverence for our inheritances. As indicated earlier, though, he holds also that "[a] race preserves its vigour so long as it harbours a real contrast between what has been and what may be; and so long as it is nerved by the vigour to adventure beyond the safeties of the past" (AI, 279). Such is the essential mandate of our practical lives—we aspire not only to live well, but to live better. And in this endeavor, we are bound irrevocably to the future available to our successors, just as our predecessors were bound to ours. Of contemporary ethicists' efforts to reproduce those excellences achieved by the Greeks, for instance, Whitehead notes: "These standards have served the Western races well. But the procedure has its disadvantages. It is backward looking, and it is limited to one type of social excellence. Today the world is passing into a new stage of its existence. New knowledge, and new technologies have altered the proportions of things. The particular example of an ancient society sets too static an ideal, and neglects the whole range of opportunity" (AI, 273).

Again, recall that Whitehead, like MacIntyre, readily acknowledges the debts we owe to our predecessors' achievements. The objective immortality that their accomplishments rightly secure we cannot dismiss, as that would contravene the aesthetic teleology from which they arose and to which they give voice. But, Whitehead reminds us, "the definition of culture as the knowledge of the best that has been said and done . . . omits the great fact that in their day the great achievements of the past were the adventures of the past" (AI, 279). Indeed, our practical enquiries must embody the "intellectual adventures" through which we construct novel ideals and ends, and thereby expand the range of goods, enjoyments, and perfections available to our successors. And to this end, Whitehead's account suggests, we bear a strict responsibility to offer our successors novel ends and ideals, to shepherd new perfections into being. That task alone discharges the debt we owe to our predecessors, a debt that we pay properly not to our predecessors, but to the future in their stead. To this extent, practical enquiry would aim to revivify the traditions MacIntyre avers. Yet it would be undertaken also under the auspices of the five virtues that characterize practical enquiries: Art, Adventure, Truth, Beauty, and Peace. For MacIntyre, the central virtues operative here would be Truth and Peace, univocal truth oriented toward securing an enduring social consensus. For Whitehead, in contrast, the practical truths we propose and the peace or consensus they secure will prove at most transiently efficacious and so transiently true. Accordingly, our practical endeavors must also include adventure and artifice, must exemplify an aesthetic perfectionism, and so must aim not to uncover a fixed telos, but to spawn that plurality of ends waiting to be born.

Now, this stark transience of our practical achievements, Whitehead grants, comes at a cost, for while our only options are "advance or decadence," we have no guarantees that our aspirations to "live better" will come to fruition. Worse, the merits of our practical proposals are evaluable, finally, only by our successors, in terms the present cannot muster. Nevertheless, we must perpetually renew our practical enquiries not only because they inhabit an aesthetic teleology, but also because that teleology enjoins them to spawn new ends as a condition for the continuation of those enquiries. Absent any guarantees that our achievements will endure, moreover, we are enjoined to undertake such enquiries if we are to discharge our obligations to the future: to expand the range of live options we offer to our successors, and so, to seed broader, more massive, traditions. To these ends, we must espouse moral systems that neither insist on the fixed truth of their foundational propositions, nor degenerate into the emotivist alternative. Rather, we must seek to develop a processive morality that is creative and adventurous. We are enjoined to do so, Whitehead's account suggests, because the "world loyalty" of our enquiries, their elemental fidelity to the aesthetic teleology they reveal, teaches us that moral truths are processive or transient, and arise amid an irreducible plurality of ends and goods. At the same time, though, that "world loyalty" teaches us that we must sustain our practical faith, that is, the optimism that we can create as well as recreate such perfections, and so discharge those obligations we bear to the future.

Whitehead would grant that the loss of practical enquiry as a social practice that the emotivist alternative implies would mark, as MacIntyre warns, "a grave cultural loss." But Whitehead's account would also suggest that MacIntyre's moral particularism stokes that emotivism, because it posits a stark dichotomy between foundational practical truths on the one hand, and the reduction of practical claims to emotive insistences on the other. That dichotomy, Whitehead suggests, undercuts the ability of our enquiries to reveal truthfully the progressive, open-ended, aesthetic teleology we inhabit. For his part, MacIntyre recognizes the limits under which our moral enquiries labor, insofar as he commends faith in dogmatic tradition as the lone viable terminus they admit. And here, Whitehead grants, barring such dogmatic recourse we might well face the emotivist crisis MacIntyre warns against. After all, if we affirm the assumption that our practical enquiries must either deliver univocal, eternal truths, or reduce to subjective insistences, then we might well wonder what purpose such enquiries serve if, as Whitehead claims, they cannot yield such eternal truths. Nevertheless, Whitehead maintains, "[i]t is always open to us, having regard to the imperfections of all metaphysical systems, to lose hope at the exact point where we find ourselves. The preservation of such faith must depend on an ultimate moral intuition into the nature of intellectual action—that it should embody the adventure of hope" (PR, 42).

Our practical enquiries properly embody "the adventure of hope," Whitehead suggests, when they reflect our world-loyalty to the aesthetic teleology we inhabit, discharge our obligation to future generations, and, in the process, cultivate a social practice wherein we retain the prospect that we may not only live well, but live better. For Whitehead, the current moral crisis that our enduring disputes generate is not the disputes themselves but the conclusion we draw from them, that is, that our enquiries must either resolve such disputes or surrender any pretense to rationality. This conclusion, Whitehead's account suggests, augurs not merely emotivism, but an amoralism wherein we dispense with the prospect that practical enquiries can propose novel, potentially enduring perfections. Our ostensible "moral crisis" then, is not emotivist, but is amoralist and even nihilistic, is predicated on the belief that we can live no better than we do now, that we, and those who will succeed us, can make no practical progress. That view contravenes the aesthetic teleology we inhabit, and so rejects our proper world-loyalty. Worse still, it exemplifies the main contemporary failing of our practical enquiries, not that they fail to secure moral consensus, but that they fail to cultivate our practical faith, our optimism in and for the future.

As aims at human perfectibility, our moral endeavors always affirm an elemental compact with a future we can but dimly discern. Whitehead, like MacIntyre, reminds us rightly that we must perpetually renew, lest we imperil, that compact. For MacIntyre, we honor that compact when we apprentice to our predecessors' practical achievements, and hand them over, largely fully formed, to our successors. Conversely, for Whitehead, we renew that compact when we cultivate our practical faith, and with it the social practices through which we might decant new perfections to hand over to our successors. To that end, though, Whitehead's account suggests, we must not only take up the practical challenges marking our era, and propose novel ends and ideals by which our successors might allay them, but we must also cultivate our successors' faith in that practice and in that endeavor, in the prospects of what Whitehead terms "intellectual action." Here, Whitehead would grant that the imperative to decant novel perfections strains the harmonizing potential of our moral enquiries. Were that not so, our practical endeavors would require neither practical faith, nor the enduring intellectual adventures that faith nourishes. We require such faith, though, not only because the ends and ideals we espouse will invariably prove finite and transient, but also because it stokes, in the face of that transience and pluralism, the optimism that our enquiries will allow us to improve upon those ends and ideals, to live as Whitehead says, not only well, but better. We face a "grave cultural loss," then, not when we fail to secure enduring moral consensus on a fixed set of ideals, but when we fail to cultivate those future-oriented aspirations of practical enquiry apart from which our moral life surrenders its mandate, its purpose, its romance.

Notes

1. Alasdair MacIntyre, *After Virtue: A Study in Moral Theory* (Notre Dame: University of Notre Dame Press, 1984). Henceforth AV.

2. Alasdair MacIntyre, *Whose Justice? Which Rationality?* (Notre Dame: University of Notre Dame Press, 1988). Henceforth WJ.

3. Alasdair MacIntyre, *First Principles, Final Ends, and Contemporary Philosophical Issues* (Milwaukee: Marquette University Press, 1990). Henceforth FP.

4. Alfred North Whitehead, *The Function of Reason* (Princeton: Princeton University Press, 1929). Henceforth FR.

5. Alfred North Whitehead, *Religion in the Making* (New York: MacMillan Press, 1933). Henceforth RM.

6. Alasdair MacIntyre, *Three Rival Versions of Moral Enquiry: Encyclopedia, Genealogy, and Tradition* (Notre Dame: University of Notre Dame Press, 1990). Henceforth TR.

7. Alfred North Whitehead, *Process and Reality,* Corrected Edition, edited by D. R. Griffin and D. W. Sherburne (New York: Free Press, 1978). Henceforth PR.

8. Alfred North Whitehead, *Adventures of Ideas* (New York: MacMillan Press, 1933). Henceforth AI.

9. Alfred North Whitehead, *Science and the Modern World* (New York: MacMillan Press, 1929). Henceforth SMW.

Part Four

Whitehead and European Philosophy

CHAPTER 7

Whitehead and Merleau-Ponty

Healing the Bifurcation of Nature

WILLIAM S. HAMRICK

The task of a philosophy of nature would be to describe all the modes of process, without grouping them under certain titles borrowed from substance thinking. Man is a mode as well as animal cells. There is no limit to the proliferation of categories, but there are types of "concrescence" which pass by shading off from one to another.

—Maurice Merleau-Ponty

When searching for "points of connection" between Whitehead and Maurice Merleau-Ponty, it matters a great deal which Merleau-Ponty we mean. For almost the whole of his philosophical career, he identified philosophy with phenomenology, the task of which was to describe the appearances as they appear in order to understand their essential meaning-structures, or essences. Whitehead, on the other hand, was a speculative metaphysician who sought to elaborate an empirically adequate and logically coherent metaphysical system to explain the nature of the basic entities that make up all that we experience. That is, Whitehead developed a philosophy of organism that revolved around microcosmic "occasions of experience" out of which everything we see is constructed, whereas the Lifeworld that Merleau-Ponty sought to describe is obviously macrocosmic. It would never have occurred to him to seek an explanation based on microcosmic entities for the world of human life. Closely related to this difference, Whitehead maintained that "[t]he study of philosophy is a voyage towards the larger generalities" (PR, 10), whereas Merleau-Ponty's interest was in the careful and patient description and appreciation (in both senses) of particulars.

Further, as a phenomenologist, Merleau-Ponty held that the only meaningful nature we encounter consists of the objects of our own experiences which are conditioned by multiple layers of sedimented cultural meanings. We are inextricably mixed up with the phenomena because a phenomenon is inherently a unity of a perceiving subject and the object perceived. As a result, our subjective activities, far from being a "high-altitude," detached thinking, are actually part of the evidence. Speaking to the *Société française de philosophie,* he stated that "[i]t is true that we discover the unreflected. But the unreflected we go back to is not that which is prior to philosophy or prior to reflection. It is the unreflected which is understood and conquered by reflection" (1964a, 19).

Therefore, if the Merleau-Ponty who identified philosophy with phenomenology had read *Process and Reality,* which he almost certainly did not, he probably would have had little sympathy with Whitehead's description of the discovery of metaphysical principles. This is particularly so for the latter's well-known simile likening the process of discovery to "the flight of an aeroplane. It starts from the ground of particular observation; it makes a flight in the thin air of imaginative generalization; and it again lands for renewed observation rendered acute by rational observation" (PR, 5). The early Merleau-Ponty would likely have characterized such method as the very sort of "high-altitude" thinking that he wished to reject.

For Merleau-Ponty another consequence of being inexorably mixed up with the phenomena is that it is a scientific myth that the world is full and complete, self-enclosed, and outside all relationships with the percipients for which that world is "already there." Rather, the scientific world is an abstraction from the Lifeworld which funds it with its basic meanings. Therefore, the task of phenomenology is to describe that Lifeworld without any scientific or metaphysical analyses and explanations which the Lifeworld itself makes possible. Whitehead, on the other hand, obviously had a higher regard for the epistemological value of science, even if in its history it had sometimes gone off the rails. What he saw as an "abstraction" consisted only of those false views of nature and our place within it, discussed below, rather than the enterprise itself.

Equally importantly, for Merleau-Ponty, perceptual objects are paradoxical because they are "in-themselves—for-us." That is, the world is "already there," independent of me, but at the same time the only world of which it makes sense to speak is the world of my experience. Effectively this position attempts to stake out a middle ground in the realism-idealism debate, though one that is easy to misunderstand. Thus, one member of the French Society of Philosophy praised him for his realism, while another appreciated his defense of idealism. Whitehead, on the other hand, was, or is usually interpreted to have been, a realist who believed that (past) reality was stubbornly fixed and objective, independent of human participation.

However, despite these substantially different assumptions about philosophical method and objectives, Merleau-Ponty's phenomenological writings do yield additional points of connection with Whitehead. Those of us who, many years ago, first began to explore those affinities, based our conclusions on three rather thin sources of evidence. The first was a meager reference to Whitehead's view of nature as "process" *("passage")* at the end of Merleau-Ponty's 1956–57 lecture course at the Collège de France on "The Concept of Nature"(1970, 87). We also knew from his other texts that he had read Jean Wahl's *Vers le concret,* the lengthy middle chapter of which discusses Whitehead, but we did not know if Merleau-Ponty had read any of Whitehead's own texts.

Second, both thinkers conceived their philosophies as therapeutic reactions against the legacy of classical modern philosophy and science, most notably the Cartesian dualism of mind and body and Galilean-Cartesian physics. This historically enduring heritage was powerful enough to frame much of the early-twentieth-century intellectual context in which Whitehead and Merleau-Ponty created their philosophies. In fact, it was in the course of discussing Laplace's contribution to this heritage that Merleau-Ponty referred to Whitehead's view of nature as "process." Among his many arguments against the Cartesian dualism, Merleau-Ponty points to abundant experimental and experiential evidence in Gestalt psychology to show that perception is not a passive response to prior stimuli that putatively structure it. On the contrary, at a prereflective, pre-thetic level—in an "anonymous" and "pre-personal" (1962, 240) fashion, and in the absence of any intellectual acts—perception actively structures a given field, and so is neither passive nor separate and distinct from the stimuli that supposedly provoke it. This means that the "subject" and the "object" of experience are not isolable, independent relata. Rather, they are inextricably mixed up with each other—dual aspects of a unitary structure of perceptual experience. But if so, "mind" and "body" cannot be what Descartes took them to be. The body turns out to be intelligent in advance of intellectual acts, and intelligence is therefore carnal. Thus, how could the eye, as a material organ, "take account of" the form of stimuli and be actively mixed up in constituting those stimuli? "It can," Merleau-Ponty concludes, "only if we introduce beside the objective body the phenomenal body, if we make of it a knowing-body and if, finally, we substitute for [a Cartesian] consciousness, as the subject of perception, existence, that is to say, being in the world through a body" (1962, 357n.).

The texts also indicated that, third, both philosophers were influenced positively, though not uncritically, by Bergson and the American pragmatists. The latter consisted mainly of William James, whose influence Merleau-Ponty felt through Husserl who had attentively studied James's descriptions of the "fringes" of consciousness, and of John Dewey.[1] Partly as a result of these common influences, and partly out of a similar reaction to classical modern philosophy and science, Whitehead and Merleau-Ponty ended up agreeing on several points. They both end up with very similar conceptions of personal identity (Hamrick 1974; Doud 1977). Their descriptions of decision making as a dialectic of spontaneity and sedimented past meanings are remarkably alike. Both stress creativity, and both detect ambiguity at the heart of free decisions (Doud, 147–48).

Likewise for both thinkers, the living human body is the point of departure and primary exemplar of their philosophical reflections. For the early Merleau-Ponty, the "phenomenal body," or "lived body" *(le corps propre),* constitutes my anchorage in the world, the necessary medium in which I gain any knowledge about the world, other people, and even myself. The lived body is not primarily an object partly because it is always "with me" (1962, 106) as my access to the world, and partly because it provides the meanings necessary to construe the body as an object in special contexts such as science. Thus, the scientific body is not totally false, but it is an abstraction from the lived body. For this reason, and because we are inextricably mixed up with the phenomena, Merleau-Ponty also resisted any purely natural interpretation of the body, particularly normative accounts that stem from one version or other of natural law theory. All our behavior owes something to biology—it is not a purely cultural construct—but it simultaneously escapes a solely biological basis through being encultured.

Whitehead similarly describes the body as point of departure and "the originative archetype for the study of reality" (Devettere 1976, 319). *Science and the Modern World* tells us that "the body is the organism whose states regulate our cognisance of the world. The unity of the perceptual field therefore must be a unity of bodily experience" (133). And even more explicitly, the discussion of "Organisms and Environment" in *Process and Reality* adds that Whitehead has, "with Locke, tacitly taken human experience as an example upon which to found the generalized description required for metaphysics" (112). On the other hand, *Modes of Thought* tells us bluntly that the body "is in fact merely one among other natural objects" (156).

I noted at the beginning that it matters a great deal as to which Merleau-Ponty we refer when we try to mark out points of connection between his work and that of Whitehead. It is now time to consider the other Merleau-Ponty. During the last five or so years of his life, Merleau-Ponty's thought took a metaphysical, or ontological, turn. Now it was no longer a matter of contrasting the lived body with the objective body, or a body-consciousness with a Cartesian *cogito.* Rather, Merleau-Ponty's later works—especially *Eye and Mind* and the incomplete, posthumously published *The Visible and the Invisible*—abandoned the primacy of these distinctions. Thus he writes: "The problems posed in *Ph.P. [Phénoménologie de la perception]* are insoluble because I start there from the 'consciousness'-'object' distinction" (1968, 200; bracketed title in the original). What was inexplicable was the relationship between the objective and lived bodies, how "a given fact of the 'objective' order (a given cerebral lesion)" could wreak havoc in one's life-world (1968, 200). The earlier phenomenology was also unable to account for the relation between consciousness and body, even the lived body, as well as the relation of ideas, the understanding, and intellectual life generally, to perception.

As a result, Merleau-Ponty's last writings developed an ontology of "flesh" *(la chair).* Flesh is neither a particular fact or entity, a mental representation, nor the point of intersection of "mind" and "body." Rather, "there is no name in traditional philosophy to designate it. . . . [F]lesh is not matter, is not mind, is not substance. To designate it, we should need the old term 'element,' in the sense it was used to speak of water, air, earth, and fire, that is, in the sense of a *general thing,* midway between the spatio-temporal individual and the idea" (1968, 139). Flesh includes my flesh and the flesh of the world. The principal mode of difference between these two modes of being is that:

> The flesh of the world is not *self-sensing (se sentir)* as is my flesh—It is sensible and not sentient—I call it flesh, nonetheless . . . in order to say that it is a *pregnancy* of possibles. . . . It is by the flesh of the world that in the last analysis one can understand the lived body *(corps propre)*—The flesh of the world is of the Being-seen, i.e., is a Being that is *eminently percipi,* and it is by it that we can understand the *percipere:* this perceived that we call my body applying itself to the rest of the perceived . . . all this is finally possible and means something only because *there is* Being. (1968, 250; italics in the original)

Furthermore, because flesh is now the primary explanatory category, the lived body is an object in nature alongside other objects, made of the "same stuff": "Visible and mobile, my body is a thing among things. . . . Things are an annex or prolongation of itself; they are incrusted into its flesh, they are part of its full definition; the world is made of the same stuff as the body" (Merleau-Ponty 1964d, 163).

This ontological shift to the primacy of flesh entails also that Merleau-Ponty will join Whitehead in rejecting another aspect of Cartesianism and its progeny. This is the bifurcation of nature into minds and bodies, values and facts, subjects and objects, and secondary and primary qualities—the former half of each pair being excluded, and the latter half included, in nature. Nature is "an object from which we have arisen" rather than a "mere accessory of consciousness in its tête-à-tête with knowledge" (Merleau-Ponty 1970, 64).

Healing the bifurcation of nature takes place through stressing our ontological identity with the rest of the world—that is, with nonhuman flesh—and Merleau-Ponty began to adumbrate their identity through the notion of the "chiasm" (1968, 130) or "reversibility" (154). This means that all flesh is such that seeing is also to be seen, touching is to be touched, feeling is to be felt, and so on. Merleau-Ponty reaches this conclusion as a result of asking questions which, as Jan Van der Veken points out, have no place in phenomenology:

> Why is it that my body is adjusted to the world? It must be that the world is somehow attuned to my body: it shares the same basic ontological structure; just as the body, the world is not just seen. The artist feels that things look at him, says Merleau-Ponty. To see/to be seen, to feel/to be felt becomes the most basic characteristic of *the flesh of the world.* The basic structure: to feel/to be felt, to see/to be seen is all pervasive. (2000, 326)

Making sense of the claim that nonhuman flesh can also be "permeated by subjectivity" (Van der Veken 2000, 326) means that we must get beyond the "highly poetic way" of stating that "Cézanne no longer knows who is seeing and who is being seen." We also need to understand how to "extrapolate (or generalize) such basic structure" (328). This requirement of philosophical adequacy will also entail for Merleau-Ponty a radical methodological change from phenomenology to descriptive generalization (see the epigraph of this chapter). Both this change in method, as well as the results that it produced, turned out to be influenced significantly by his reading of Whitehead.

In the unfinished text of *The Visible and the Invisible,* Van der Veken is clearly right to say that "Merleau-Ponty is mainly exploring intuitions" which his untimely death prevented from becoming a "full fledged conceptuality" (2000, 328). However, the 1994 publication of expanded and annotated student notes from Merleau-Ponty's lectures at the Collège de France from 1956–60 contains a thirteen-page essay on "The Idea of Nature for Whitehead," and this essay shows that the "full fledged conceptuality" at the end of Merleau-Ponty's route very probably would have taken on a strongly Whiteheadian cast. The works on which Merleau-Ponty based his appreciation of Whitehead were *Science and the Modern World* and *The Concept of Nature.* He also referred several times to Wahl's *Vers le concret,* the long middle chapter of which discusses Whitehead.

I have described elsewhere in some detail the main themes from this essay (Hamrick 1999). Here I will give a briefer account and then make some remarks about their implications for drawing Whitehead and Merleau-Ponty together in a stereoscopic vision. Taking them in the order in which Merleau-Ponty himself discusses them, the first is Whitehead's rejection of the Laplacian concepts of space and time already mentioned above. But here we learn that Merleau-Ponty is attracted to Whitehead's criticisms because they attack Laplace's "simple location" of supposedly nonoverlapping, nonencroaching spatial and temporal quanta (1994, 154). Merleau-Ponty praises instead Whitehead's view of overlapping, encroaching relationships (1994, 157) between instances of process that are temporally thick instead of a series of "flash points" (CN, 173) or atomistic "nows" (1994, 154).

Second, Merleau-Ponty agrees with, though he did not fully understand the meaning of, Whitehead's view that nature contains an "internal activity" (CN, 54). What particularly interests Merleau-Ponty is that, whatever this "internal activity" might be, it is not an idealistic passage from Nature to Spirit (1994, 155). Therefore, activities of process are what is given to us. "There is no Nature at an instant: all reality implies 'an advance of nature' *(moving on)*" (1994, 155, citing CN, 54; italics in the original). Nature is a creative advance in which an object becomes "only an abbreviated way to note that there has been an ensemble of relationships" (1994, 158). Furthermore, third, in these relationships, there is no bifurcation between primary and secondary qualities (1994, 158).

From this refusal of bifurcation Merleau-Ponty draws three conclusions. (1) "The unity of events, their inherence in each other, appears here as the correlative of their insertion in the unity of the thinking being" (1994, 159). This language is very close to the passage from *Science and the Modern World* cited earlier, namely that "[t]he unity of the perceptual field therefore must be a unity of bodily experience" (91).

As with the phenomenal, or lived body described above, (2) the mind is not, as Descartes and Laplace would have it, outside of nature. On the contrary, "[i]ts awareness shares in the passage of Nature" (1994, 159, citing CN, 67 [but Whitehead does not capitalize "nature"]). A corollary of this fact is that, despite misleading connotations of the "aeroplane" simile cited above, Whitehead himself would also have refused the "high-altitude" thinking of the detached observer rejected by Merleau-Ponty. Nature is an "operative presence" (1994, 163, citing CN, 73), because of the indissolubility of creator and creature. Likewise, the course of nature cannot be reduced to "'the history of matter' . . . 'the fortunes of matter in the adventure of nature'" (1994, 157, citing CN, 16).[2]

(3) In what would later be the language of chiasmatic reversibility, natural process and our "inherence in the Whole" (1994, 159) give birth to a unity of body and nature and create the framework of relationships that constitute intersubjectivity. Since the body, even the lived body, is now considered to be a part of nature, what is true for me is also the case for everyone else as well: "I am a part of Nature and function as any given event of Nature: I am, through my body, part of Nature, and the parts of Nature admit between them relations of the same type as those that my body has with Nature" (1994, 159).

The fourth major theme from Whitehead's writings that Merleau-Ponty endorses is that knowledge and causality are dual aspects of these relations. He believes that Whitehead is correct to point out that the flaw in Hume's epistemological premises consisted in limiting his account of experience to the data of "presentational immediacy." Hume did not grasp the "infrastructure, behind the immediate, of which our body gives us the feeling" (1994, 159). The "push of duration" in the creative advance of nature is not an accidental property of nature, but rather belongs to it essentially and to all its diverse presentations. The creative advance of nature, like a wave, is global rather than fragmented (1994, 163). What does individuate it is the "natural passage of time" (1994, 162). For Merleau-Ponty, Whitehead correctly describes a Gestalt structure of temporality in which any given occasion of experience prereflectively retains its predecessors and makes a (present) decision about them in the light of what sort of future it protentively intends. Merleau-Ponty rejects, as he correctly reads Whitehead as rejecting, the line of thought from Augustine to Bergson that made temporality an aspect of subjectivity as over against matter (1994, 160). Rather, the "natural passage of time, the pulsation of time which is not a pulsation of the subject, but of Nature . . . is inscribed in our body as sensorality" (1994, 162). We participate in this natural time because "Whitehead always maintained the idea of a 'concrescence' of Nature in itself which is taken up by life. . . . The unity of Nature, according to Whitehead, is founded on this, that all nature is 'concrescence'" (1994, 165).

It follows from this passage that Merleau-Ponty also finds in Whitehead's views of our relations with nature support for what he refers to as the immanence and transcendence of nature. Immanence means that we are immediately present to nature rather than being mediated by representational thought. Transcendence means that nature "is complete in any of its appearances, but is not exhausted by any of them" (1994, 160). Merleau-Ponty considers that these closely linked properties of nature follow directly from the rejection of simple location, the bifurcation of mind from nature, and, once more, the detached spectator. Thus, he cites approvingly Whitehead's statement (at CN, 14–15) that "[t]here is no way to stop Nature in order to look at it" (1994, 160). It therefore also follows that Merleau-Ponty would not in the end have thought Whitehead guilty of endorsing "high-altitude thinking."

For Merleau-Ponty, Whitehead does not provide a "definitive clarification" of what nature is. It is neither merely an object of thought nor subject, and for the same reason: "its opacity and envelopment. It is an obscure principle" (1994, 162). Nevertheless, he does believe that Whitehead has taken a decisive step in providing positive content for the concept of nature. Then, in the last paragraph he arrives at the passage cited as the epigraph of this paper (1994, 165). He concludes by noting that Whitehead has refused the double dangers of mechanism and vitalism, while holding on to the view that "life is not substance" (165). As for the epigraph, it is remarkable how, without ever having read *Process and Reality,* he could have come so close to expressing what *Process and Reality* would turn out to be.

However, it is not so remarkable, given the themes of the Whitehead essay briefly described above, that at least six traces of Whitehead's thought would be inscribed in Merleau-Ponty's last writings, particularly *Eye and Mind* and *The Visible and the Invisible.* First and perhaps most obviously, flesh as an "element" has the same global, nonfragmented character as does nature for Whitehead. Also, characterizing nonsentient things as "flesh" because they present us with a "*pregnancy* of possibles," along with Merleau-Ponty's description of nature as events (1968, 200, 208), converges on what Merleau-Ponty appreciated in Whitehead's notion of concrescence and in his description of the way that acts of process prehend their past actual worlds.

Second, the Whiteheadian rejection of "simple location" manifests itself in Merleau-Ponty's descriptions of the chiasmatic relationships between our flesh and that of the world, between my body and those of others, and between my objective and lived body. Since my body, just as all the things around me, are modes of the same flesh, "this flesh of my body is shared by the world, the world *reflects* it, encroaches upon it and it encroaches upon the world. . . . [T]hey are in a relation of transgression or of overlapping" (1968, 248). "Encroachment" *(empiètement)* and "overlapping" *(enjambement)* are the same words that Merleau-Ponty uses in *La Nature* to characterize Whitehead's rejection of Laplace.

For example, Merleau-Ponty writes that "[w]e speak of 'inspiration,' and the word should be taken literally. There really is inspiration and expiration of Being, action and passion so slightly discernible that it becomes impossible to distinguish between what sees and what is seen, what paints and what is painted" (1964d, 167; see also 1968, 138). In the same way Whitehead asks: "Where does my body end and the external world begin? . . . . [T]he breath as it passes in and out of my lungs from my mouth and throat fluctuates in its bodily relationship. Undoubtedly the body is very vaguely distinguishable from external nature" (MT, 155, 156).

The denial of simple location is also inscribed in Merleau-Ponty's last account of intersubjectivity, now termed intercorporeity. My experience of my own body and that of the other are two sides of the same reality of flesh. The other's sentience is implied in our own because "to feel one's body is also to feel its aspect for the other" (1968, 245). I and the other "belong to the same system of being for itself and being for another; we are moments of the same syntax . . . we belong to the same Being" (1968, 245).

Third, Merleau-Ponty's descriptions of this envelopment of flesh as one of "intertwining" and "chiasm" embody not only a denial of simple location, but also the trace of Whitehead's assertion (at CN, 54) that nature is an "internal activity." As Merleau-Ponty construes it, concrescence occurs when "a bit of matter coils up on itself [and] prolongs the 'passage of Nature'" and unifies it (1994, 162). Merleau-Ponty uses this same imagery of "coiling" to describe the chiasmatic reversibilities of flesh. It is "the coiling over of the visible upon the seeing body, of the tangible upon the touching body, which is attested in particular when the body sees itself, touches itself seeing and touching the things" (1968, 146).

Fourth, the chiasm is temporal as well as spatial. Merleau-Ponty holds, just as does Whitehead, that the past is immediately present to the present, and that, as noted above, through these internal relations, a present act or decision begins with the retention of the past. Thus, Whitehead could have written for both of them when he noted that "[f]eelings [in the new act of concrescence] are 'vectors'; for they feel what is *there* and transform it into what is *here*" (PR, 87). The chiasm gets enacted in the becoming of the concrescence through the receptivity of feelings of causal efficacy. The data of a given experience must always be in the past, if only the immediate past, because, as Whitehead pointed out, one cannot perceive exact contemporaries. There is always some temporal divergence, which is what Merleau-Ponty calls an *"écart,"* between the experience and its data—touching and touched, seeing and being seen, and so on. Merleau-Ponty in fact agrees: the chiasmatic reversibility between touching and being touched "is always imminent and never realized in fact" (1968, 147). If I attempt to see my eyes seeing, I can either see or be seen, but the attempt to unite them in a single experience always miscarries at the last moment. As a result, awareness of the chiasm always depends on having at least two separate noncontemporary occasions of experience.

Fifth, just as "[t]he experience of my own body and the experience of the other are themselves two sides of the same Being" (1968, 225), so also are mind and body, idea and flesh. "There is a body of the mind, and a mind of the body and a chiasm between them" (1968, 259), he writes, and ideas, rather than being the contrary of the visible, are, as Proust had the merit of showing us, "its lining and depth" (1968, 149). Each speech-act is literally an incarnation, words made flesh. Or, as Whitehead put it in *Religion in the Making,* "Expression is the one fundamental sacrament. It is the outward and visible sign of an inward and spiritual grace" (RM, 127).[3]

One also finds the same relationship of the visible and the invisible in nonhuman nature. Meaning is carnal and organic; it is the in-visible within the visible which creates the style of the thing displayed as its latency and possibility. Thus, Merleau-Ponty writes: "As the vein bears the leaf from within, from the depths of its flesh, ideas are the texture of experience, its style, first mute, then uttered. Like every style, they are elaborated within the thickness of being" (1968, 119; translation altered). The style expresses the thing's "unique manner of existing" (1962, xviii). It is the ideality of the flesh which is not a mere property among others, but a "conceptless presentation of universal Being" (1964d, 182) or, as he said in the Whitehead essay, nature "is complete in any of its appearances, but is not exhausted by any of them" (1994, 160).

Sixth, it is also the case, as Merleau-Ponty noted of Whitehead, that ideas as meanings are not first provided us by representational thinking. Nor do they emerge from an idealistic sort of constituting consciousness: "[T]he relation between a thought and its object, between the *cogito* and the *cogitatum,* contains neither the whole nor even the essential of our commerce with the world" (1968, 35). Whitehead put the matter more simply when he said that "I contend that the notion of mere knowledge is a high abstraction" (AI, 225–26). For Whitehead, an idea is any pattern of definiteness that achieves ingression into an actual occasion of experience. They are also in-visible for Whitehead in all the ways that definiteness can manifest itself. These encompass not only the objective form under which past actual occasions are prehended, but also the subjective form of the present occasion which expresses the way that it prehends, and it is the subjective aim that expresses how it wants to be perceived by future occasions. In short, both the "objective" and "subjective" species of eternal objects (PR, 291) are in-visible, carnal ideas in Merleau-Ponty's sense. They are part of the way that Whitehead could have argued that he had met Merleau-Ponty's ontological requirements for the inseparability of creator and creature, the installation of potentiality and internal activity in nature, and escaping the bifurcation of primary and secondary qualities.

There is at least one other point of connection between these two thinkers that does not appear in the Whitehead essay. It is philosophical humility and what might be called, for lack of a better phrase, philosophical commitment. Merleau-Ponty's method of descriptive generalization was structured through interrogation rather than dogmatic pronouncements. It was open, rather than closed. It was humble to the point of diffidence about claiming success for hard-won insights rather than being hermetically sealed in self-congratulatory pride or smug assurances. It was also driven by a commitment to consider all the evidence while maintaining a sensitivity to the ambiguity of that evidence.

Whitehead shares the same philosophical humility and commitment. Three times in the first twenty pages of *Process and Reality* he warns his readers about expecting too much from speculative philosophy. The penultimate paragraph of his "Preface" tells us that "[t]here remains the final reflection, how shallow, puny, and imperfect are efforts to sound the depths in the nature of things. In philosophical discussion, the merest hint of dogmatic certainty as to finality of statement is an exhibition of folly" (xiv). To this caution he adds that "[p]hilosophers can never hope finally to formulate these metaphysical first principles" (PR, 4) and that "[i]n particular, there are no precisely stated axiomatic certainties from which to start. There is not even the language in which to frame them" (PR, 13).

Likewise, Whitehead shares Merleau-Ponty's commitment to consider all the evidence. "The chief danger to philosophy," the first sentence of Part V of *Process and Reality* tells us, "is narrowness in the selection of evidence" (337). Nothing can be excluded because of bias, special pleading, idiosyncrasy, diffidence, or arbitrariness. In short, "Philosophy may not neglect the multifariousness of the world—the fairies dance, and Christ is nailed to the cross" (PR, 338).

What conclusions, then, should we draw from comparing Whitehead's process metaphysics with Merleau-Ponty's earlier phenomenology and his later ontology of flesh? First, as regards the phenomenology, I have already pointed out that their reactions to the same set of philosophical and scientific doctrines created common ground in their views of the body, perception, and personal identity. Furthermore, Merleau-Ponty's descriptions of the lived body and the Lifeworld remedy a substantial lack of "macrocosmic" detail which Whitehead neglected in constructing his scheme of metaphysical categories. But Merleau-Ponty's earlier insistence on the distinction between the lived body and nature, or between human existence and natural objects, created a dualism of sorts which was never overcome phenomenologically and, on Merleau-Ponty's own grounds, probably could not have been. Thus, the method, although illuminating and necessary for the full comprehension of human being, is insufficient by itself.

Another way to say this is that, as we have seen, (phenomenological) description for Merleau-Ponty should precede analysis and explanation. But it does not follow from this that we cannot explain what has been described and that explanation is not an equal philosophical necessity. Merleau-Ponty obviously perceived this inadequacy because of his earlier inability to explain the relationship between the objective, scientific body and the lived body, and because he himself sought to unify the two by making them both modes of flesh.

As for the later Merleau-Ponty, final conclusions must necessarily be more tentative in the light of the fact that he had only begun to develop his ontology of flesh when death overtook him. Even with the appended "Working Notes," it is impossible to know how far and in what direction his method of descriptive generalization would have taken him. But we do have one clue. At the end of "An Unpublished Text," which he wrote while a candidate for the Collège de France, he expressed what I believe would have been the goal, or at least one of the main goals, of his new ontology. In relevant part he stated:

> [T]here is a "good ambiguity" in the phenomenon of expression, a spontaneity which accomplishes what appeared to be impossible when we observed only the separate elements, a spontaneity which gathers together the plurality of monads, the past and the present, nature and culture into a single whole. To establish this wonder would be metaphysics itself and would at the same time give us the principle of an ethics. (1964a, 11)

Notice that such a project would have entailed reworking his phenomenology of the social world in the light of the completed ontology.

What that might have looked like is of great interest to many contemporary Merleau-Ponty scholars.

I think it fair to say that, although it is impossible to demonstrate here, what he did state clearly, as well as what he was struggling to express, in *The Visible and the Invisible,* can be explained adequately within Whitehead's process metaphysics. It does not follow that no other metaphysics could explain it, so a Whiteheadian scheme is not a necessary condition of explicating his emerging ontology. But it is, I would argue, a sufficient condition and, given his rejection of substance thinking, it is difficult to imagine any other serious contenders.

Moreover, an ontology of "flesh" still has lessons to teach a speculative metaphysics such as that of Whitehead. There are at least two reasons for this. First, flesh expresses in a particularly meaningful way my macrocosmic relationships with other people, things around me, and other forms of sentient life, and the ecosystem in general. I open myself to them through my five senses and through much less precise, deeper bodily resonances, and they do likewise to me. We share in one flesh because of the ways in which my flesh intertwines with, has a reversibility with, all other entities that make up this active element of nature. Second, through its chiasmatic reversibilities flesh serves as an explanatory principle for our unity with nature. I have tried to show in this chapter what Merleau-Ponty absorbed from Whitehead in working out the notion of flesh, and Merleau-Ponty's writings about Whitehead show that he was not opposed to thinking of process beneath the level of the life-world, at the level of animal cells. Perhaps in time he would have arrived at Whitehead's actual occasions of experience—those spatially and temporally chiasmatic, internally related and active, nonsubstantial, unities of creator and creature, actuality and potentiality, *logos* and nature.

Notes

1. Several thinkers have noted similarities between Dewey and Merleau-Ponty, but the latter told Herbert Spiegelberg during a 1953 interview in Paris that he had not read Dewey (personal communication from Herbert Spiegelberg).

2. As the editor of *La Nature* notes, Merleau-Ponty paraphrases here Whitehead's statement that "[t]he course of nature is conceived as being merely the fortunes of matter in its adventure through space" (1994, 157, n. 5).

3. I am indebted to Jan Van der Veken for this reference.

Works Cited

Devettere, Raymond J. 1976. "The Human Body as Philosophical Paradigm in Whitehead and Merleau-Ponty," *Philosophy Today* 20, no. 4/4: 317–26.

Doud, Robert E. 1977. "Whitehead and Merleau-Ponty: Commitment as a Context for Comparison," *Process Studies* 7, no. 3 (Fall): 145–60.

Edie, James M. 1984. "Merleau-Ponty: The Triumph of Dialectics over Structuralism," *Man and World* 17: 299–312.

Hamrick, William S. 1974. "Whitehead and Merleau-Ponty: Some Moral Implications," *Process Studies* IV, no. 4 (Winter): 235–51.

———. 1999. "A Process View of the Flesh: Whitehead and Merleau-Ponty," *Process Studies* 28, no. 1–2 (Spring–Summer): 117–29.

Merleau-Ponty, Maurice. 1962. *Phenomenology of Perception.* Trans. Colin Smith. London: Routledge. Originally published as *Phénoménologie de la perception.* Paris: Gallimard, 1945.

———. 1964a. "The Primacy of Perception and its Philosophical Consequences." In *The Primacy of Perception and Other Essays,* ed. James Edie. Evanston: Northwestern University Press. Originally published as "Le Primat de la perception et ses conséquences," *Bulletin de la Société Française de Philosophie* LXI (1947) (séance du 23 novembre 1946).

——— .1964b. *Signs.* Trans. Richard McCleary. Evanston: Northwestern University Press. Originally published as *Signes.* Paris: Gallimard, 1960.

———. 1964c. *Sense and Non-sense.* Trans. Hubert L. and Patricia Allen Dreyfus. Evanston: Northwestern University Press. Originally published as *Sens et non-sens.* Paris: Nagel, 1948.

———. 1964d. *Eye and Mind.* Trans. Carleton Dallery. Evanston: Northwestern University Press. Originally published as *L'Œil et l'esprit.* Paris: Gallimard, 1964.

———. 1968. *The Visible and the Invisible.* Text established by Claude Lefort and trans. Alphonso Lingis. Evanston: Northwestern University Press. Originally published as *Le Visible et l'invisible.* Paris: Gallimard, 1964.

———. 1970. *Themes from the Lectures at the Collège de France 1952–1960.* Trans. John O'Neill. Evanston: Northwestern University Press. Originally published as *Résumés de Cours, Collège de France 1952–1960.* Paris: Gallimard, 1968.

———. 1973. *The Prose of the World.* Trans. John O'Neill. Evanston: Northwestern University Press. Originally published as *La Prose du Monde.* Text established by Claude Lefort. Paris: Gallimard, 1969.

———. 1994. *La Nature, Notes Cours du Collège de France.* Text established and annotated by Dominique Séglard. Paris: Éditions du Seuil.

Wahl, Jean. 1932. *Vers le concret.* Paris: J. Vrin.

Whitehead, Alfred North. 1920. *Concept of Nature.* Cambridge: Cambridge University Press.

———. 1933. *Adventures of Ideas.* New York: The Macmillan Company.

———. 1938. *Modes of Thought.* New York: The Macmillan Company.
———. 1960. *Religion in the Making.* New York: Meridian Books.
———. 1967. *Science and the Modern World.* New York: The Free Press.
———. 1978. *Process and Reality.* Corrected edition. Edited by David Ray Griffin and Donald W. Sherburne. New York: The Free Press.

CHAPTER 8

Points of Connection in Whitehead's and Nietzsche's Metaphysics

JANUSZ A. POLANOWSKI

To claim that Alfred North Whitehead and Friedrich Nietzsche hold disparate opinions on the intellectual profitability of metaphysical speculations is equivalent to proclaiming that water is wet. No other two modern philosophers have such contradictory ideas about the value of metaphysical reflections, despite the fact that their philosophies were undoubtedly influenced by the same social, economic, intellectual, and scientific changes.

We all know of Nietzsche's charismatic proclamation of himself as an "anti-metaphysician."[1] He is one for whom the pursuit of Truth, that is, the sort of knowledge that resides beyond the world of appearances, is merely an exercise in philosophical futility: "The 'true' world is an idea which is no longer good for anything, not even obligation—an idea which has become useless and superfluous—consequently, a refuted idea: Let us abolish it."[2] As far as the German philosopher is concerned, all metaphysical systems from Ancient Greek thought through medieval philosophies to modern rationalistic speculations have been motivated by the most basic human need for epistemological certainty, a certainty that will lull us into the illusion that ours is a world that can be, if correctly approached, not only understood but also manipulated to afford us predictability and control, resulting in an illusory existential security. Nietzsche himself eloquently makes this point:

> There are schematic minds, those which hold a thought complex to be *truer* when it can be inscribed in previously designed schemes or tables

> of categories. There are countless self-deceptions in this field: almost all great "systems" belong here. But the *fundamental prejudice* is: the order, perspicuity, system must belong to the *true being* of things, conversely that disorder, the chaotic, incalculable appear only in a false or incompletely known world—is an error in short—: which is a moral prejudice derived from the fact that the truthful, trustworthy man is wont to be a man of order, of maxims, and in general something calculable and pedantic. But it is quite indemonstrable that the nature of things behaves according to this recipe for a model official.[3]

Whitehead, on the other hand, whose process philosophy exemplifies one of the greatest instances of speculative, systematic thought in the annals of philosophical ruminations, finds himself standing on the other side of this great philosophical divide staring straight into Nietzsche's eyes and boldly challenging his repudiations of metaphysics. For Whitehead metaphysics is "the endeavor to frame a coherent, logical, necessary system of general ideas in terms of which every element of our experience can be interpreted";[4] and, unlike Nietzsche, he not only emphasizes the epistemological value of pursuing metaphysical work but also maintains that metaphysical speculations are so fundamental to our thinking about the world that rejecting them as intellectually fruitless is to miss their importance. In other words, behind every statement we make about reality rests the scaffolding of metaphysical presuppositions that are the manifestations of our general comprehension of the world; and unless we allow ourselves to engage in the explicit examination of these presuppositions, we will never be certain whether our ideas about the world are presupposing the same or disparate understandings of existence, which can result in holding contradictory ideas about the world and making our utterances about it philosophically effete. Therefore, Whitehead believes that anyone aspiring to say anything meaningful about the world must first endeavor to work out a well-grounded metaphysics in order to avoid all the epistemological inconsistencies that often prohibit us from attaining as comprehensive an understanding of the world as possible.

I propose to argue, however, that despite Nietzsche's and Whitehead's fundamental philosophical disagreements about the value and usefulness of metaphysical speculation, some philosophical commonalities exist in their respective thinking about the world. Perhaps those aspects of traditional metaphysical projects that Nietzsche finds philosophically questionable are what Whitehead endeavors to address in his speculative philosophy, as though striving to mollify his German colleague's uneasiness with metaphysics. The philosophical commonalities that link Whitehead's philosophy with Nietzsche's thinking about the world can be summed up in their mutual exaltation of novelty, complexity, creativity, multiplicity, and adventurousness, and at the same time their incontrovertible rejection of ontological duality, essentiality, finality, certainty, simplicity, and sterility. To a great extent the speculative philosophy that Whitehead proposes for us to consider not only attempts to address Nietzsche's criticisms against the traditional metaphysical systems but also parallels Nietzsche's own metaphysical speculations. This is not to say that had Nietzsche had an opportunity to expose himself to Whitehead's process philosophy he would have unreservedly endorsed it; he feared the philosophical dogmatism that seems to suffuse almost all metaphysical systems. He was weary of any metaphysical proclamations in principle, which by definition are designed to tell us how the world is apart from how it appears to us. Such a division of reality in Nietzsche's mind is philosophically insupportable.

To understand the points of connection between Whitehead's thinking and Nietzsche's ruminations about the nature of reality, we first need to review the criticisms that Nietzsche offers of traditional speculative philosophies and then determine whether the concerns he raises find both an echo and a response in Whitehead's process philosophy.

Nietzsche has a nonsystematic approach to philosophical discourse; that is, Nietzsche's philosophical reflections are replete with seeming contradictions that puzzle those who think more systematically about reality. Indeed, because of his nonsystematic manner of doing philosophy, some critics claim that Nietzsche is properly viewed as a literary figure rather than as a serious philosopher.[5] Nietzsche himself does not hide the fact that his writings evade easy philosophical classification. His philosophical corpus is full of vicious criticisms of a wide variety of philosophies and does not permit us to assign Nietzsche a comfortable place in any philosophical camp.

Whether we classify Nietzsche's philosophy as antisystematic and devoid of coherence or we seek in his philosophical ruminations some overarching metaphysical structure, albeit invisible to the uninitiated philosophical eye, the fact remains that one genuine preoccupation permeating his writings is a concern to depict reality as it presents itself to us as living, breathing organisms. Nietzsche believes it a great mistake to create philosophical systems that at their core are either marginally interested in, or completely unappreciative of, the ways the world unfolds in our experience. He reasons that if we are going to involve ourselves in philosophical speculations about the nature of the world, we need to start from the point that is most accessible or familiar to us, namely, our experiences. Too often philosophers have had a predilection to spawn their respective metaphysical speculations with little concern for human experiences of the world. This neglect can be traced back, Nietzsche maintains, to Ancient Greece, and particularly to Plato. He blames Plato's influence on successive generations of metaphysicians for the flaws that permeate our philosophical tradition.[6]

How does Plato's influence manifest itself? It reveals itself in the assumption of a metaphysical duality between how the world is in itself and how it appears to be to us. The task of metaphysics has been to uncover the true nature of a reality that is masked by appearances. A traditional metaphysician desires to rip the mask of appearance off the world's face and exclaim, "Aha . . . this is how you are when appearances are dropped!"

So what is required to erect this epistemological bridge between the world of appearances and the real world, that is, the world as it-is-in-itself? We need to make two fundamental assumptions: (1) There is such a thing as the real world that is independent of our experiences, and (2) This true world can in principle be accessible to its seekers. If, however, neither assumption can be sustained, the value of traditional metaphysics evaporates.

The assumption that there is a real world, that is, the world that resides behind appearances, is rooted in the idea that knowledge is capable of dealing only with aspects of reality that are immune to change. In other words, for metaphysicians to make the claim that knowledge about the world is in principle attainable means that they have to posit the type of existence that, unlike the world of appearance, is not subject to change. Regarding this issue Nietzsche writes: "A world in a state of becoming could not in a strict sense be 'comprehended' or 'known,'"[7] for ". . . logic deals only with formulas for 'that which remains the same': . . . 'the world in a state of becoming' is 'unformulatable,' and knowledge and becoming exclude one another."[8] Hence, the argument that knowledge can depict only that which is unchangeable functions as an argument for postulating the existence of another realm, for example, the Platonic realm of ideal forms. The realm of forms transcends the world open to the human senses and can be approached only through reason. This is the realm where change is the forbidden guest.

This Platonic account of reality casts a long epistemological shadow over metaphysical reasoning in general, Nietzsche contends. Nietzsche's philosophical hammering against metaphysical projects produces its most destructive blow when he accuses metaphysicians in general, and Plato in particular, of postulating the existence of a world of Forms and a world of appearance without good reasons. He maintains that such a deep metaphysical presumption regarding the duality of reality is philosophically unjustifiable: "In short: the essence of a thing is only an opinion about 'the thing.'"[9] "The 'in-itself' is even an absurd conception; a 'constitution-in-itself' is nonsense; we possess the concept of 'being,' 'thing,' only as a rational concept."[10] Thus, what Nietzsche challenges is the ontological dualism, which proclaims that what dwells behind appearances and is immutable is the real and is consequently knowable by our intellect whereas that which mutates is not worth our epistemological concern.

Even though many metaphysicians join Nietzsche in his rejection of any form of ontological dualism, they still face his intellectual wrath for maintaining, nonetheless, what could be referred to as "epistemological dualism." Why does Nietzsche view epistemological dualism as intellectually unpalatable? The answer lies in his view of knowledge. He asserts that only two positions regarding the possibility of the human mind's attaining knowledge are possible: either the mind can never acquire an objective knowledge of the world because there is no mind-independent world, or there is objective knowledge, for "there is a world out there beyond the mind, and the mind can contact that world in various ways, [which in turn] gives us truth about the world,"[11] where "truth" is understood as a set of propositions, which we can produce about the world, that correspond to or reflect "how the world is in-itself."[12] In this view, the world is divided into two parts. The first is constituted of an immense variety of things, which make up the world and with which we come into contact; and the second consists of human minds that entertain certain beliefs about those things, that is, that there is an intimate connection between the basic categories of reason and the structures of reality.[13]

Nietzsche believes this type of theory of knowledge to be philosophically indefensible. He opines that in order for us to determine the epistemological correctness of the correspondence theory of truth, we are expected to assume "God's point of view," which would permit us to attain absolute knowledge so that we could compare things as they-are-in-themselves in the world apart from our experiences of them with the beliefs that we hold about them. The difficulty that arises with this sort of theory, Nietzsche observes, resides in its epistemological nonverifiability. That is, as conscious human beings, we can never put ourselves in a situation in which we are able to step outside our minds and perform a comparison between things-in-themselves and our beliefs about those things and see whether what we believe about them coincides with how things are; these circumstances render the correspondence theory philosophically unverifiable.[14]

We could argue that just because we are deprived of "God's point of view" does not mean that our knowledge of the world is incorrect or flawed. Nietzsche, nonetheless, urges that the above-adduced weakness of the correspondence theory is a sufficient reason to doubt all alleged human knowledge. If the process of attaining knowledge necessarily involves placing us in a relationship with something that we are endeavoring to acquaint ourselves with, then by definition it is impossible for us to put ourselves in a position to know those things apart from the relationship we hold with those things when we are investigating them. Nietzsche suggests that in our coming to know the world, the world becomes conditioned by our knowing.[15] That is, knowledge gaining is not merely a process of passive activity involving the mind's reflecting the world outside it; instead, it is the process of epistemological generation during which the mind in its process of world apprehension imposes its own structures rendering the world-in-itself not only forever beyond its grasp but simply nonexistent: "Ultimately [Nietzsche muses] man finds in things nothing but what he himself imported into them."[16] "The world that we have not reduced to terms of our own being, our own logic, our psychological prejudices and presuppositions does not exist as a world at all"; "the world is fabricated solely from psychological needs."[17] Hence, "Truth" is not something that is out there in the world waiting to be unearthed by us; it is not a Platonic or semi-Platonic form or a category that dwells behind appearances: "The biggest fable of all is the fable of knowledge. One would like to know what things-in-themselves are; but behold, there are no things-in-themselves!"[18] "Truth" is of our own making, always teetering on an error and never granting us epistemological certainty: "But what after all are man's truths?—They are his *irrefutable* errors."[19] Hence, epistemological certainty is nothing more than a philosophical illusion rooted in a Platonically infected idea of metaphysical dualism that divides reality into the world of change and the world of being.

Nietzsche wants to abandon the entire distinction between the world of appearance and the world in-itself and unify what Plato has sundered. He wants to commence metaphysical speculations by focusing his attention on the aspect of human experience that is most evident and puzzling, namely change.

Looking at Nietzsche's critical evaluation of traditional theories of knowledge, we could conclude that he is a skeptic who finds cosmological speculation philosophically nugatory. He writes, "It is true that there *might* be a metaphysical world; the absolute possibility of it is hardly to be disputed. . . . But there is nothing to be done with it, much less is it possible to let happiness, salvation, and life depend on the spider-thread of such a possibility. For nothing could be said of the metaphysical world but that it would be a different condition, a condition inaccessible and incomprehensible to us; it would be a thing of negative qualities."[20]

However, drawing such a conclusion from his epistemological ruminations would go against his own assessment of skepticism. "Scepticism," he opines, "is a result of decadence"[21] for it is "the most spiritual expression of a certain many-sided physiological temperament, which in ordinary language is called nervous debility and sickliness."[22] In other words, he encourages us to engage our intellectual powers to describe the world to the best of our abilities, even if such pursuit would ultimately result in the generation of another set of errors. What he exhorts us to do is to reevaluate our old metaphysical philosophies in the light of our own new understanding of reality: What does this mean? It means the rejection of Platonic and Christian philosophies as well as metaphysical systems that one way or another possess a proclivity to seek the "Truth," for as we have already seen they can no longer withstand the scrutiny of reason. Instead, he proposes to erect a theory of the universe that reflects the world we inhabit. As Paul Carus points out:

> Nietzsche's main desire was to live the real life and make his home not in imaginary Utopia but in this actual world of ours. He reproached the philosophers as well as the religious leaders and ethical teachers for trying to make mankind believe that the real world is not purely phenomenal, [and] replacing it by the world of thought which they called "the true world" or the world of truth. [Plato] and all his followers are accused of hypocrisy for making people believe that "the true world" of their own fiction is real and that man's ambition should be to attain to this true world (the world of philosophy, of science, of art, of ethical ideals), built above the real world.[23]

Therefore, on the most elementary level, Nietzsche's depiction of the universe is rooted in his rebellion against transcendental metaphysics in favor of his reluctant embrace of some form of monism, where monism is broadly understood as "preference for the Whole over the parts, with a consequent denigration of individual things to the benefit of the Whole."[24] In his metaphysical thinking, the only part of reality that enjoys a certain sense of endurance is the Whole whereas the parts constituting the Whole are in a perpetual state of flux, that is, they are fugacious and temporal, which in turn makes our "predicates for individual parts of the universe . . . unsteady, temporary, subjective, perspectival."[25]

Hence, what emerges from Nietzsche's metaphysical monism is the world divested of substance, as that in which the properties characterizing the world inhere. In this respect the German philosopher follows the steps of such eminent empiricists as John Locke and David Hume. Recall Locke's perceptive observation that "the general name 'substance' being nothing but the supposed, but unknown, support of those qualities we find existing, which we imagine cannot subsist *sine re substance*, without something to support them"[26] nonetheless having "no idea of what it [substance] is, but only a confused, obscure one of what it does,"[27] as well as Hume's emphatic assertion that "the idea of a substance . . . is nothing but a collection of simple ideas that are united by imagination and have a particular name assigned to them."[28]

Like his British predecessors, Nietzsche employs a similar line of argumentation regarding the reality of substance. He questions whether behind the idea of "substance" is any genuine content, for if we strip any "object" of its particular qualities that impact us as their observers, then are we left with anything perceptible that stands apart from these characteristics? The answer is no, for "if I think of a muscle apart from its 'effects,' [Nietzsche writes] I negate it . . . [because] a 'thing' is the sum of its effects, synthetically united by a concept, an image."[29] Therefore, the reason we take the notion of substance as referring to something real is anchored in our language: we allow ourselves to be cozened by our grammatical constructs into thinking that apart from the effects, powers, and mutable qualities that characterize a particular object, there is some fixed, inalterable foundation in which the thing's qualities dwell. "There is no such *substratum*. There is no 'being' behind the doing, working, becoming; 'the doer' is a mere appanage to the action. The action is everything. In point of fact, the people duplicate the doing when they make the lightning lighten, that is a doing-doing. They make the same phenomenon first a cause, and then, secondly, the effect of that cause."[30]

Consequently, Nietzsche's theory of the universe is not rooted in the notion of substance. As indicated at the beginning of this chapter, Nietzsche opposes the traditional metaphysical projects partly because of their "hostility to the transience, contradictoriness and pain of human experience,"[31] that is, he accuses traditional metaphysicians of ignoring human experiences of life and instead contriving universal theories that fail to make any substantially meaningful sense out of human existence. As he puts it, an overman "conceives reality *as it is:* he is strong enough for this—he is not estranged or far removed from it, he is that reality himself,"[32] whereas the metaphysical types seek "salvation in their imaginary worlds that are supposedly the true reality."

What is it that is so paradigmatic about human life that Nietzsche applies it to his universal theory of the world? The answer is "mutability." Change is the aspect of reality that cannot be ignored and has to be the foundation upon which our apprehension of reality needs to be erected.

Following the footsteps of Heraclitus, Nietzsche reasons that if there is anything self-evident about existence, it is that "everything has its origins in time and history, and consequently everything in the world is finite and destined to be destroyed." Change is the "language" of reality, and any attempt to abandon this language in our discourse about the nature of reality in favor of the metaphysical language of Being or essence is merely an exercise in philosophical illusions.

Consequently, Nietzsche banishes "Being" and "Essence" from his metaphysical vocabulary. He considers the essentialist conceptuality highly inadequate to the task of depicting the malleability of existence because "he sees 'the character of the world in a state of becoming.'"[33] Accordingly, he assays to generate a new way of addressing the nature of reality. The concepts of "force" and "energy" are harnessed by Nietzsche to reflect the evolutionary nature of the world: "[The] world may be thought as a definite quantity of force and as a certain number of centers of force."[34] Hence, the ontology of existence that he proposes is the ontology of a process that suffuses all levels of existence:

> This world: a monster of energy, without beginning, without end; a firm, iron magnitude of force that does not grow bigger or smaller, that does not expend itself but only transforms itself. . . . Out of the simplest form striving toward the most complex, out of the stillest, most rigid, coldest forms toward the hottest, most turbulent, most self-contradictory, and then again returning home to the simple out of this abundance, out of the play of contradiction back to the joy of concord, still affirming itself in this uniformity of its courses and its years, blessing itself as that which must return eternally, as a becoming that knows no satiety, no disgust, no weariness. . . .This world is the will to power.[35]

Reality is a cauldron of throbbing, evanescent energy that is in a perpetual state of existential transitoriness.

Indeed, Nietzsche's philosophical analysis of nature goes even further, for he views this "magnitude of force" as being constituted of individual events that he labels "quanta of powers": "No things remain but only dynamic quanta."[36] In order, however, not to get lost in his somewhat poetically imbued philosophical renderings of the world, we need to push farther what he means by "quanta." So, the question that presents itself next is, what does Nietzsche mean by "dynamic quanta of power" or "the centers of energy"?

The quanta of power are the most elementary building blocks of which the world is composed. What, then, can be said about the nature of these quanta? The answer lies in Nietzsche's criticism directed toward traditional metaphysics. As we recall, one reason that Nietzsche abandons the traditional metaphysics is that he wishes to describe the world by starting from the point that is the most accessible to us, namely ourselves. He proposes to view the world through this prism: "Supposing that nothing else is 'given' as real but our world of desires and passions, that we cannot sink or rise to any other 'reality' but just that of our impulses—for thinking is only a relation of these impulses to one another:—are we not permitted to make the attempt and to ask the question whether this which is 'given' does not *suffice,* by means of our counterparts, for understanding even the so called mechanical (or material) world."[37]

Employing his reflections on human nature, Nietzsche embarks on depicting the quanta in terms of the same sort of impulses that govern human activities. Simply put, quanta are driven by "will," desire for control. In their process of self-creativity, these centers of power strive to exert their control over the environment in which they come to instantiate themselves: "[A quantum of power] strives to become a master of all space, to extend its power to, and to thrust back everything that resists it."[38] As one of Nietzsche's most famous axioms sums it up, "The innermost essence of being is will to power."[39] Without that will, there would be no world.

Because this world consists of multiplicities of quanta striving to assert their wills on the world, then it is pertinent to apprehend the relationships that these centers have vis-à-vis each other. We may be inclined to think that these energetic centers endure self-contained lives divested of any connectivity with others unless they engage each other in a struggle for existence. But the fact remains, Nietzsche opines, that ultimately the world is one big continuum of energy: it is the ocean of energy whose unity is the only real thing whereas the drops constituting that ocean are the momentary "waves" of creativity that establish their delimited existences as rapidly as they relinquish them. Furthermore, the constitutive many establish their reality in terms of the relationships that they hold with each other in the matrix of their co-dependency. In other words, quanta can never enjoy the independence of being "a thing-in-itself" that is separated from others. To extricate a thing from its relationship is to condemn it to nonexistence. To employ a human paradigm, it would be like trying to understand a particular human being apart from the relationship she maintains with others and the world in general. Remove all those relationships and you have removed her from the world: no relations, no willing, no existence. Permanence finds no reality in multiplicity, Zarathustra proclaims, because "everything goeth, everything returneth; eternally rolleth the wheel of existence. Everything dieth, everything blossometh forth again; Eternally runneth on the year of existence."[40] The only thing that retains any stability is the Universe as a whole.

It is evident that Nietzsche's development of his metaphysical schema is guided by his desire to avoid relying on such concepts as "being" or "essence" in order to escape his criticisms directed against traditional metaphysics. The only thing that is essential about the Nietzschian universe is its willful mutability. We could say that Nietzsche elevates change to the level of "essence." Things come into existence and then vanish out of existence in order to let the elements constituting these things find a new way of reconstituting, redefining, and transcending themselves. "In general, Nietzsche declares, the deepest desire of life is 'to create beyond and above itself,' thereby perishing; where that is lacking, there is decadence."[41] Creativity and a pursuit of novelty are the defining characteristics of the will to power. The quanta reveal their existential essence in terms of the effects they produce and resist vis-à-vis each other and the world as a whole. Indeed, the case is that various quanta of power in their life-generating exercise of will to power, in their "[strife] to become master[s] over all space, to extend [their] forces, and to thrust back all that resist [their] extension,"[42] they necessarily find themselves in conflict with other quanta, and the struggle for dominance unfolds.

Because the principle governing all existence is the pursuit of as much power as is possible, it often occurs that quanta not only engage in the competitive struggle against each other but also in the practice of a self-enlightened cooperation, so to speak, in order to acquire a greater amount of power. Because individual quanta reveal themselves in terms of the relationships they maintain with others, they "continually encounter similar efforts on the part of other bodies [quanta] [and thus] they come to an arrangement with those of them that are sufficiently related to [them]: [and] they conspire together for power."[43] This self-enlightened conspiring together gives rise to social organizations in the form of cooperative units that in turn generate the existential complexity that we encounter in the world in the form of living and nonliving complexities.

What differentiates living from nonliving cooperative units? It is their organizational morphology that determines whether a particular union is organic or inorganic. The constitutive members of inorganic unions are concerned merely with extending their individual powers through cooperation without surrendering their individual wills to power to the societies in which they participate. They strive to retain their own identities while engaging in cooperation. The quanta that are members of inorganic unities "do not, except in a 'loose and popular' sense, attain diachronic identity."[44]

The members of organic complexities, on the other hand, acquire their power by generating much more complex organizational units in which some quanta become subsumed within their cooperative systems in order to increase the power of the entire organizations of which they are members. In other words, they become absorbed into the whole by relinquishing their own wills whereas others are elevated to the level of dominant forces within the unit and consequently are responsible for extending the power of the whole as well as integrating the "intermediate" quanta into the whole.

We can immediately see, therefore, that Nietzsche's employment of such terms as *will, struggle, desire, novelty, complexity, mutability,* and *cooperation* gives us a glimpse into his comprehension of the nature of reality in general and puts his metaphysical thinking on a parallel path with Whitehead's thinking about the world. If we consider Nietzsche's criticisms of metaphysics and his own rudimentary metaphysical system, we cannot escape the impression that his philosophical ruminations find their resounding echo in Whitehead's metaphysical speculations about the world. Keeping in mind Nietzsche's philosophical reservations regarding Plato's influence on metaphysical speculations, we may reasonably imagine that if Nietzsche had been granted an opportunity to acquaint himself with *Process and Reality,* he probably would have been critical of certain Platonic themes in Whitehead's philosophy. We are all aware of Whitehead's appreciation of Plato's influence on the Western philosophical tradition, which, on the other hand, irritated Nietzsche so much that he took upon himself to vehemently oppose the Greek philosopher at every turn.

However, despite the obvious differences between Nietzsche's and Whitehead's philosophical thinking, the metaphysical intuitions regarding the nature of reality that these two intellectual giants share with each other are quite astonishing. The first connection between Whitehead and Nietzsche arises in their rejection of thinking about the world in terms of substances. So, despite their intellectual disparities regarding the value of Plato's philosophy, both Nietzsche and Whitehead begin their metaphysical speculations about the world at the same point; namely, they reason that any metaphysical speculation must commence its speculative process from the vantage point most accessible to us, namely, human experiences. "The true method of discovery is like the flight of an aeroplane [Whitehead writes]. It starts from the ground of particular observation; it makes a flight in the thin air of imaginative generalization; and it again lands for renewed observation rendered acute by rational interpretation."[45] Hence, like Nietzsche, who calls upon us "only to posit such modes of being as we are most sure of in the way of [our] actual experience,"[46] Whitehead urges us to launch our philosophizing through the analysis of the way we come to "know" the world. "In order to discover some of the major categories under which we can classify the infinitely various components of experience, we must appeal to evidence relating to every variety of occasions."[47]

Furthermore, both philosophers initiate their respective philosophies by following the spirit of Heraclitus's observation about the world that "the sun is new every day."[48] They readily accept an empirically confirmed observation that the world's most essential feature is its continuously transfomative nature. As Nietzsche succinctly puts it, "'Change' belongs to the essence,"[49] and Whitehead wholeheartedly accedes: "To be actual is to be a process. Anything which is not a process is an abstraction from process, not a full-fledged actuality."[50]

Because both philosophers view the fundamental nature of reality in terms of its mutability, they first set out to repudiate the notion of substance, which undergirds much of Western philosophical thinking. Indeed, we have already seen Nietzsche's decisive rejection of thinking about the world in terms of substance, hence his resolute proclamation that "Boscovich has taught us to abjure the belief in the last thing that 'stood fast' of the earth—the belief in 'substance,' in 'matter,' in the earth-residuum and particle-atom."[51]

Similarly, Whitehead directs his thinking toward abandoning the notions of substance and matter in our reflections on nature. One of the driving forces behind Whitehead's reasoning is his attempt to solve the mind-body problem so luminously projected upon the metaphysical scene by the Cartesian philosophy. While Nietzsche battles Platonic dualism as well as Christianity, Whitehead sets out to deal with the Cartesian dualism. Indeed, both of them seek the monistic understanding of nature, for the Cartesian substance dualism is the outgrowth of Platonic philosophy, which has gone through the centuries of intellectual reformulations from Aristotle to neo-Platonists to Sebastian Basso[52] and his followers.

Without going too deeply into the history of dualism, it is enough to say that within Plotinus's metaphysical schema, there is a separation drawn between the soul—the part of reality that is immune from change or becoming—and the physical aspect of reality, whose primary characteristic is its mutability. However, by the time the Middle Ages expire and the seventeenth century arrives, Plotinus's view of human nature undergoes a significant intellectual rethinking: Basso and his followers take upon themselves the task of reversing Plotinus's view of nature by elevating matter to the level of the ultimate "in contrast and opposition to the antecedent conception of the physical as composite of form and matter."[53]

Descartes is not long in apprehending the philosophical consequences of Basso's reformulation of the physical. Since the physical becomes equated with matter and matter no longer admits forms—as its qualitative determinants because forms are no longer part of the new metaphysical picture—the matter establishes itself as qualitatively immutable and undifferentiated and thus expressed only in terms of primary qualities.

In like manner, the conception of the soul experiences its own reformulation from the Aristotelian conceptuality through the neo-Platonic one and culminating with the Cartesian ontological separation into matter and the soul, *res cogitans*. Hence, the metaphysical image of the world that emerges out of the Cartesian philosophy is still dualistic in nature with the difference that in the Aristotelian world, the soul is a part of the physical whereas under the modern view it acquires its own ontological independence.

Despite the initial enthusiasm associated with Descartes's philosophical progress, many started to question his metaphysical framework. The positing of two ontologically independent substances yields so many philosophical problems for the comprehension of nature that before Descartes's soul departs this world, he is forced to search—albeit unsuccessfully—for answers to questions dealing with the relationship between *res extensa* and *res cogitans*.

Nietzsche and Whitehead come to "reject [not only] the modern doctrine of the physical as immutable matter"[54] but also the entire metaphysical schema underlying the modern scientific view of the world. Listen to Nietzsche: "Physicists believe in a 'true world' in their own fashion: a firm systematization of atoms in necessary motion, the same for all beings—so for them the 'apparent world' is reduced to the side of universal and universally necessary being which is accessible to every being in its own way. But they are in error [Nietzsche inveighs]."[55] Why are they in error? They are in error, Whitehead replies, because of "the fallacy of simple location," which declares the belief that a thing "can be said to be here in space and here in time, or here in space-time, in a perfectly definite sense which does not require for its explanation any references to other regions of space and time."[56] In other words, both Whitehead and Nietzsche rebuff the metaphysical view of the universe based on the Newtonian physics, which affirms "the independent individuality of each bit of matter"[57] that lives a solitary life internally unrelated to all other parts of the universe. As Whitehead asserts,

> Modern physics has abandoned the doctrine of Simple Location. The physical things which we term stars, planets, lumps of matter, molecules, electrons, protons, quanta of energy, are each to be conceived as modifications of conditions within space-time, extending throughout the whole range. There is a focal region, which in common speech is where the thing is. But its influence streams away from it with finite velocity throughout the utmost recesses of space and time. Of course, it is natural, and for certain purposes entirely proper, to speak of the focal region, thus modified, as the thing situated there. But difficulties arise if we press this way of thought too far.[58]

Simply put, Whitehead maintains that in the Einsteinian age as well as in the quantum physics age, any metaphysical system presupposing that the world is made up of unchanging substances with changing attributes clearly goes against the empirical evidence furnished by scientific reasoning.

Hence, as though following Nietzsche's call to arms to apprehend the world as a pulsating and continuously evolving structure, Whitehead grounds his system not in terms of immutable bits of matter that are in motion and are solely related to each other externally, but rather in terms of centers of becoming that he labels "actual occasions" or "actual entities." "The actual entities . . . are the final real things of which the world is made up."[59] Just as Nietzsche posits his most elementary building blocks of the universe as quanta of power, which are characterized by their creative mutability, so Whitehead follows the same path in making actual occasions "the primary actual units of which the temporal world is composed."[60] Both philosophers, therefore, approach their task of capturing the fundamental nature of the universe by postulating its constitutive parts as centers of power that are driven by their own transformative natures. These centers are involved with each other in the universal matrix of co-dependence where no entity can either stand apart from other entities or be understood outside the relationships in which it participates.

When Nietzsche proposes quanta of power as the universal elements of existence, he addresses them as "the will to power." "This world is the will to power—and nothing besides! And you yourselves are also the will to power—and nothing besides!"[61] He thinks, therefore, that we can understand the internal lives of quanta by reflecting on our own experiences: "The centers of energy . . . according to Nietzsche, inwardly experience essentially the same kind of impulses as man experiences within himself, albeit the experiences or impulses vary enormously in degree of development."[62]

By the same token, "drops of experience," or actual occasions, are the result of Whitehead's analysis of our own experiences of the world. What does it mean to experience the world? From a human point of view, it means to find ourselves involved in the complexity of relations that characterize the universe. In this respect, our own lives are quite comparable to the lives of actual occasions, which also can find themselves engaged in an infinite number of relations with other occasions. As in the case of all living organisms, both history and social context play essential roles in determining the character of actual entities: "There is nothing which floats into the world from nothing,"[63] or as Nietzsche says, "Everything has its origins in time and history, and consequently everything in the world is finite and destined to be destroyed."

It is essential, however, to bear in mind that even though Whitehead is using human experience as the model for describing actual entities, he "is not claiming that there is no difference between [human] moments of experience and that of an electron."[64] What he does seek are those aspects of experience that we do share with other animals and plants as well as inanimate objects. That is why he rejects the notion that all experience necessarily entails consciousness. In *Modes of Thought,* Whitehead points to the vast number of our own experiences that normally remain unconscious: "We experience more than we can analyze. For we experience the universe, and we analyze in our consciousness a minute selection of its details."[65]

Once again Whitehead's denial of the primacy of consciousness in experience seems to closely reflect Nietzsche's own thinking about the place of consciousness in nature. When Nietzsche talks about the centers of power as being driven by instinct rather than conscious activity, he relies on similar reflections regarding our conscious processes:

> We could in fact think, feel, will, and recollect, we could likewise "act" in every sense of the term, and nevertheless nothing of it all need necessarily "come into consciousness." The whole of life would be possible without its seeing itself as it were in a mirror: as in fact even at present the far greater part of our life still goes on without this mirroring,—and even our thinking, feeling, volitional life as well, however painful this

> statement may sound to an older philosopher. *What* then is *the purpose* of consciousness generally, when it is in the main *superfluous?*[66]

So as Whitehead "ascribes consciousness only to those few complex occasions of high mentality capable of sustaining intellectual feelings . . . [i.e.,] there are no degrees of awareness below [a certain] threshold [of existence],"[67] likewise Nietzsche believes that conscious activities are delimited to a narrow plain of existence. In fact, he diminishes or dismisses the value of consciousness by stating, "Formerly it was thought that man's consciousness, his 'spirit' offered evidence of his high origin, his divinity. . . . Here again we have thought out the thing better: to us consciousness, or the 'spirit,' appears as a symptom of a relative imperfection of the organism, as an experiment, a groping, a misunderstanding, as an affliction which uses up nervous force unnecessarily—we deny anything can be done perfectly so long as it is done consciously."[68] As far as Nietzsche is concerned, the perfection of the activity of an organism lies in its instinctive behavior.

One of the reasons behind their depictions of the most fundamental blocks of existence in terms of becoming lies in Nietzsche's and Whitehead's recognition that any metaphysical system that strives to describe the world as it is has to take into account creativity as an undeniable aspect of the universe. We recall Nietzsche's objections against the traditional philosophies that either flatly deny the reality of creative change or neglect to furnish an adequate account of its reality; and consequently, he describes the quanta of power in terms of their activities designed to leave their mark on the world. These centers seek to establish their own reality by the effects they produce and resist; their existential reality is bound up with others. Hence, if there is any constant to reality, that constant is mutability, creative becoming, perpetual inventiveness, for the world is a "self-generating work of art that gives birth to itself."[69]

Whitehead, no less than Nietzsche, is interested in providing an adequate account for "creativity" as the essential aspect of reality. Without creativity, there could be no novelty, and without novelty there would be no actuality: "'Creativity' is the principle of novelty. An actual occasion is a novel entity diverse from any entity in the 'many' which it unifies. Thus 'creativity' introduces novelty into the content of the many, which are the universe disjunctively. The 'creative advance is the application of this ultimate principle of creativity to each novel situation which it originates.'"[70] And so creativity is the dimension of reality that assures that the present becomes the past by being transcended and transformed into the future, for without this creative impulse, with which all the concrescing occasions are endowed, there would be no creative advancement of the world.

While Nietzsche defines quanta of power in terms of their will to power, Whitehead analyzes concrescing occasions in terms of their prehensive processes: "The essence of an actual entity consists solely in the fact that it is a prehending thing."[71] We could employ Nietzsche's language of will to power to describe the prehensive process guiding the emergence of actual occasions. Actual occasions seek to impose their own "will" on the universe through the power of their own self-instantiation: "[H]ow an actual entity becomes constitutes what the actual entity is."[72] An actual entity not only leaves a mark on the universe, it also pushes it into the future: "The universe is thus a creative advance into novelty. The alternative to this doctrine is a static morphological universe."[73]

Another concept that connects itself with creativity and novelty is freedom. It is impossible to overestimate the importance of freedom in both Whitehead's and Nietzsche's metaphysics. Nietzsche addresses the notion of freedom by questioning the validity of the concept of causality. In his critical evaluation of causal relationships, Nietzsche follows Hume's analysis of causality by maintaining that causal explanations that we attribute to the world are nothing more than perspectival misapprehensions of reality that we impose on the world: "Necessity is not a fact but an interpretation."[74] He attributes man's invention of causality to his need or desire not only to control the world but also to feel secure within the world. "Causality is created only by thinking compulsion into the process. A certain 'comprehension' is the consequence; we have made the process more human, 'more familiar': the familiar is the familiar habit of human compulsion associated with the feeling of force."[75] If the events that constitute the world can be classified in terms of repeatable causal relationships among those events, Nietzsche argues, then we can continue to work under the grand illusion that the world can be mapped out by discovering these causal relations.

The fact, however, remains that when we engage in the process of causal delineation of the world, we engage in a process of perspectival interpretation of reality, which is based on the mistaken assumption that the cause and effect that we extricate out of the continuum can give us a real understanding of reality: "Cause and effect: there is probably never any such duality; in fact there is a *continuum* before us, from which we isolate a few portions;—just as we always observe a motion as isolated points, and therefore do not properly see it, but infer it. . . . There is an infinite multitude of processes in that abrupt moment which escape us."[76] Simply put, Nietzsche argues against the idea of causality on the basis of the immensity of the processes characterizing the world; and he believes that the idea of causal relationships presupposes the existence of discrete things, which he understands as myth.

Similarly, Whitehead rejects any form of simple-minded causality, for as Victor Lowe tells us, Whitehead is motivated to solve an age-old dilemma of reconciling the apparent contradiction between the mechanical causality of science and the human intuition of freedom:

> The older dualism, following the lead of Immanuel Kant, held that to the scientist every event, inanimate or human, is bound to appear mechanically caused in its entirety; yet the moralist is bound to think of right and wrong as freely done; and the two beliefs do not really conflict, they are merely asserted from different points of view. . . . Whitehead believed that this is a bogus solution. Our life is one life; you cannot parcel it out to thinkers sworn not to interfere with each other. Causality and freedom, like all fundamental contrasts, are in existence itself. You cannot reconcile them by distinguishing points of view, but only by finding a way to think them together.[77]

So in order to resolve the aforementioned dilemma regarding man's place within the naturalistic world of causal relations, Whitehead sets out to confront what he dubs "scientific materialism," which interprets the unfolding events in the world in terms of "mechanical materiality," where matter is understood as composed of indivisible particles interacting with each other in space and time and consequently giving rise to greater complexities that are subject to mutability.

What is important to bear in mind is that from the perspective of "scientific materialism" the world experiences change on the level of complex entities while on the most basal level of existence particles enjoy thorough immutability, that is, matter in itself is "inert, i.e., without activity, and thus completely unable to initiate locomotion: matter is moved, it does not move itself."[78] This, in turn, means that when the particles of matter come in contact with each other, they establish their connections in terms of external relations, and consequently the notion of freedom in its richest understanding is slowly but surely choked out of the system. As Whitehead explains, the "assumption that I call 'scientific materialism' presupposes the ultimate fact of an irreducible brute matter, or material, spread throughout space in a flux of configurations. In itself such a material is senseless, valueless, purposeless. It just does what it does, following a fixed routine imposed by external relations which do not spring from the nature of its being."[79] Newtonian physics, for instance, falls under this category of "scientific materialism," for its analysis of the world "is based upon the independent individuality of each bit of matter."[80]

By rejecting both the underlying idea of "simple location" as well as its notion of causality based on the externality of relationships among the bits of matter, Whitehead endeavors to escape a simple-minded determinism of scientific materialism by positing the existential lives of actual occasions in terms of their prehensive processes, thus allowing freedom in his metaphysics as that aspect of reality that opens new routes to both expected and unexpected novelties as essential parts of his philosophy. Even on such an elementary level as ultimate individual entities, spontaneity is the engine powering the present into the unpredictable future. Therefore, when Whitehead asserts that "the concrescence of each individual actual entity is internally determined and externally free,"[81] he very successfully preserves freedom without disengaging the past. When he proclaims that an "actual entity is internally determined," he is very much aware of the fact that the concrescing entity, in one sense, is confined by particular conditions and limitations imposed by the prehended data under which a new occasion achieves satisfaction; but in another sense, the emerging entity is endowed with freedom, which permits that occasion to exercise its own unique way of appropriating past data through positive and negative prehensions. The manner in which a subject approaches and incorporates the prehending data is referred to as "the subjective form"; "the subjective form is the immediate novelty; it is how that subject is feeling that objective datum."[82] Whitehead's solution is ingenious in resolving the apparent problem of the coexistence of genuine novelty with the determining past when he asserts that

> [the] process of the synthesis of subjective forms derived conformally is not settled by the antecedent fact of the data. For these data in their own separate natures do not carry any regulative principle for their synthesis. The regulative principle is derived from the novel unity which is imposed on them by the novel creature in process of constitution. Thus, the immediate occasion from the spontaneity of its own essence must supply the missing determination for the synthesis of subjective form. Thus the future of the Universe, though conditioned by the immanence of its past, awaits for its complete determination the spontaneity of the novel individual occasions as in their season they come into being.[83]

Hence, beginning from relatively elementary levels of reality, the complexity of choices and decisions involved is already present. The existence of actual entities, and subsequently all existing things, is due to the decision processes that shape reality, in which we are the manifestation of freedom.

Considering Nietzsche's preoccupation with the idea of freedom, we cannot escape the impression that he would have liked Whitehead's rich account of freedom within his system. Whitehead manages to strike a tenuous balance between "hardcore" determinism, which dissolves any meaningful place for genuine freedom to take root, and a thoroughgoing rejection of scientific knowledge.

Another point of connection between Nietzsche's and Whitehead's metaphysical visions of the world resides in their attempts not merely to describe the most fundamental building blocks of reality in terms of self-creative activities, but also in terms of a thrust of those building blocks to generate composite entities of ever greater complexities. Both Whitehead and Nietzsche employ their categorical schemata to explicate how, out of the rudimentary microcosmic actualities characterizing the lowest levels of existence, there emerges the world of macrocosmic complexities that we come to experience and know as objects in the world. Recall that Nietzsche suggests that the elemental centers of power define themselves not only in terms of the resistance that they project vis-à-vis each other, but also in terms of their cooperative efforts that result in the generation of greater existential complexities, leading to the need for the distinction between organic and inorganic structures. Likewise, Whitehead extends his metaphysical analysis to greater complexities. In fact, we can venture to say that his examination of these "societies," to employ Whitehead's vernacular, is much richer and more detailed than the analysis of his German colleague.

To elaborate, Whitehead introduces the notion of societies as the way of accounting for all these complexities of actual occasions that we encounter in the macrocosmic world as everyday objects. "The Universe achieves its values by reason of its coordination into societies of societies, and into societies of societies of societies. Thus an army is a society of regiments, and regiments are societies of men, and men are societies of cells, and of blood, and of bones, together with a dominant society of personal human experience, and cells are societies of smaller physical entities such as protons, and so on, and so on."[84] So stones, plants, animals, people, etc. are those groupings of occasions that attain their reality because their component entities share some common characteristics with each other, regardless of the differences that separate them in some other respects. So even though all occasions are morphologically unique, that is, no two occasions are exactly the same in the manner they prehend the world, the fact remains that they do come to share some aspects of reality, which in turn causes them to find themselves in relationships with each other that give rise to greater complexities. Whitehead writes, "The members of the society are alike because, by reason of their common character, they impose on other members of the society the conditions which lead to their likeness."[85] In other words, "a set of entities is a society in virtue of a 'defining characteristic' shared by its members, and in virtue of the presence of the defining characteristic being due to the environment provided by the society itself."[86] Whereas Nietzsche's analysis of the bundles is limited to their division into organic and inorganic, Whitehead's examination of the societies, on the other hand, leads him to introduce various forms of social organizations. Hence, he talks about "personal societies" as opposed to "non-personal societies" and "living societies" vis-à-vis "non-living societies."

To give some examples, a blade of grass would be classified as a living, nonpersonal society because as a living society, it is characterized by both the relative shortness of its existential endurance in comparison to nonliving societies, which can exist for very long periods of time, and its much greater intensity of subjective experiences during which the mental poles of the constitutive occasions play a greater role in their prehensive processes. In other words, the occasions of living societies are much more "interested" in utilizing their mental poles in order to pursue novelty than are the occasions of nonliving societies in which physical poles play the predominant role, a role that is characterized by retention of as much conformity to their past as possible. As Whitehead tells us, "'life' is the origination of conceptual novelty, novelty of appetition."[87]

Indeed, Whitehead's analysis of societies progresses even further when he asserts, "In the case of single cells, of vegetation, and of the lower forms of animal life, we have no ground for conjecturing living personality. But in the case of higher animals there is central direction, which suggests that in their case each animal body harbours a living person, or living persons."[88] Simply put, despite the fact that the constitutive occasions of societies of societies of blades of grass, for example, enjoy the heightened intensity of their experiences because of their increased coordination and their pursuit of novelty in their prehensive processes, these experiences do not reach the level of highly complex living societies, in which the bodily organization of these organisms can provide an environment for the emergence and sustenance of "nonsocial" strands of the personally ordered occasions, whose capacity for heightened intensity of feelings is the result of a much wider background of inheritance, namely the whole living organism.[89]

Our discussion of Nietzschean connections with Whitehead's process philosophy would be incomplete if we did not mention Nietzsche's eternal recurrence theory in light of Whiteheadian process philosophy. It would appear that the cosmology present in the "eternal recurrence" theory would posit a possible challenge to Whitehead's philosophy of creativity. We would be inclined to think that the eternal recurrence theory would not be a philosophical nexus in which Whitehead could find intellectual presence with Nietzsche. As a matter of fact, we could say that the eternal recurrence theme would be an alien theory even to someone such as Nietzsche whose philosophy is geared toward stressing a creative mutability of reality.

Before we establish whether Nietzsche's eternal recurrence theory parts ways with Whitehead's metaphysics, it is important to point out that unlike Whitehead, who has a profound apprehension of ideas driving modern scientific thinking, Nietzsche has a rather limited scientific background, and his delimited scientific knowledge reveals itself in his misapprehension of "the relationship between the heat death and the mechanical world view."[90] In a sense we could argue that no matter how philosophically challenging Nietzsche's cyclical theory of nature is to Whitehead's metaphysics, the fact remains that Whitehead's cosmological reflections are as much informed by his philosophical intuitions as they are by his extensive scientific knowledge.

When in the middle of the 1880s the mind of Nietzsche stumbles on a theory of eternal recurrence, his intellectual reflection wanders into a philosophical world in which Parmenidean being and Heraclitean becoming no longer stand as irreconcilable opposites that cannot be simultaneously embraced; rather, they become necessary characters defining the nature of reality. As Nietzsche tells us, the doctrine of eternal recurrence is rooted in his realization that "if the world may be thought of as a certain definite quantity of force and as a certain definite number of centers of force . . . it follows that in the great dice game of existence, it must pass through a calculable number of combinations. In the infinite time, every possible combination would at some time or another be realized."[91] In other words, Nietzsche presupposes that in a world in which time is eternal, space is infinite, and the number of atoms that fill space is finite and determined, it is unavoidable that the number of configurations that these atoms achieve throughout the infinite time span must not only be limited but also inevitably repetitious.

Indeed, Henri Poincaré,[92] a contemporary of Nietzsche, confirms this idea of repetition: he argues that regardless of the complexity of a mechanical system, if that system consists of a finite number of parts and is allowed to function long enough without any outside disturbance, sooner or later all the configurations that had been attained by the system in the past are going to be repeated.

Hence, Nietzsche's eternal recurrence theory seems to add the principle of permanency as a guarantor of existence to his view of the world as an eternal monster of energy that is in continuous flux, for without it pure change would be impossible. The world in which things are deprived of any form of endurance in all respects would be the world of no existence, for if everything is in continuous change and there is nothing that endures, then what is it that changes? Nothingness could give rise only to nothingness.

What appears to be troubling, nevertheless, about the eternal recurrence theory is not that it endeavors to recognize some form of permanence in reality, but that this principle of permanence seems to entirely dislodge the genuine novelty from the world's creativity. If everything happened in the past and the past is bound to be reproduced, then the ostensible pursuit of novelty that both Whitehead and Nietzsche so strongly embrace is genuinely impossible. Simply put, Nietzsche's eternal recurrence theory seems to deny Whitehead's insistence on novelty as a driving force behind the world's change. For if indeed Nietzsche is correct about his theory of continuous repetition, then reality is anything but a superficial expression of novelty.

Of course, the question that arises is whether the eternal recurrence theory that Nietzsche proposes necessarily denies the possibility of genuine novelty. We could, however, argue that if Nietzsche were a supporter of classical atomism, or what Whitehead refers to as scientific materialism—which holds that "fixed scientific cosmology which presupposes the ultimate fact of an irreducible brute matter, or material, spread throughout space in a flux of configurations . . . [that are governed by] a fixed routine imposed by external relations which do not spring from the nature of [their] beings"—then it would be quite difficult to understand how Nietzsche could talk about the presence of genuine novelty in light of this theory.

However, as we have already discussed, Nietzsche, like Whitehead, rejects mechanistic theories of explanation as a way of understanding the world. He replaces immutable atoms that are involved in a dance of mechanistic aggregations with quanta of energy whose external relationships with each other are dictated by their own internal creativity that Nietzsche delineates in terms of will to power. The static materiality of the atomic world gets to be supplanted with dynamism of energetic centers internally involved with each other.

So how are we to resolve this apparent contradiction between Nietzsche's unending infatuation with the continuous mutability of everything that exists and his eternal recurrence theory that seems to dwell on the circularity of events? If Whitehead's notions of metaphysics as an "endeavor to frame a coherent, logical, necessary system of ideas" is correct, then we can imagine his arguing that we have to place the theory of eternal recurrence within Nietzsche's larger understanding of the world as "the will to power." We can hear Whitehead asserting that if we accept Nietzsche's full commitment to mutability and novelty as the guiding principles of reality, then the only way to make sense out of his eternal recurrence theory is to shift its hermeneutics away from maintaining that the recurrences pulsating through reality are the result of mechanistic repetitions replaying themselves to the smallest minutia of detail, as they had unfolded in the past,[93] to recognizing that the dynamic world of Nietzschian metaphysics is the world of infinite energetic creativity in which the quanta of power achieve their novelty through the repetition of their own will to power without replaying the same events ad infinitum. As Nietzsche rhetorically asks us, "Is not the existence of *any difference at all,* rather than perfect repetitiveness, in the surrounding world enough to impugn the idea of a uniform cycle of existence?"[94] Repetition lies not in the content of unfolding events but in the activity from which these events emerge. As there would be no concrescing occasions without their prehensive processes, so there would be no quanta of power without their will to power: same activities, different outcomes. Or as Nietzsche eloquently advises, " Let us believe in the absolute necessity of the whole but beware of maintaining, with respect to any law, even though it may be a primitive mechanical law derived from experience, that such a law is dominant in this whole and is an eternal property."[95]

As indicated at the beginning of this chapter, Whitehead and Nietzsche find themselves maintaining contrary ideas regarding the intellectual value of metaphysical speculations. Whitehead is a quintessential metaphysician: his entire philosophical pursuit is a reflection of his deep philosophical commitment toward speculative philosophy. His preoccupation with coming to apprehend reality through metaphysical categories is so complete and thoroughgoing that no matter what aspect of our experiences of the world he chooses to engage in his thinking—be it science, literature, education, religion, art—his metaphysical speculations bleed through his philosophical reflections.

Nietzsche, on the other hand, approaches metaphysics with a healthy skepticism driven by his rebellion against the traditional metaphysical projects. He is so frustrated and appalled by their intellectual "high-mindedness" that he assumes the role of the Antichrist in order to demolish their foundations and turn them into palaces of ruin.

Yet, we can clearly perceive a certain sense of intellectual ambiguity underlying Nietzsche's "philosophizing with a hammer," for as he destroys the transcendental palaces of traditional metaphysics, he immediately searches to resurrect in their places his own metaphysics of change and becoming. It is as though Nietzsche is fully aware of Whitehead's philosophical admonition that if we wish to engage in philosophical discourse about the world, then we cannot elude metaphysical speculations, and thus we may as well become clear about them by erecting our own systems.

Notes

1. Friedrich Nietzsche, *The Gay Science,* translated by Walter Kaufmann (New York: Vintage Books, 1974), 283.

In *Nietzsche* (Princeton: Princeton University Press, 1968), 204, Walter Kaufman writes about Nietzsche that "he looked upon himself as an experimental philosopher who wished to break with the tradition of 'unlimited ambition.' For the delusion of the metaphysicians that they might be able 'to solve all with one stroke, with one word' and thus become 'unriddlers of the universe,' Nietzsche proposed to substitute 'the small single questions and experiments.'"

2. Friedrich Nietzsche, *Twilight of the Idols,* "How the True World Finally Became a Fable," selected and translated with an introduction, preface, and notes by Walter Kaufman in *The Portable Nietzsche* (New York: The Viking Press, 1954), 485.

3. Quoted by George Allen Morgan Jr. in *What Nietzsche Means* (Cambridge: Harvard University Press,1941), 21.

4. Alfred North Whitehead, *Process and Reality,* corrected edition, edited by David Griffin and Donald W. Sherburne (New York: Free Press, 1978), 3.

5. A. J. Hoover, *Friedrich Nietzsche: His Life and Thought* (Westport: Praeger, 1994), 25.

6. Stephen Houlgate explains in *Hegel, Nietzsche, and the Criticism of Metaphysics* (Cambridge: Cambridge University Press, 1986), 233, Nietzsche considers all past philosophers to a certain extent to be metaphysicians.

7. Friedrich Nietzsche, *The Will to Power* (New York: Random House, 1967), 281.

8. Quoted by R. J. Hollingdale, "Theories and Innovations in Nietzsche" in *Nietzsche: A Critical Reader,* edited by Peter R. Sedgwick (Blackwell, 1995), 115.

9. Nietzsche, *The Will to Power,* 302.

10. Ibid., 313.

11. Hoover, 31.

12. Ibid., 31.

13. Ibid., 31.

14. Friedrich Nietzsche, *The Will to Power,* vol. II, Book III, translated by Anthony M. Ludovici, in *The Complete Works of Friedrich Nietzsche,* edited by Oscar Levy (New York: Russell and Russell, 1964), 329.

15. Nietzsche, *The Will to Power,* 301.

16. Ibid., 327.

17. Ibid., 13.

18. Ibid., 301.

19. Friedrich Nietzsche, *The Joyful Wisdom,* translated by Thomas Common, in *The Complete Works of Nietzsche,* edited by Oscar Levy (New York: Russell and Russell, 1964), 208.

20. Friedrich Nietzsche, *Human, All-too-Human,* translated by Helen Zimmern, in *The Complete Works of Friedrich Nitzsche,* edited by Oscar Levy (New York: Russell and Russell, 1964), 20–21.

21. Friedrich Nietzsche, *The Will to Power,* edited by Oscar Levy, in *The Complete Works of Friedrich Nietzsche* (New York: Russell and Russell, 1964), 34.

22. Friedrich Nietzsche, *Beyond Good and Evil,* translated by Helen Zimmern, in *The Complete Works of Friedrich Nietzsche,* edited by Oscar Levy (New York: Russell and Russell, 1964), 144.

23. Paul Carus, *Nietzsche: And Other Exponents of Individualism* (New York: Haskel House Publishers,1972), 18–19.

24. Hoover, 60.

25. Ibid., 60.

26. John Locke, *An Essay Concerning Human Understanding,* in *The Works of John Locke* (London: 1823), II, xxiii, 4.

27. John Locke, *Concerning Human Understanding* (Oxford: The Clarendon Press, 1934), II, iii, 19.

28. David Hume, *A Treatise of Human Nature* (Oxford: The Clarendon Press, 1978), 16.

29. Nietzsche, *The Will to Power,* 296.

30. Friedrich Nietzsche, *On the Genealogy of Morals,* translated by Horace B. Samuel, in *The Complete Works of Friedrich Nietzsche,* edited by Oscar Levy (New York: Russell and Russell, 1964), 46.

31. Houlgate, 38.

32. Friedrich Nietzsche, *Ecce Homo,* translated by Anthony Ludovici, in *The Complete Works of Friedrich Nietzsche,* edited by Oscar Levy (New York: Russell and Russell, 1964), 137–38.

33. Houlgate, 90.

34. Nietzsche, *The Will to Power,* 549.

35. Ibid., 550.

36. Ibid., 339.

37. Nietzsche, *Beyond Good and Evil,* 51. Nietzsche continues: "I do not mean as an illusion, a 'semblance,' a 'representation' but as possessing the same grade

of reality as our emotions themselves—as a more primitive form of the world of emotions, in which everything still lies locked in a mighty unity, which afterwards branches off and develops itself in organic processes . . ."

38. Nietzsche, *The Will to Power,* 550.

39. Ibid., 369.

40. Friedrich Nietzsche, *Thus Spake Zarathustra,* translated by Thomas Common (Mineola: Dover Publications, 1999), 153.

41. George Allan Morgan, *What Nietzsche Means* (Cambridge: Harvard University Press, 1941), 63.

42. Nietzsche, *The Will to Power,* 340.

43. Ibid., 340.

44. Steven D. Hales and Rex Welshon, *Nietzsche's Perspectivism* (Urbana: University of Illinois Press, 2000), 65.

45. Whitehead, *Process and Reality,* 5.

46. A. Wolf, *The Philosophy of Nietzsche* (London: Constable and Co., 1915), 59.

47. Alfred North Whitehead, *Adventures of Ideas* (New York: Free Press, 1967), 226.

48. Quoted in W. K. C. Guthrie's, *History of Greek Philosophy,* vol. 1 (Cambridge: Cambridge University Press, 1962), 484.

49. Nietzsche, *The Will to Power,* 547.

50. Whitehead, *Process and Reality,* 22.

51. Nietzsche, *Beyond Good and Evil,* 19.

52. For more detailed discussion of the evolution of Platonic dualism look to Ivor Leclerc, "Whitehead and the Dichotomy of Rationalism and Empiricism," in *Whitehead's Metaphysics of Creativity,* edited by Friedrich Rapp and Reiner Wiehel (New York: State University of New York Press, 1990), 2–4.

53. Ibid., 2.

54. Ibid., 5.

55. Nietzsche, *The Will to Power,* 339.

56. Alfred North Whitehead, *Science and the Modern World* (New York: Macmillan, 1925), 69.

57. Alfred North Whitehead, *Adventures of Ideas* (New York: Macmillan, 1933), 200.

58. Ibid., 201–202.

59. Whitehead, *Process and Reality,* 18.

60. Alfred North Whitehead, *Religion in the Making* (New York: Macmillan, 1974), 88.

61. Nietzsche, *The Will to Power,* 550.

62. Wolf, *The Philosophy of Nietzsche,* 61.

63. Whitehead, *Process and Reality,* 244.

64. Thomas E. Hosinski, *Stubborn Fact and Creative Advance* (Lanham: Rowman and Littlefield, 1993), 21.

65. Alfred North Whitehead, *Modes of Thought* (New York: Free Press, 1929), 89.

66. Nietzsche, *The Joyful Wisdom,* 296.

67. Lewis S. Ford, *The Emergence of Whitehead's Metaphysics* (Albany: State University of New York Press, 1984), 3.

68. Friedrich Nietzsche, *The Antichrist* (New York: Alfred A. Knopf, 1918), 60.

69. Nietzsche, *The Will to Power,* 419.

70. Whitehead, *Process and Reality,* 21.

71. Ibid., 41.

72. Ibid., 21.

73. Whitehead, *Process and Reality,* 339–40.

74. Nietzsche, *The Will to Power,* 297.

75. Ibid., 350.

76. Nietzsche, *The Joyful Wisdom,* 158.

77. Victor Lowe, *Understanding Whitehead* (Baltimore: John Hopkins University Press, 1966), 21.

78. Randall Morris, *Process Philosophy and Political Ideology* (Albany: State University of New York Press, 1991), 68.

79. Whitehead, *Science in the Modern World,* 24.

80. Whitehead, *Adventures of Ideas,* 200.

81. Whitehead, *Process and Reality,* 27.

82. Donald W. Sherburne, *A Key to Whitehead's Process and Reality* (Chicago: The University of Chicago Press, 1981), 12.

83. Whitehead, *Adventures of Ideas,* 328.

84. Ibid., 264.

85. Whitehead, *Process and Reality,* 89.

86. Ibid., 89.

87. Ibid., 102.

88. Ibid., 107.

89. See for further discussion: Donald W. Sherburne, "Whitehead's Psychological Physiology," *The Southern Journal of Philosophy* 7 (1970): 401–407.

90. For the detailed discussion of the connection between Nietzsche's eternal recurrence theory and its scientific foundations refer to Stephen G. Brush, "Nietzsche's Recurrence Revisited: The French Connection,"*Journal of the History of Philosophy* XIX, no. 2 (1981): 235–38.

91. Nietzsche, *The Will to Power,* 549.

92. Stephen G. Brush, "Nietzsche's Recurrence Revisited: The French Connection," *Journal of the History of Philosophy* XIX, no. 2 (1981).

93. Harold Bloom, ed., *Modern Critical Views: Friedrich Nietzsche* (New York: Chelsea House, 1987), 82. Gilles Deleuze asks and answers the question: "Why is mechanism such a bad interpretation of the eternal recurrence? Because it does not necessarily or directly imply the eternal return. Because it only entails the false consequence of a final state. This final state is held to be identical to the initial state and, to this extent, it is concluded that the mechanical process passes through the same set of differences again. The cyclical hypothesis, so heavily criticized by Nietzsche, arises in this way. Because we cannot understand how this

process can possibly leave the initial state, re-emerge from the final state, or pass through the same set of differences again and yet not even have the power to pass once through whatever differences there are. The cyclical hypothesis is incapable of accounting for two things—the diversity of coexisting cycles and, above all, the existence of diversity within the cycle."

94. Quoted by Karl Jaspers, *Nietzsche: An Introduction to the Understanding of His Philosophical Activity* (Tucson: The University of Arizona Press, 1965), 355.

95. Ibid., 356.

Part Five

Whitehead on Nature and Technology

CHAPTER 9

Thinking with Whitehead about Nature

John B. Cobb Jr.

The Ecological Crisis

Awareness of the ecological crisis has brought into being a type of writing about nature that had been largely absent in the past. Of course, the biological and physical sciences dealt intensively with particular features of nature as it could be known to empirical observation and through experiment. But most of this study focused, as does science in general, on recurrent patterns and the formulation of laws about them. It said little about the changing condition of the actual natural world.

Within the biological sciences ecology existed as a specialization. It was not, in principle, more temporally oriented than other branches of science, but field ecologists could not but notice the deterioration of the systems they studied. They saw that most of this deterioration resulted from human acts. Some became alarmed, and ecologists played a major role in alerting the rest of the world to the destructive consequences of human actions. That the environmental crisis as a whole is so often called the ecological crisis testifies to their special role.

Although most scientists continue to look for timeless patterns, some, along with other thoughtful people, now attend to the changes that are taking place in our environment, especially those that result from human activity. Vast quantities of information have been accumulated, much of it deeply troubling.

Much of this literature is ordered to concerns as to what people should do about the these matters. Most of this is technical discussion of proposals from the scientific, technological, economic, and managerial points of view. There is no doubt about its importance.

But the shape of these proposals and the extent to which they are adopted or ignored depends in part on deep-seated beliefs and attitudes about human beings and about the natural world. Those concerned that humanity is not responding adequately to the threat ask questions about these beliefs and attitudes. They propose what they regard as better beliefs and attitudes.

Much of this discussion is religious. We have come to understand that the great religious traditions arising in the first millennium B.C.E. focused attention on human salvation in a way that withdrew attention from the human relation to the natural world. The Christian form of this anthropocentrism paved the way for the objectification of nature that made rapid progress in technology and science possible. Because this progress greatly expanded human use of nature without concern about its effects on nature, it brought about a crisis. Christians are reformulating their faith so as to emphasize God's concern for the whole creation and human responsibility in that context. Other religious traditions are engaged in similar reformulations.[1]

Philosophical Responses

Most philosophers, like most practitioners of other academic disciplines, have gone about their business little affected by this new attention to nature. But some have brought their philosophical approaches to bear on this topic, and a few have specialized in what has come to be called environmental ethics. For many the approach to nature has been indirect, because they stand in traditions that have denied its independent existence.

Since Kant, the creative role of the human mind in constituting everything we can know as nature has been emphasized. In extreme formulation this could imply that the problems identified in nature could be rectified simply by a change in thinking. With respect to the human body this conclusion has been drawn from idealistic premises quite frequently, but I am not aware of a published statement of this sort with respect to the whole natural world.

Still, an emphasis on the social construction of reality has been brought into the discussion of nature. It is held that all that is meant by "nature" is a construction of human minds or language. The meaning is not imposed by an independently given reality. Diverse cultures, and diverse groups in the same culture, construct "nature" differently. Those who gain from the status quo are maintaining the present construction.

Our task is to expose this fact and take from them the power to construct our world. Only so will collective behavior improve.

Thus far there has been less attention to what "social construction" should succeed the present one. The focus is on power relations. It seems to be assumed that if the oppressed, or people as a whole, gained power, the social construction of nature that would follow would be satisfactory. In any case, the net effect of this analysis is to return attention to social relations and how power corrupts them.

Marxists have a more realistic view of the natural world. But they, too, believe that improvements in human relations to that world depend on changes in social relationships. Changing the attitudes about nature of the powerless does not help. Unless the exploitation of people is ended, there is no way to end the exploitation of nature. The major response of socialism to ecological thought has been the social ecology of Murray Bookchin and his Institute for Social Ecology.[2]

The majority of the philosophers who have entered into discussions of the natural world in light of the ecological crisis want change in general beliefs and attitudes. Among them there is a further split. Some believe that the dualism of the human and the natural along with the anthropocentrism that dominates the philosophical tradition must be overcome. Others affirm the dualism and anthropocentrism and work within the traditional frame of reference.

Those who are content with a dualistic and anthropocentric approach see the need as greater attention to human dependence on the natural environment and to the finite character of that environment. The problem has been that people have taken the environment and its capacity to support human life for granted. Attitudes formed in a time when human activity played a minor role in shaping the environment persisted when it became a major determinant of nature's condition. People must learn to pay close attention to the consequences of their actions, recognizing that they can destroy the capacity of the Earth to support them. But this does not require any basic change in ontology, anthropology, value theory, or ethics.

An important representative of this position is John Passmore. In his book *Man's Responsibility for Nature: Ecological Problems and Western Traditions*[3] he argued that to extend rights to nonhuman entities would bring an end to civilization, the creation and preservation of which is humanity's unique responsibility.[4] Rights are not applicable to nonhumans since there is no community of mutual responsibility between humans and nonhumans,[5] although it is appropriate to restrict human rights *over* animals.[6] Humans have moral responsibilities with regard to nature, but these are not responsibilities *to* nature. Human responsibility is only to other human beings.

This dualistic and anthropocentric position dominates writing about the ecological crisis in general, but not that in environmental ethics. Precisely because those who hold it judge that no really new philosophical problem is posed by the ecological crisis, awareness of the problem evokes little writing of this kind. Those who do see the need for changes in the understanding of humanity and nature dominate the philosophical literature.

Among these, also, there is a major division. On the one hand, there are those who are especially concerned to overcome the doctrine that humans have no responsibilities to other animals. These writers emphasize the extension of moral considerability from individual human beings to individual animals. On the other side are those who focus on ecological issues. They are concerned that people think in systems terms, recognizing that human beings are part of the system.

Peter Singer and Tom Regan are the best-known advocates of the animal welfare position. They stand in a philosophical tradition, going back at least to Bentham,[7] that rejects the dualism between human beings and nature. At least the higher animals are subjects of pleasure and pain like ourselves and deserve consideration in much the same way. Treating humanity as if it were an exception to animal life generally is "speciesism."[8]

Singer argues that any being that has interests is worthy of equal consideration. Any being that is capable of suffering and enjoyment has interests. Therefore, all sentient beings are equally objects of moral consideration. Obviously, such moral consideration does not lead to the same consequences in each case, but it does have the consequence that it is wrong to inflict suffering on sentient beings.

The case against painless killing is less unequivocal.[9] Singer works on this case elaborately and concludes that mammals, at least, are likely to have the characteristics of personhood that make it wrong to kill them. These characteristics are rationality and self-consciousness.[10] Regan argues directly from the possession of interests to the right to life.[11]

Regan and Singer did not have the ecological crisis in view as they worked to break down the boundary in philosophical ethics between human beings and other animals. But the connections with other moves in this direction brought the two discussions into close relationship. Much of it was friendly, but some of it was not.

In an article published in *Environmental Ethics* in 1980,[12] J. Baird Callicott argued that the ethical debate was not only between those who denied moral considerability to animals and those who affirmed it. Environmentalism spoke with a third voice, extending moral considerability to the natural world in a very different way. Callicott's appeal was to Aldo Leopold's "land ethic," according to which "a thing is right when it tends to preserve the integrity, stability, and beauty of the biotic community. It is wrong when it tends otherwise."[13] The criterion is thus the well-being of the community as a whole rather than the pleasure of individual creatures.

This ethical principle, like that of the supporters of animal welfare, denies that only human beings are to be given moral consideration. Indeed, it goes much farther in its critique of anthropocentrism. Human well-being is to be subordinated to that of the community as a whole. But the well-being of the community is not reducible to that of individual people or other animals. Benefiting the biotic community leads, for example, to efforts to restrict human population.[14] It also promotes the killing of animals that threaten the health of the biotic community and protects those that are needed by it with no regard to their respective degree of sentience.

Callicott recognized that animal welfare thinkers had very different concerns from those of Leopold. They focused on what human beings did to domestic animals, especially on factory farming and laboratory experimentation, whereas Leopold was concerned with the wild. There might be no necessary contradiction between them. Strictly, Callicott's argument was that one could not build up an overall environmental ethic out of extending moral consideration to nonhuman individuals. But in his original article Callicott showed virtual indifference to what happens to domestic animals or to the suffering and death of wild ones. It seemed that the land ethic was to replace concern for individual animals.

Regan responded by calling this kind of environmentalism "environmental fascism."[15] He argued that the concerns of environmentalists for biological communities could be met by extending rights to each creature within the community. "Were we to show proper respect for the rights of individuals who make up the biotic community, would not the *community* itself be preserved?"[16]

Later Callicott expressed regret for the polemical character of his essay and affirmed a complementary relation between the two approaches to nature.[17] He did not, however, accept Regan's individualist proposal, which fails to recognize that societies cannot be understood as simple additions of individuals and ignores the fact that the health of the biotic community depends on such things as the predator-prey relationship. Instead, he recognizes that human beings are members of more than one community. Just as awareness of the biotic community and its nature draw us to value its well-being, so our recognition of our community with domestic animals can lead us to value their well-being.

The animal welfare debate continues, but since Callicott clarified the sharp distinction between it and environmental philosophy, the latter has largely developed independently. Most environmental philosophers have judged that the primary question is the rights or value of species and ecosystems.

The attribution of intrinsic value to the higher animals in animal welfare literature is not difficult to understand. In the utilitarian tradition experiences of pleasure and pain have intrinsic value, positive and negative. This is not based on the private judgments of the observer. But it is difficult to know what attributing intrinsic value to species or biotic communities means.

Callicott recognizes the technical problem. He accepts the view that "there can be no value apart from an evaluator, that all value is as it were in the eye of the beholder."[18] Since the beholders in question are human beings, he acknowledges that, in one sense, his environmental ethics is anthropocentric. But what the beholder values depends on how the beholder understands the world. Now that people understand the world in terms of biotic communities, it is at least psychologically likely that they will value their well-being. When they do so, they will appraise all things in terms of the contribution they make to this whole.

Many environmental philosophers have a strong sense of the integrity of the natural world, of the importance of its being free to be itself, of the wrong that is done when it is defaced by human beings. They struggle with the question of whether this simply reflects human valuing or whether it is a response to values that are objectively there. The question is often discussed in terms of intrinsic value.

The obstacle to affirming the intrinsic value of nature is the principle enunciated by Callicott, a principle that dominates value theory generally. Value depends on subjects. In different schools of thought it does so in two ways. For utilitarians such as Singer and Regan, value is found in the objective condition of the subjects. Pleasure is good; pain is evil. It is not dependent on how an observer values pleasure and pain. For other philosophers, as in the quote from Callicott, value is a function of the subject's valuation. In his words, it is in the eye of the beholder.

Callicott struggles against the tendency of his subjectivism to lead to a relativism of taste. He argues that as people come to understand biotic communities they will experience them as supremely valuable. Indeed, he claims that natural objects can have "intrinsic value" without being subjects. "An intrinsically valuable thing on this reading is valuable *for* its own sake, *for* itself, but it is not valuable *in* itself, i.e. completely independently of any consciousness, since no value can in principle . . . be altogether independent of a valuing consciousness."[19]

Callicott explains this by asserting that this value is projected onto nature. The projection is grounded in human feelings, but these feelings are brought into being by the impact of the object. The occasion for the projection of intrinsic value is objective. But he knows that this theory captures only half of what is usually meant by intrinsic value. The term usually denotes value not only in itself but also for itself. This would require attributing to nature the status of subject, and Callicott does not do this.

One of those who seek a more objective view of the intrinsic value of nature is Holmes Rolston III. In part he does so by objecting to the subject/object dualism that underlies modern value theory. Subjects arise out of the objective in a continuous process. He points out that contemporary science has greatly weakened this distinction,[20] and that in the study of the natural world people discern projects that are analogous to human ones. These natural projects are quite as objective as any other feature of what is going on. The sharp distinction of fact and value does not work.

Based on considerations of this sort, Rolston emphasizes a continuum between human subjective values and those in nature. The projective element serves to unite them all. Continuous with the values in human subjectivity are those in other animal subjectivity. These are continuous with the projects to be found in other parts of the natural world.[21] The human values are the fullest, but they do not exhaust the intrinsic value of the world. Intrinsic value is located in species and ecosystems as well as in individuals.

Callicott continued to struggle with the issue of intrinsic value. Like Rolston, he saw contemporary science, especially quantum theory, as helpful.[22] On the one hand, as Rolston noted, the subject/object distinction is broken down. On the other hand, quantum theory displays the way in which all things are deeply interconnected. One who understands this latter fact can see that the intrinsic value that inheres in the human subject must now be recognized as shared by all the other entities that participate in constituting that subject.

Some environmental philosophers find all these positions still too anthropocentric. They argue that until there is a a more radical change of consciousness about who we are and how we are related to the rest of the natural world, there will be insufficient change in our behavior. Those who adopt this view often call themselves deep ecologists. Arne Naess has worked with George Sessions to define this group as a school. They appreciate the land ethic of Leopold, but are not satisfied with it.[23]

Callicott's recent writings come close to deep ecology, but he fails to emphasize the need for a change of consciousness.[24] Rolston has done much to encourage a richer sensibility in the awareness of the particulars of nature, and he agrees with most of the eight points by which Sessions and Naess define deep ecology.[25] But there are two features of the standard account that separate it from Rolston.

First, deep ecology holds to biocentric equality. "The intuition of biocentric equality is that all things in the biosphere have an equal right to live and blossom and to reach their own individual forms of unfolding. . . ."[26] Second, the change of consciousness for which deep ecology calls differs from anything considered by Rolston. It has strong affinities with Buddhism. Whereas most of our thinkers have been locked into separate subjectivities, deep ecologists call for giving up ego-selves in favor of true selves. The sense of being a separate ego with private desires is false. The true self is inclusive of all. What is required is "self-realization," by which deep ecologists understand that "'no one is saved until we are all saved,' where the phrase 'one' includes not only me, an individual human, but all humans, whales, grizzly bears, whole rain forest ecosystems, mountains and rivers, the tiniest microbes in the soil, and so on."[27]

Deep ecology is generally more interested in resituating understanding of humanity and nature than in solving theoretical problems as posed by modern philosophy. Rolston's effort to rethink the subject/object duality of modern thought can qualify as deep ecology. One thinker who has made particularly interesting contributions to rethinking the relation of human beings to nature, and who is claimed as a deep ecologist even though he does not affirm all its features,[28] is Paul Shepard.

Shepard presents the hunting and gathering society as that form of life in which human psychological needs and outward behavior were in harmony and humans were also well related to the environment.[29] He traces the history of domestication of plants and animals, the building of cities, the development of religions and philosophies, and modern secularization as one long, complex history of growing alienation from nature in general and human nature in particular. Shepard has a rich appreciation of how each distinct landscape shapes consciousness and language. As with deep ecologists in general, he does not believe the ecological problem can be rightly addressed apart from deep-seated inner changes which, for him, require recovery of the understanding of animals and landscapes that civilization took from humanity.

At this point deep ecology makes contact with postmodern environmental ethics in its deconstructive form, at least in its representation by Jim Cheney.[30] Cheney draws extensively on Shepard's work. He dates the beginning of modernity with the shift from mythical narrative, which he understands as situated discourse, to theory, which he describes as totalizing discourse. He locates this shift at the same point at which Shepard sees the beginning of alienation from nature. He sees the breakdown of this modern period as beginning only in this century with its abandonment of totalizing language and return to situated discourse. He speaks with approval also of how Rolston suggests that we understand Aldo Leopold's new ethical principle as "deeply embedded in [Leopold's] love for the Wisconsin sand counties."[31] Understood in this way it can avoid being totalizing language and play the role of situated discourse.

Whitehead

Whitehead did not address the ecological crisis or develop an environmental ethic. Nevertheless, his cosmology has obvious relevance to a range of the relevant issues. Because it is a cosmology, its relation to environmental issues is, in some ways, more like that of the traditional religions than like philosophical ethics.[32] Religions, also, describe the way they understand the world to be and draw conclusions from that understanding about how to live in it. Classical philosophy took something of this form as well. Questions of fact and value, is and ought, are not sharply distinguished in Whitehead or in these traditions.

In modern times, on the other hand, individual philosophical problems are treated more or less independently. Ethics is a distinct field. It is preoccupied with a set of standard questions about values, rights, duties, and so forth. There are several established schools of thought on these questions. If there are cosmological commitments involved, these are not highlighted.

It is difficult to locate the implications of Whitehead for ethics in the present context. Indeed, his thought raises questions about the wisdom of the fragmentation of philosophy into separate divisions. With respect to environmental ethics this leads to formulations that clash with important principles in social ethics.[33] One point of contact between Whitehead and some of those philosophers who have dealt with the ecological crisis is this recognition that the questions about how to respond cannot be answered when formal ethics is abstracted from a larger context of thinking.

Whitehead disagreed with Kant's way of responding to Hume and proposed an alternative that recovered a relation to the real world. But Whitehead's alternative, like Kant's, affirmed a large contribution to the content of experience on the part of the subject. He distinguished between perception in the mode of causal efficacy, in which the world enters into us and forms us, and perception in the mode of presentational immediacy, in which we present to ourselves an ordered world of colors and sounds. He agrees with Kant that our sense of space is largely formed in this mode, but he believes that our awareness of time comes to us from the way the world imposes itself on us in causal efficacy.

No two events occur in just the same place and time. Accordingly, the actual world of each occasion is unique to it. Every experience grows out of a different world. Hence the idea that all that we feel and think is conditioned by our location is directly derivable from Whitehead's cosmology. The rich development of the understanding of social location of more recent times is congenial to this vision, but neither Whitehead nor his followers led in its development. Hence, a Whiteheadian can be appreciatively informed by the discussion of the social construction of reality developed by other thinkers.

On the other hand, Whitehead is a realist. People construct their world out of data given them by that world. This imposes limits on construction. All experience is selective and interpreted, but it is not invented. Unlike idealists, Whiteheadians struggle to discriminate what the world is like apart from human interpretation from the way it is interpreted. We seek more accurate interpretations. This is a never-ending effort, but a crucial one.

For example, Whiteheadians believe that there either is, or is not, a hole in the ozone layer and that it is, or is not, increasing in size. There is always room for interpretation, and interpretations affect the way the evidence is read. But the answers are not simply a matter of social construction. If we wish to stop the growth of the hole, we must take specific actions dealing with the physical world. Changing our social construction of the world will not solve the problem.

Deconstructing bad interpretations is important, as is understanding who has the power to impose interpretations. It is also important to construct interpretations we believe to be better. This has been a major part of the project of Whiteheadians. We have been less effective in analyzing the power relations that shape the dominant constructions.

The Whiteheadian response to Marxists is similar. They are right about the importance of overcoming human oppression. But it is one-sided to argue that social change is primary and that only when it is accomplished can nature be liberated. It is also true that unless alienation from nature is overcome, human liberation cannot be achieved.

Based on these judgments, followers of Whitehead prefer to keep the discussions of human liberation and of the liberation of nature closely related. In the real world, global capitalism is oppressing both humanity, especially the poor, and the other creatures. Nevertheless, this does not mean that there is no need for direct reconsideration of nature and the human relation thereto.

Passmore represents the anthropocentrists who teach that human beings are responsible *for* nature *to* other people. This responsibility is real. For example, responsibility to future generations is an important motivation for change. But that humans have no responsibility *to* nature and that nature can have no rights is not evident to Whiteheadians.

The term *rights* is not one that plays a significant role in Whitehead. Passmore is certainly correct that it was developed in an anthropocentric context. It also has a strongly individualistic cast. Rights are often thought of as correlative to duties, and nature has no duties toward us. But as many philosophers have noted, the language of "rights" is also used in cases where there is no reciprocity. For example, people are inclined to attribute rights to a dying person after there is no further possibility of reciprocation. I have proposed that whenever it can be said that we ought to treat someone or some thing in a particular way, we can also say that it has the right to be treated in that way.[34] With this understanding, I have no difficulty attributing rights to nonhuman creatures. But this dispute with Passmore could be terminological.

On the other hand, the extent to which Passmore draws a line between humanity and nature raises issues that cannot be reduced to terminology. Not only does he deny rights to other creatures, he asserts that people can have no responsibilities to them. Whiteheadians cannot agree. We see human beings as one species among others, whatever its distinctiveness. The overall relation of humans to nature should reflect the continuity and kinship with other creatures and the common belonging to a single world. It should also reflect the fact that all are internally related to all. This means that each is damaged when others are damaged.

Whiteheadians are supportive of the concern for animal welfare. We share the view that moral considerability applies to animals. The enormous suffering inflicted on the animals raised for meat and on those on which people experiment is morally outrageous. Some Whiteheadians draw practical conclusions similar to those of Regan and Singer.[35]

Nevertheless, there are philosophical differences that also affect the practical outcome. Both Regan and Singer think of rights in either/or terms. They are not sure where to draw lines above which certain rights apply, but the line is important, because everything above it deserves equal consideration, and what falls below it deserves none at all.

For a Whiteheadian there are practical questions about whether to give such consideration in a particular instance, but in principle, everything warrants *some* moral consideration. Questions are better couched in terms of how much weight to give to what with regard to any particular issue rather than absolute either/ors.

Consider the question of killing animals. A Whiteheadian sides with Singer in seeing the infliction of suffering as a clearer moral evil than killing. But Singer wants a strict rule against killing as well. Singer justifies it by first identifying the characteristics of human beings that forbid their being killed. He identifies self-consciousness and the awareness of identity through time. He then shows that this characteristic applies to at least some nonhuman animals. That it applies much more clearly to some than to others does not matter. If it applies at all, then the rule applies equally. He argues from this to not killing, and therefore not eating, mammals.

The requisite characteristics are clearly present in chimpanzees and gorillas. The case against killing them is strong. These characteristics seem to play a much smaller role in sheep. Accordingly, although sheep deserve moral consideration, this fact does not by itself answer the question whether a sheep may be killed for food. The practical argument for vegetarianism is much stronger when the treatment of animals raised for food is emphasized.

This is not the place to go into detailed practical judgments. The relevant point is only that for Whitehead a variety of considerations come into play and their weight varies. Singer is looking for clear lines and absolute rules. Whiteheadians do not inhabit a world in which these can be found.

Callicott's appeal to Leopold's land ethic also has deep resonance in Whitehead. Things are ordered in societies. In many instances the good of the society as such is extremely important. As people learn more about the environment, they discover that this is the case with biotic communities. Acting for the benefit of the biotic communities that make up our living environment makes a great deal of sense.

On the other hand, we disagree with some of the features of Callicott's argument. He seems to juxtapose the community to individuals quite sharply. We agree that the community cannot be understood as the sum of individuals as they would be apart from the community. Hence, as he says, expanding animal rights, individualistically conceived, to include all creatures would still not work. But to juxtapose to that the well-being of the community as virtually independent of the individual well-being of its participants is also wrong. Regan is not altogether wrong to associate this neglect of individuals with fascism.

Whitehead proposes a third way beyond individualism and holism, based on his idea that all the entities in the community are internally related to one another. None are in fact what they would be in separation from the community. Each is what it is by virtue of its membership in the community. The community is, in a sense, the sum of the members, each of which is what it is by virtue of participating in that community.

This means that the community is benefited either by benefiting individual members or by improving the system as a whole. In a biotic community the best approach will normally be systemic. The members will be better off as the system improves. As Callicott knows well, the improvement to the whole may involve the suffering and death of some, but any effort to prevent that, or even hesitation to kill animals when that is needed, reduces the total value realized in and through the individual participants. This position is closer to Callicott's than to Regan's, but in some cases, the well-being of particular individuals, especially but not only human ones, should receive a weight in moral decisions that is ignored in the holistic approach. The sorts of considerations Singer introduces against killing chimpanzees cannot be simply set aside by ecological or systemic arguments.

There is a second feature of Callicott's position with which Whiteheadians disagree. We share the view that value depends on subjects. But whereas Callicott puts the weight on the subject's valuing something else, we agree with Regan and Singer that there is value in the subject's own experience. Further, Callicott seems to suppose that the only subject capable of significant valuing is the human one. This is related to the other point. If valuing is a conscious act of judging something external, it may be that subjects other than human ones are limited. But if intrinsic value lies simply in the enjoyment of being, as Whitehead believed, then there is no reason to restrict value so narrowly. On the contrary, there is every reason to assume that living things in general enjoy living and want to continue living.

Their enjoyment is quite objective to human subjects. Whether people value it or not, it occurs—or does not occur. Hence, value in nature is quite objective. We do not need to project it. This objective value is intrinsic in the full sense of being a value not only in itself but also for itself.

Whitehead does not draw a line below which there is no intrinsic value at all. Even among creatures such as human beings where there is some conscious enjoyment of being, much of the enjoyment, and therefore the value, is nonconscious. Also, the value in unified animal experience is largely derived from values in the cells that make up the body. These are, presumably, not conscious at all, but they are subjects nonetheless. They are both patients and agents. They are acted upon and they act. Being acted on is feeling the world in a certain way, it is a subject receiving its data into itself. Hence, attributing value to all actual entities is not separating value from subjectivity.

Nevertheless, there are great differences in the amount of enjoyment of which creatures are capable. In some cases the capacity for enjoyment is so slight that moral considerability fades off to negligible levels. In other cases, even excluding human ones, it is quite weighty. In most cases, dealing with the community systemically will best increase the value in the biotic community. In some cases, systemic considerations must be balanced against the effects on the enjoyment of individual creatures.

This view provides a richer account of the intrinsic value of nature than Callicott's, but it does not gainsay the point he makes. People do also project value on many things independently of judgments about what creatures with what capacities are present. The impact that a landscape makes on human beings may inspire that kind of projection. What is objectively present in nature should not be called "intrinsic" value, but what has moved one person is likely to move others as well. It should not be tampered with. This judgment of value is about features of nature that objectively have the capacity to evoke this richness of enjoyment in human beings.

In principle this value can be in tension with intrinsic value. That is, there are situations in which the enjoyable activity of animals might mar a feature of nature that could give humans great enjoyment. People might decide to fence an area off to protect this feature, thereby harming the biotic community. Whiteheadians judge that there are many values to be considered and that actual judgments are not derived from any single rule.

Callicott's projection theory allows him to attribute what he calls "intrinsic" value to species and landscapes and biotic communities as well as to individual things. But because the value remains projected, Rolston is not satisfied. Rolston believes the value is in nature and found there by humans. The values he finds include those of animal enjoyment that Whitehead emphasizes, but he finds no reason to posit subjectivity below the level of sentience. That means that a great deal of the world, even the living world, lacks subjectivity. Its intrinsic value for Rolston cannot be connected with the status of subject.

Here is a fundamental divide between Whiteheadians and most ethicists. The attribution of nonconscious subjectivity to every individual event appears counterintuitive and even silly to many. Even those who are open to the possibility want to discuss ethical issues without committing themselves to such doubtful metaphysical speculation. One reason Whitehead's thought is so little discussed in the context of philosophical ethics is that he brings cosmological ideas into the discussion of values.

A second objection from Rolston is that Whitehead's value theory entails a sharp duality between the values that are in nature independently of human experience and those that humans project on it. With regard to a landscape, its overall beauty is in the experience of the human observer. Only the causes of that experience are objectively in nature. Also, in a tree the intrinsic values are only in the individual cells. What those values are depends on the social organization of the cells into a tree, but the tree does not have a separate intrinsic value of its own.

Rolston, on the other hand, sees natural processes as working in a quasi-purposeful way at many different levels. These seem to him to have values that are continuous with those realized in conscious subjectivity. Whiteheadians cannot give an account of this that is satisfactory to him.

From a Whiteheadian point of view, Rolston's own account is somewhat vague and philosophically confusing despite its rich promise. The projects he finds in nature seem to require a status that is not purely objective. Sometimes his formulations suggest that what is purely objective generates what is purely subjective—a greater metaphysical puzzle than the attribution of subjectivity to all events. At other times he seems to resolve the problem by denying the subject/object duality. That direction would bring him closer to Whitehead, for whom every unit event is both subjective and objective.

Deep ecology is also attractive to Whiteheadians. We are deep ecologists if that means that we reject dualism and anthropocentrism and believe that new sensibility and vision are needed. We, too, deconstruct the isolated ego and understand ourselves to be products, moment by moment, of the whole world. But we are not consistently welcomed by leaders of the movement.

There are two sticking points. The first is the same problem that Rolston finds with our thought. Deep ecologists find intrinsic value in systems and landscapes more than in individuals. They are more critical than are we of the concern for the well-being of individual animals.

The second is that, like Rolston, we do not accept biocentric equality. Like him we see a particularly rich achievement of value in human experience, and we see grades of value in other creatures. That every creature is of equal value seems to us false.

Sessions has criticized us quite severely. The extension of value from human beings to other creatures is a mistake. Sessions writes: "This attempt to apply Whiteheadian panpsychism, while positing various degrees of intrinsic value to the rest of Nature, nonetheless merely reinforces existing Western anthropocentrism, and thus fails to meet the deep ecology norm of 'ecological egalitarianism in principle.'"[36] This is a criticism Whiteheadian ecological ethics receives also from some eco-feminists, Buddhists, and followers of Schweitzer.

We have two responses. First, although we do believe that there are grades of intrinsic value and that this is very important, this is not the only relevant consideration in evaluating other entities. I have already mentioned two others. One is that there are systemic considerations. On the whole, the entities most important to the biological community are those with less intrinsic value. This does not mean that every entity has equal value either intrinsically, or in its role supportive of community, or in balancing these two considerations. But it does mean that intrinsic value should not be overplayed in ethical considerations. The other is that the contribution of entities to human aesthetic value is quite distinct from either of the above considerations.

In addition to these valuations there is another that is quite central to Whitehead's thought. This is the role of contrast. In any experience some of the diverse influences are integrated into contrasts. In the contrast, their distinctness is maintained, but a new and more valuable pattern emerges through the way they are related. This requires the emergence of novelty. For this kind of value to arise in an occasion, such as in a human experience, there must be diversity in its world. The greater the diversity that is integrated through contrast, the greater the resultant value. This is a strong argument for maintaining biodiversity as well as a diversity of ecosystems and landscapes.

Whiteheadians find this plurality of considerations a better basis for making ethical judgments than "egalitarianism in principle." Little follows from that as long as it is not taken seriously for practical purposes. But if it were taken seriously, the consequences could be terrible. The already prominent calls for drastic population reduction, for example, could lead to ignoring the needs of threatened people (as Garrett Hardin recommends) on the grounds that the resultant population reduction would improve the quality of life for those who remain and also reduce pressure on the habitat of other species. Much as I (as one deeply concerned for the whole system and the biodiversity within it), would like to see an end to population growth achieved through birth control, my valuation of human life is such that callousness toward mass deaths seems utterly wrong.

Paul Shepard's thinking has been a challenge to my Whiteheadian sensibilities for many years. Whitehead uses the term *civilization* to name his fully developed value system.[37] Shepard shows that civilization was a long step in the alienation from nature that sickens us and destroys the environment. One may rightly reply that the meaning of the term is not the same in the two cases, but this does not remove the problem. Whitehead's understanding of historical progress was nuanced, but he saw an overall advance where Shepard sees decline. This appears clearly in Whitehead's notorious comment in *Science and the Modern World:*

> The North American Indians accepted their environment, with the result that a scanty population barely succeeded in sustaining themselves over the whole continent. The European races when they arrived in the same continent pursued an opposite policy. They at once cooperated in modifying their environment. The result is that a population more than twenty times that of the Indian population now occupies the same territory, and the continent is not yet full.[38]

One might suppose that this sensibility and judgment can be separated from the philosophy as such. In large part, fortunately, this is true. Our present understanding of the North American Indians undercuts Whitehead's statement in a number of ways. Contemporary Whiteheadians know the destructive consequences of humans "filling" a continent in the European fashion, as Whitehead, seventy-five years ago, did not. We also know that the Native American population was much larger than supposed at the time Whitehead wrote.

But built into Whitehead's philosophy is a notion of the achievement of greater value through creative transformation of what is given. This notion directs us necessarily toward a historical process. It celebrates our ability to criticize our situation and rise above it. Change is not always progress, but it is needed for zest.

Shepard, on the other hand, regards history as disaster. A healthy condition is one in which values and ways of being in the world are learned through socialization, generation after generation. Of course, there are changes. But changes are not to be canalized so as to become the basis of further changes.

My own solution to this problem has been to treat Whitehead and Shepard as a contrast. There is truth in both. Domestication has been both positive and negative; so was the rise of civilization. The question of whether history has been worth it is not yet settled. At present prospects are not good, but we should not despair. In any case, what we now need is the kind of creative transformation Whitehead celebrates. Without it, the values Shepard persuasively affirms cannot be realized.

Jim Cheney's postmodernism renews some of the same challenge. It calls for a return to primal patterns in a way that devalues all achievements of the past ten thousand years. Whitehead affirms change, but also continuity. Sometimes one is more important than the other, and the twentieth century may have been one of those times. But the new grows out of the old. To reject old values for the sake of the new is dangerous. What is needed is transformation through contrast.

Cheney sets up alternatives as sheer oppositions. Either we return to situated discourse that makes no claim to relevance beyond its immediate place, or we continue with hegemonic language. But surely postmodernist statements about situated discourse arose from situated discourse and were generalized. Furthermore, granting that all thought and speech is situated, does this preclude the idea that from different perspectives wisdom may arise that is worth sharing more broadly?

Are all attempts to gain an overview necessarily hegemonic? May we not develop an overview that encourages situated discourse and local knowledge? Is that not what postmodernism is itself doing?

Whiteheadians prize Whitehead's cosmology for the overview it supplies. Hence, these questions are important. We can understand that many systems of thought have been oppressive. The dominant modern view of the world, which still determines so much thought today, is oppressive. Neo-liberal economic thought is oppressive. We propose Whitehead's cosmology as a way to liberate from these and other oppressions. We have even thought of Whitehead's philosophy as itself postmodern.[39] Now other postmodernists tell us that what we meant for liberation is nothing but another form of oppression. This is a serious challenge to our self-understanding.

Clare Palmer has formulated a deconstructionist critique of Whitehead in the conclusion of her book, *Environmental Ethics and Process Thinking*.[40] In the book as a whole she recognizes that the ethical implications of Whitehead's thought cannot be equated with any one traditional system but can be related to several. Her presentation is fair, and sometimes insightful.

This is true also of most of the concluding criticisms. They are similar to ones mentioned above. Palmer wants an environmental ethic that is more egalitarian than Whitehead's. She believes that a Whiteheadian ethic gives too much weight to human interests. But she proposes adjustments that would make a Whiteheadian ethics more acceptable to her in these respects.

None of this prepares the reader for the devastating critique with which she ends, when she attacks the whole approach from a deconstructive postmodernist perspective. In doing so she appeals to Cheney.

The attack is threefold. First, it condemns any cosmological system whatsoever. Such systems are inherently totalizing and colonizing. That is, they generalize from theories generated in one locale to what is true always and everywhere. Their application in other locales replaces the ideas that are germane to those places. Second, even if there may be some ways of generalizing that can be justified, Whitehead's cannot. It does not allow difference to stand, but instead regards everything as like human experience. It is "familiarizing." Third, the view of human experience that it generalizes is "Western liberal white male."[41]

I will respond to these criticisms in reverse order. The third is the least fair. Palmer bases it on lifting up Whitehead's generalization of the "self-actualizing, self-creative aspect of the actual occasion."[42] To be fair, she would have to note that Whitehead generalizes equally its receptive character and stresses the occasion's primarily emotional nature. That feeling is so much more fundamental than thought in Whitehead, that, indeed, thinking is a form of feeling, is not a distinctively Western liberal white male view.

The second objection raises more serious issues. Central to the Whiteheadian project is the overcoming of dualism. It is the success in doing this that has commended Whitehead's thought for environmental ethics. Now postmodernists are objecting to this achievement. They are saying that instead of seeing humanity as continuous with nature and recognizing its kinship with other creatures, we should let their otherness simply stand, accept and appreciate it.

For Whitehead, too, otherness is important. Without it there would be no contrasts, and contrasts are the soul of value. But for Whitehead, to think of sheer otherness is not to think at all. For nature to be simply other would return it to the status to which it descended in Hume and Kant when it lost all functions whatsoever and disappeared from human concerns. This is not, of course, what Palmer wants. She follows Cheney in wanting local knowledge grounded in the particularities of nature in every place. That makes sense for Whiteheadians also. But it does not explain what the "nature" is that takes on these particular forms. Whiteheadians do not know any nonvacuous way to think of that nature without attributing subjectivity to it. We do not know any meaning we can give to subjectivity that is not derivative from our experience of subjectivity. In short, we do not know what the meanings are that underlie the objections at this point. That does not warrant their dismissal. But it does invite the critic to clarify the alternative. Simply calling for local knowledge and the affirmation of otherness does not accomplish this.

These comments relate to the first objection as well. This objection is to the cosmological enterprise as such. In Whitehead's version one begins locally, generalizes from local experience, and then tests the generalizations in other locales.[43] This is different from the image of colonizing. Nevertheless, it *is* a quest for successful generalizations that can be adopted by people in many locales. And when one approaches a new locale in this way, one does not do so with sheer openness. One brings hypotheses of a general nature to be tested. This is different from allowing local knowledge in each place simply to be itself with no claim to general relevance.

There is a very deep question as to whether inclusive vision is desirable or not. Postmodernists say no, yet in the process of doing so they seem to propose their own inclusive vision. The insistence that nature should be allowed to stand in its sheer otherness does not arise spontaneously in all locales! Still, the postmodernists claim that their vision is of the independent development of local knowledge everywhere. Its normative principle is the rejection of the custom of abstracting from local knowledge and imposing the abstraction on others.

A Whiteheadian must ask that this vision, which also arises from situated thinking, be laid alongside the vision of a body of hypotheses growing out of situated knowledge in many places and coordinating that knowledge. The rejection of this latter vision by deconstructive postmodernists has thus far been too facile and ad hominem. But Whiteheadians must intensify their sensitivity to the danger that the effect of presenting a completed system, rather than involving people in the process of its construction, can be all too much as described by their critics.

Notes

1. See, e.g., Stephen C. Rockefeller and John C. Elder, eds., *Spirit and Nature: Why the Environment is a Religious Issue* (Boston: Beacon Press, 1992); and Mary Evelyn Tucker and John A. Grim, *Worldviews and Ecology* (Lewisburg, Pa.: Bucknell University Press, 1993). Under Tucker's leadership the Center for the Study of World Religions at Harvard University held a series of ten conferences each on one of the world's religious traditions. Each conference is resulting in a volume of essays.

2. Murray Bookchin, *The Modern Crisis* (Philadelphia: New Society Publishers, 1986).

3. John Passmore, *Man's Responsibility for Nature: Ecological Problems and Western Tradition* (London: Duckworth, 1974).
4. Ibid., 178–79.
5. Ibid., 116–17.
6. Ibid., 115.
7. Jeremy Bentham, *Introduction to the Principles of Morals and Legislation,* chapter xvii.
8. Peter Singer, "All Animals Are Equal," in *Animal Rights and Human Obligations,* edited by Tom Regan and Peter Singer (Englewood Cliffs: Prentice-Hall, 1976), 154. Singer expresses his indebtedness to Richard Ryder for the term *speciesism.*
9. Ibid., 155.
10. Peter Singer, *Practical Ethics,* second edition (Cambridge: Cambridge University Press, 1993), 110–11.
11. Tom Regan, "Do Animals Have a Right to Life?" in Regan and Singer, op. cit., 197–204.
12. J. Baird Callicott, "Animal Liberation: A Triangular Affair," republished in J. Baird Callicott, *In Defense of The Land Ethic: Essays in Environmental Philosophy* (Albany: State University of New York Press, 1989), 15–38.
13. Aldo Leopold, *Sand County Almanac* (New York: Oxford University Press, 1949), 224–25.
14. Callicott, 27–28. Callicott refers to Garret Hardin's lifeboat ethics with approval.
15. Tom Regan, *The Case for Animal Rights* (Berkeley: University of California Press, 1983), 362.
16. Ibid., 363.
17. J. Baird Callicott, "Animal Liberation and Environmental Ethics: Back Together Again," in Callicott, op. cit., 49–59.
18. Callicott, "Animal Liberation," 26.
19. J. Baird Callicott, "On the Intrinsic Value of Nonhuman Species," in *The Preservation of Species,* edited by Bryan G. Norton (Princeton: Princeton University Press), 142–43.
20. Holmes Rolston III, *Philosophy Gone Wild: Essays in Environmental Ethics* (Buffalo: Prometheus Press, 1986), 93–94.
21. Holmes Rolston III, *Environmental Ethics: Duties to and Values in the Natural World* (Philadelphia: Temple University Press, 1988), 216.
22. J. Baird Callicott, "Intrinsic Value, Quantum Theory, and Environmental Ethics," *Environmental Ethics* 7 (1985).
23. Bill Devall and George Sessions, *Deep Ecology: Living as if Nature Mattered* (Salt Lake City: Gibbs M. Smith, 1985), 85–86.
24. See Michael Zimmerman, "Quantum Theory, Intrinsic Value, and Panentheism," in *Postmodern Environmental Ethics,* edited by Max Oelschlaeger (Albany: State University of New York Press, 1995), 277–308.
25. Ibid., 70.

26. Ibid., 67.
27. Ibid.
28. Ibid., 72–74.
29. See especially Paul Shepard, *Nature and Madness* (San Francisco: Sierra Club, 1982).
30 Jim Cheney, "Postmodern Environmental Ethics: Ethics as Bioregional Narrative," in Oelschlaeger, op.cit., 23–42.
31. Ibid., 29.
32. Whitehead's cosmology is included alongside traditional religious ones in Tucker and Grim, op.cit. See David R. Griffin, "Whitehead's Deeply Ecological Worldview," 190–206.
33. The negative reaction to the North American discussion by Third World writers is at least partly a response to the one-sidedness of environmental ethics separated from social ethics. See Ramachanda Guha and Juan Martinez-Alier, *Varieties of Environmentalism: Essays North and South* (London: Earthscan, 1997), especially chapter V.
34. John B. Cobb Jr., *Matters of Life and Death* (Louisville: Westminster/John Knox, 1991), 16.
35. An example can be found in Daniel A. Dombrowski, *Hartshorne and the Metaphysics of Animal Rights* (Albany: State University of New York Press, 1988). Jay McDaniel has also written extensively about animals. See, e.g., *Of God and Pelicans: A Theology of Reverence for Life* (Louisville: Westminster/John Knox, 1989).
36. Devall and Sessions, 236.
37. Alfred North Whitehead, *Adventures of Ideas* (New York: Macmillan, 1933), Part IV.
38. Alfred North Whitehead, *Science and the Modern World* (New York: Macmillan, 1925). Paperback 1967, 205–06.
39. The term is suggested by Whitehead's objectification of the "modern" world in *Science and the Modern World* and his view that William James had initiated a new epoch in philosophy. Influenced by Whitehead, I, personally, have used the term since the sixties. See, for example, "From Crisis Theology to the Post-Modern World," *Centennial Review* 8 (Spring 1964).
40. Clare Palmer, *Environmental Ethics and Process Thinking* (Oxford: Clarendon Press,1998).
41. Ibid., 221.
42. Ibid.
43. See Alfred North Whitehead, *Process and Reality: An Essay in Cosmology*, corrected edition edited by David Ray Griffin and Donald W. Sherburne (New York: Free Press, 1978), 5. Whitehead is thinking more of areas of modern knowledge than of local knowledge, but the model applies equally well in the latter case.

CHAPTER 10

Whitehead and Technology

FREDERICK FERRÉ

Alfred North Whitehead was not explicitly a philosopher of technology. Nevertheless, his rich insights into the uses of reason, the needs of society, and the slow, uncertain advances of civilizations, can help philosophers and plain citizens alike—any who try to reflect on the deep character of the artifacts by which humans transform their lifeworlds and make new worlds possible—clarify their thoughts. His insights can even help guide responsible choices about which technologies to resist, and which to foster. In our current technological society, such guidance is obviously of urgent importance for the future of humanity and of the planet we restlessly occupy. Technology provides one of the key points of contact between abstract worldviews and concrete worlds. This chapter will try to sketch how these come together in Whiteheadian perspective.

The Character of Technology

Despite a sprinkling of references to "technologies" and "technology" in his later works, Whitehead offers no formal definition of this term. Still, he makes it clear in context that he has nothing especially arcane in mind. He is content with commonsense usages. Technologies are implements that provide human beings physical help, forming part of the "outfit" that people over the millennia have created as an enhanced environment for human living. Our inborn capacities for thought are probably no greater than those of our naked ancestors, but "there has been an immense expansion of the outfit which the environment provides for the service of thought."[1] Examples include "modes of communication . . . writing . . . preservation of documents, variety of modes of literature, critical thought, systematic thought, constructive thought . . . mathematical symbolism," and, finally, "improved technology providing physical ease" (AI, 60–61).

By distinguishing technology from such mental methods as "mathematical symbolism" and from "critical, systematic, and constructive" thought as such, Whitehead implies the quite normal view that technology needs to be embodied, somehow, not simply left "in the head." Technologies need not be "high tech," but they do need to be situated squarely in the physical order. At the time of the Black Death in Europe, for example, "soap, water, and drains were the key to the situation" (AI, 94). Since they were not available, millions suffered and died. Malthusian misery was forced on other, non-European civilizations, not by some iron law but by habitat and inadequate technology. "Now India and China are instances of civilized societies which for a long period in their later history maintained themselves with arrested technology and with fixed geographical location. They provided the exact conditions required for the importance of the Malthusian Law" (AI, 93). But, Whitehead suggests, more advanced technology could have changed those conditions, making the grim "Law" inapplicable and freeing countless persons from their suffering.

Such a linkage between technology and freedom is, for Whitehead, exactly the fundamental point. Famously, the horrible institution of slavery was in large part undermined by the rise of technologies, such as the cotton gin, that could replace forced human labor. But this point demands generalization. Considered deeply, "the essence of freedom is the practicability of purpose" (AI, 84). Freedoms of the press, of speech, of religion, and the like, come quickly to mind in modern liberal democracies. Important as these are, however, it would be a mistake to define freedom in their terms. They are social, civic freedoms. Beneath them, the human species has had to wrestle free from "the massive habits of physical nature, its iron laws," which for most of human history, and still for most persons, "determine the scene for the sufferings of men" (AI, 84).

> Birth and death, heat, cold, hunger, separation, disease, the general impracticability of purpose, all bring their quota to imprison the souls of women and of men. Our experiences do not keep step with our hopes. The Platonic Eros, which is the soul stirring itself to life and motion, is maimed. (AI, 84)

Relief of suffering, then, is the main mission of technology, broadly understood as the embodied implementation of practical purpose. "Mankind has chiefly suffered from the frustration of its prevalent purposes, even such as belong to the very definition of its species. . . .

Prometheus did not bring to mankind freedom of the press. He procured fire, which obediently to human purpose cooks and gives warmth. In fact, freedom of action is a primary human need" (AI, 84).

The physical embodiment of our tools, implements, and artifacts gives them a solidity, a weight, that can be coercive—for good or ill—in the pursuit of someone's purposes, not always our own. Whips and thumbscrews can be effective means for the control of slaves, embodying the practical purposiveness of mastery over an oppressed population. An office building sets in concrete the patterns of commerce, employer-employee relations, work conditions, and much more entailed in modern economic and social institutions. Practical purposes are expressed, but not in ethereal, abstract ways. Purposes embodied in major technologies tend to dominate. We may willingly cooperate, or we may resist. Either way, the technologies we find surrounding us in our culture's "outfit" reflect the ubiquity of compulsion. Neither in nature's world of massive regularities nor in the human world of embodied purposes can compulsion be escaped.

From a Whiteheadian perspective, this is not by any means always a bad thing. The ancient Greeks recognized the important role of νάγχη in the physical and moral structure of the universe. Like them or fight them, there are implacable forces in the universe to which humans must bend. When they are coordinated, we may refer to them as forces of "compulsion"; when sporadic they appear as "violence" (AI, 6).

Both loosen the grip of the status quo. Just as Roman cities crumbled before the sporadic violent onslaughts of barbarians ravening at their gates, so, with equal inevitability, pastoral Europe gave way to the coordinated compulsion of the steam engine: in factories, over rail lines, and on the sea. And although this certainly caused much suffering, such was the price to be paid for advance. In this universe there is no such thing as standing still. Advance or decay are our only choices.[2] Technology sometimes serves the cleansing role of destroyer to force advance. Whitehead chooses "Steam," in parallel with the ancient "Barbarians," to designate the "senseless agencies driving their respective civilizations away from inherited modes of order" (AI, 6). Often human beings perceive the technologies of their time as "senseless agencies." Any accurate descriptive phenomenology of technology will need to record this widespread fact of feeling.

Still, senselessness is far from the full reality of the matter. We have already noted that technologies are the embodiment of purposes. Purposes are led by values, hopes, or fears, and are therefore far from simply "senseless." Whitehead himself quickly recognizes that we are here dealing in matters of degree, not in absolutes. The violence of the barbarians was perceived by the Romans as senseless, but from the viewpoint of the Huns there were abundant purposes, aspirations, and pleasures. "To Attila and his hordes their incursion into Europe was an enjoyable episode diversifying the monotonous round of a pastoral life" (AI, 7). Even more obviously, the steam engine itself is far from "senseless," since it was a product of intelligence, thoughtfully invented with a blending of theoretical and practical reason by James Watt (1736–1819) and his colleagues. As an agent of compulsion it broke old social patterns and freed ideal aspirations of democratic thought to eliminate slavery and shape new institutions, but as a product of purpose it was itself bipolar. One pole consists in the massive physical regularities of the natural order in which, for example, water becomes gas at a certain temperature, gases expand with heating, metals have reliable properties, and the like. The other pole consists in the mental powers of human persons to devise and manipulate symbols, make diagrams, contemplate and refine abstract possibilities, discriminate anticipated outcomes, sustain positive valuations of certain of these outcomes, and arrange physical devices according to conscious preferences. Without both poles interacting, there would have been no steam engine. As Whitehead acknowledges, "[T]he age of coal and steam was pierced through and through by the intellectual abilities of particular men who urged forward the transition" (AI, 8–9).

Causal compulsion and mental evaluation are present at all levels of reality, natural and social, for Whitehead. The mix, the relative importance of the two poles, is what varies. Seen from a certain perspective, technology can appear remorseless, inhuman, coercive. It can dash hopes and frustrate purposes. It can arm and perpetuate tyranny; but equally, it can undermine cruel institutions, shatter a decaying status quo, and release fresh ideals to create new social realities. Thus, seen from another perspective (as by paleontologists) technology emerges as exciting evidence of effective mentality entering a world bare of tools. It can empower aspiration; it can create new facts, new possibilities, new dangers, and new satisfactions. It can be seen as mentality making a difference, as intelligence and values becoming incarnate in the environment.

The Functions of Technological Intelligence

Intelligence comes in many degrees of more and less, and in a variety of modes. These overlap in ways that make it impossible to answer the "more or less" questions without first specifying the sort of intelligence we are examining. In humans, a high degree of practical cleverness may coexist with a low degree of discriminating reflectiveness. Brilliant abstract intelligence may be exhibited by a social dolt. Animals, too, of different species, may be gifted in quite different ways. Within the same species different individuals may prove to be less or more capable of manifesting that species' special kind of brightness.

This recognition of pluralism should not be overstated. There must be some overarching trait or traits that are key to "intelligence" in general, or we would not know why we are using the same word in different contexts. What are they? One pervasive but variable trait is *flexibility,* the capacity to adjust to changing circumstances, whether these be new premises in an argument or new facts in the environment. A second is *quickness* in response; a euphemism for limited intelligence is "slow." A third general trait allowing of more or less is *discrimination,* the variable capacity to make significant distinctions, whether these be in the jungle, at a cocktail party, or in a mathematical calculation. A fourth trait is the ability to make more or less remote *inferences,* moving several steps from the immediately given to what is not yet obvious, as in the learned capacity to "read" coming weather from present signs or the ability to plan several moves ahead, in chess or politics or war, or to draw conclusions from theoretical postulates. A fifth trait is the greater or lesser capacity for *synthesis,* the ability to pull disparate elements together into a meaningful whole, as a detective might synthesize scattered clues in solving a crime, a child might suddenly "put together" what her birthday surprise will be, or a metaphysician might construct a worldview. A sixth variable trait of intelligence is *effectiveness,* the capacity to direct attention and action toward contextually defined appropriate goals, whether these are practical, aesthetic, social, theoretical, or other. These capacities, combined in one way or another, are functions that may sometimes conflict with each other (keen discrimination of differences may make synthesis more difficult), but they are all recognizably functions of intelligence throughout its different modes. I would add one more, though I realize there is less consensus on it: namely, the capacity to *compare and evaluate ends.* It is a mark of high intelligence, I believe, to be able to reflect on the relative importance of contextually possible but mutually incompatible goals. Sometimes, at least at certain highly developed levels of responsible agency, the unexamined goal is not worth pursuing. Then even high degrees of flexibility, quickness, discrimination, inferential power, synthetic capacity, and instrumental effectiveness may only serve stupidity.

Whitehead's approach to thinking can make sense both of the *variety* of these modes and yet the fundamental *unity* of intelligence—or of "Reason," as he preferred to call it. Both this variety and this unity characterize technology, the embodiment of intelligent purposes. There are important differences between the "high" technology of recent times and the ancient craft technologies that coevolved with the human species. These differences are so important that some insist that only "high" technology is "real" technology. Whitehead, as I intend to show, would not agree to such discontinuities. Real differences demand acknowledgment, but not at the expense of seeing what still fundamentally unites the hand ax and the atom bomb within the variegated technological family.

Whitehead's way of helping us see both the differences and the continuities in technology through the ages is through an examination of the functions of intellect. Mentality, for Whitehead, is pervasively present in the universe as one of the two poles animating every event as it becomes actual. But for most of the universe, the mental aspect is not much in evidence, since the overwhelming bulk of the universe is dominated by its immediate past environment, with precious little scope for spontaneity or innovation. When small pockets of complexity in the environment develop, however, allowing some nearby entities to take account of interesting alternatives, the mental poles of these entities are energized, becoming more important in proportion as real possibilities for novelty increase. Novelty appears when the pressure to conform to settled habits is released; this, in turn, is triggered by increased variety and complexity in the environment, stimulating increases in the ability of mentality to take account of new possibilities not already physically present in the here and now.

Mentality itself is the capacity to transcend the immediate environment, to take meaningful account of the physically absent through imagination or symbol. It may not be widely distributed through the universe, but it certainly functions strongly in humans. Daydreaming of an absent lover, worrying about a future attack, hoping for food—these are normal capacities of men and women, old and young, rich and poor. Mere daydreaming, worrying, and hoping, however, bake no bread. They could even pose a danger, distracting or paralyzing an agent at the very moment when focused effort is most needed. Or, worse, they could, by virtue of their escape from control by the here and now, foster a condition of dangerous anarchy leading to personal and social disintegration, confusion, and death.

Against this destructive side effect of mental freedom, mental discipline is needed. Fortunately, mentality is demonstrably capable of imposing controls upon itself. Whitehead calls this mental capacity to control its own anarchical tendency, "Reason."

At its least sophisticated, it may just be a clutch of methods used to get out of difficulties. This could be pretechnological; for example, what a naked person in the desert might employ to keep from dying of thirst. Mentality, undisciplined, might attend so frantically to what is not actual in the environment, water, that such a person could waste precious energy and time rushing randomly around under the hot sun, looking now here, now there, for the precious liquid. But suppose that something works. A certain type of cactus, let us say, at first gnawed at merely as part of a desperate series of trials of everything and anything, releases cool moisture on this person's cracked lips. Mentality's capacity to recognize and remember this success as a *type* of behavior, involving a certain *type* of plant, gives rise to a rudimentary *method.* A method is a general pattern for doing something. Taking account of general patterns, of abstract features, is just what mentality does. Physical pushes and pulls are always particular and local. Insofar as methods are repeatable they are abstract and universal, in the domain of the mental. Thus, when the naked person in the desert recognizes a type or pattern of behavior as useful in satisfying the craving for moisture and begins to repeat it, directing attention toward a few general types of cacti, focusing activity, saving energy—employing a simple *method*—there is the emergence of practical Reason.

Although this example must be classed as pretechnological, since there are no implements involved, it highlights the fertile ground of method, from which technology springs. It is not a long step, after all, to such simple but fully artifactual methods as taking long sticks to retrieve honey from hollow trees or using stones to crush rabbits' heads.

Early technology of the craft variety is continuous with the methods-generating practical Reason that Whitehead calls the "Reason of Ulysses," in honor of Homer's champion escape artist, who goes from scrape to scrape, always finding some clever method for survival (FOR, 37). This kind of intelligence is as old as our species and, Whitehead speculates, much older. In developing methods for coping with practical challenges in their environments, animals too have manifested mentality in this mode, at least in the fortunate discovery of a method before habit and instinct resume their rule. As Whitehead put it, "The history of the practical Reason must be traced back into the animal life from which mankind emerged. Its span is measured in terms of millions of years, if we have regard to the faint sporadic flashes of intelligence which guided the slow elaboration of methods" (FOR, 40). Even quite elaborate crafts, such as metallurgy and glassmaking, constitute complex, internally nested methods resulting from happy accidents noticed, remembered, and repeated. That a certain metal will melt under one kind of heating method, while another requires heating in a different type of furnace, count as important facts, painfully learned, and precious to any society built, for example, on bronze or iron. Much later, but still in the ancient crafts tradition, the guilds of medieval Europe were organized to protect and perpetuate the memory of these fortunate findings. The recipes on which civilization rests need to be passed down through the generations. They need not be understood, but they need to be remembered.

In addition to Ulysses—never one to pause in his adventures to try to understand the general principles of his successes—Whitehead identifies another hero of Reason, Plato, patron of understanding for its own sake. But how different the speculative Reason of Plato is from the practical Reason of Ulysses! On first look, they seem to have nothing in common. Rather, they seem grounded in fundamental conflicts of aim and style.

Practical Reason is always "interested" in an outcome, aiming at something it wants to gain or avoid; speculative Reason in principle is, by contrast, "disinterested" and willing to follow an argument wherever it may lead, taking truth, not advantage, as its goal. Practical Reason is satisfied when a method works; speculative Reason wants to know *why* a method works and is not satisfied until it understands. Practical Reason is impatient with detail and tries to "keep it simple" as long as it works; speculative Reason revels in detail, unpacking complexity for its own sake. Practical Reason does not argue with success; speculative Reason is self-critical, since "good enough" is no guarantee of the best. Practical Reason is ad hoc, operating without explicit principles; speculative Reason is systematic and as explicit as possible so that everything can be endlessly reexamined and criticized. To Ulysses, the standards of Plato look unmotivated, obsessive, patrician, and masochistically self-flagellating. From Plato's viewpoint, the tricks of Ulysses are ignoble, thoughtless, lazy, and self-defensively uncritical. The wonder is that these two modes of Reason ever joined forces in what became modern high technology!

Science, until the sixteenth century in Europe, had indeed been patrician and mainly impractical; the crafts had been plebeian and mainly unsystematic. For centuries, practical and speculative Reason had been practiced by different classes of people. But in Europe of the sixteenth century, each mode of Reason came to mate with the other and the offspring were modern technologically implemented science and modern theory-led technology.

The mating itself was made fruitful by the fact that, for all their striking differences, practical and speculative Reason are both, at bottom, simply modes of Reason, with much more in common, as Whitehead shows, than appears on the surface. Practical Reason, we remember, is mentality grasping at possibility while disciplining itself by method. Once served by a method, the initial appetition can apparently be satisfied by endless repetitions of the method—and that is just the danger! Practical Reason's refrain, "If it ain't broke, don't fix it," becomes a damper on improvement and a invitation to the staleness and loss that mere repetition brings. What is needed is continuing restlessness, new appetitions for still better possibilities, in which mentality can criticize its own successful methods, asking "why" and insisting on understanding the whole in which the entire technological enterprise is set. Mentality grasping possibilities is still active, but the appetitions are new. *Understanding* is the satisfaction now sought, for its own sake, by mentality in its Speculative mode. This is a much more recent phenomenon than practical Reason, Whitehead points out: "It belongs to the history of civilization, and its span is about six thousand years" (FOR, 40). But speculation alone is not yet fully speculative Reason. To earn the title "Reason" requires that the anarchical liberties of mentality be brought somehow under discipline, not by the oppressive weight of here and now, not even by the successes or failures of practical methods, but by purely mental methods of self-criticism and control. Whitehead gives credit to the ancient Greeks. "Their discovery of mathematics and of logic introduced method into speculation" (FOR, 40). Logic is to the Reason of Plato as practical technique is to the Reason of Ulysses. Both are modes of mentality governing the thirst for "more" than is given in the here and now.

But for hundreds of years they merely paralleled one another, in uneasy isolation. Craft technologies grew by accretion and retention, as they always had; science, philosophy, and theology continued to weave skeins of great ideas on looms of logic. And then came the marriage that changed science as much as it changed the crafts. As Whitehead put it:

> The enormous advance in the technology of the last hundred and fifty years arises from the fact that the speculative and the practical Reason have at last made contact. The speculative Reason has lent its theoretic activity, and the practical Reason has lent its methodologies for dealing with the various types of facts. Both functions of Reason have gained in power. The speculative Reason has acquired content, that is to say, material for its theoretic activity to work upon, and the methodic Reason has acquired theoretic insight transcending its immediate limits. (FOR, 40–41)

Science was always logical; it was transformed, however, by becoming implemented with instruments through practical methods. Technology was always implemented; it was transformed, however, by becoming logical, tuned into theoretical possibilities that could make for new appetitions only accessible by going through science. Galileo's telescope is a good example of the transformation of science. Glassmaking was a well-developed craft tradition in the sixteenth century. Lenses for eyeglasses had been known and used for generations before Galileo put them into his viewing tube to explore the heavens. With the instrument, new data poured into awareness. The logical arguments of Galileo's opponents were no longer enough. A new kind of science was born.

The radio, in contrast, is a good example of the transformation of technology. Without the speculations of James Clerk Maxwell (1831–79) on invisible electromagnetic waves, and the experimental laboratory work of Heinrich Hertz (1857–94), Guglielmo Marconi (1874–1937) could not have imagined, must less patented, senders and receivers of such waves. But with "logic" in the lead, appetition was given new domains of possibility to yearn in, and a new kind of theory-led technology was born. We still live surrounded by the residues of craft traditions that would have been recognizable hundreds of years ago; yet, even more definitively, we live in a technosphere of implements made imaginable only by a transformed science born of the union between practical and speculative Reason. This is what finally distinguishes our modern age: that our civilization's key technologies are no longer matters of luck and memory; they have been sired on method by speculative thought. That is, human intelligence has deliberately opened new ranges of possibilities, for better or for worse, which otherwise would literally have been beyond conception. In showing this, Whitehead's analysis helps to clarify the source and challenge of our historical condition.

Choosing a Wise Technological Future

History is changed in two simultaneous but opposing ways, for Whitehead. The greatest events in human affairs, like the smallest individual events of concrescent actuality, are pushed by compulsion and pulled by aspiration. As seen in our earlier example, the "steam" of the industrial revolution and the "democracy" of high ideals jointly led to the end of institutionalized slavery in the United States. Sometimes aspiration is frustrated by compulsion; sometimes aspiration may gradually alter factual circumstances so that new causal realities may emerge in institutions of civilization.

> We notice that a great idea in the background of dim consciousness is like a phantom ocean beating upon the shores of human life in suc-

> cessive waves of specialization. A whole succession of such waves are as dreams slowly doing their work of sapping the base of some cliff of habit; but the seventh wave is a revolution—'And the nations echo round.' (AI, 23)

Technology, as a historical force, shares just this bipolar nature. As we saw in the first section, it is something that begins in aspiration but ends, for better and for worse, in the domain of causal compulsion. The physical embodiment of the automobile, for example, actually fulfills aspirations for joyful mobility—wind in the hair—and also actually frustrates perspiring commuters in traffic jams. Sometimes, that is, technology serves to liberate and extend purposes; sometimes it serves to imprison and limit. Much also depends on whose purposes and what aspirations are being implemented by which artifacts.

The key conditions of modern life, as we saw in the previous section, now reflect "theory-led technology" embodying the exciting but dangerous freedoms of speculative Reason. Is there a "logic" that can provide constructive internal controls over potentially anarchical mentality, now armed with the power to generate novel technological possibilities? Whitehead gives general guidance on such a logic for the assessment of purpose and aspiration, applicable to technological choices that must be made in any postmodern age. Going back to basics, he identifies the fundamental function of Reason—prior to all its distinctions into various modes—in terms of his famous invocation of "a three-fold urge: (i) to live, (ii) to live well, (iii) to live better" (FOR, 8). The ultimate standard, that is, Whitehead urges, is life itself. "In fact the art of life is *first* to be alive, *secondly* to be alive in a satisfactory way, and *thirdly* to acquire an increase in satisfaction" (FOR, 8). If these hints can be unpacked, they may suggest the needed self-disciplinary standards for human speculative Reason in order to choose postmodern technologies wisely.

What is it "to be alive"? Firstly, at a minimum, we find *metabolism*—interfacing with the nonliving physical environment in ways we might roughly call "eating and excreting"—and *reproduction,* of some sort, as the two features that define all living things, from microbes through plants and animals. Aristotle chose these two basic functions as characterizing the "vegetative soul," forming the first building block in the pyramid of functions found also in animals and human beings (*Psychology,* translated by Philip Wheelwright [New York: Odyssey Press, 1951], 125–32). Secondly, if we continue to follow Aristotle, the next functions of being alive, as animal rather than plant, are *sensation* and *locomotion,* that is, powers of gaining information about one's environment and of finding one's way about in it. Thirdly, human beings manifest all the above functions in our own way of being alive but also, as part of adult normal behavior, evince the functions of *calculation* and *reflection* as well. These latter penetrate and transform all the others, constituting our "rational soul."

In another forum, it would be worthwhile to examine the various ways in which plants and animals practice the "art of life" in their various ways of expressing the urge to survive, thrive, and go on and on flourishing in ever-richer ways. In this chapter on technology, however, we are mainly focused on technology in human life, where Reason—mentality disciplined by mentality—plays its multidimensional role in advancing the art of life. First, practical Reason, noticing and refining methods, identifies technologies to help us *survive.* The use of fire and pelts helped our ancestors retain the bodily warmth required for metabolism to continue; hoes and spears helped provide food, drawing the necessary energy from the environment to sustain metabolism. Dugout canoes and snowshoes helped human mobility in search of food or safety, or in search of mates for the propagation of new generations. And so on. Second, practical Reason can function beyond the level of survival to help us *"live well."* The satisfactions of secure homes, well stocked with extra provisions for future needs and comforts, social arrangements for mutual protection, and community projects aimed at satisfactions beyond any individual's capacity alone, all are well within the reach of traditional practical Reason.

Science-led "high tech" developments are in principle the continuation of the urge of life to "*live better.*" The restlessness of mentality, with its endless appetitions beyond the actual, criticizes each plateau of human achievement. This, Whitehead reminds us, occurs with or without science, as long as the gadfly of mentality is allowed to buzz. But once speculative Reason—free mentality disciplined by logic—has succeeded in weaving scientific theory-structures, fed and disciplined by advanced instruments, then the creative freedoms and perils of theory-led technological innovation become qualitatively different from anything that humankind has known.

Freely inventing technologies for the sake of living, living well, and living better raises ethical issues to a new pitch as well. Unlike our distant ancestors, we are more sharply aware of what we are doing, what we are aspiring toward. And in this new mode of deliberate technological Reason, our technological inventions are set into a theoretical context in which wider practical consequences and deeper questions of right and wrong rise in advance of implementation—something to which our species has not been long accustomed. New scientific ecological understanding, for example, makes it clear how intimately all living organisms are related to one another and how profoundly our species' long-term satisfactions depend on the continued flourishing of the biological networks in which we exist as fellow-members. Considerations of distributive justice and wider environmental health force us out of the anthropocentric myopia that has long clouded human consciousness. Such science-based considerations expand our awareness of the ethical stakes, give us far more information about what once might have been ignored as "side effects," and yet do not lead to sentimentalism. Ecological understanding vividly alerts us to the food chain of which we are a part. Just as everything is related to everything else, so everything eats and everything is eaten. Even the primary producers, energized by sunlight, draw nourishment from the soil. Everything else alive lives only by feeding on other organisms or their products. "Life is robbery,"[3] as Whitehead bluntly put it. But then comes the ethical challenge: "It is at this point that with life morals become acute. The robber requires justification" (PR, 105).

Postmodern *food* technology makes an absorbing ethical topic, especially as the numbers of humans needing nourishment increases, especially in the regions of the world least able to afford complex, expensive techniques. Genetic engineering, cloning, aquaculture of Earth's open seas—all these and more offer themselves as new possibilities generated by theory but not yet fully assessed by the larger logic implicit in the "art of life." Assuming that all of these entail "robbery," how should they be justified, if at all?

Whitehead would urge weighing the needs of survival, then of satisfaction, then of flourishing—not only in terms of the sustainable well-being of the wider biotic community but also in terms of the special qualities of satisfaction available to human persons, thanks to the rich complexity of personal mental powers. This suggests that there should be no reflex rejection of new technologies (as "Frankenfoods," or the like) but equally no thoughtless embrace without the restraining logic of wider considerations.

Similar life-centered, mentality-honoring methods of assessment could be applied, from the Whiteheadian perspective, to all the fundamental technologies of living, living well, and living better. Continuing with Aristotle's pyramid of living functions, postmodern technologies of human (and nonhuman) *reproduction* would demand close examination by the logic of the art of life. These issues would include such theory-led possibilities as cloning—both animal and human cloning—and would carefully spell out the zones of ethical justification and lack thereof. When norms and limits come into effective play, questions whether and how to limit human reproduction to an optimum rather than maximum level will also be addressed, for the sake of increasing individual human satisfactions and general organic flourishing in a world in which the web of life must not be deformed by excess reproduction by any species, including our own.

The logic of the art of life will need to be applied also to the basic animal functions of sensation and locomotion, in which humans share. Each of these constitutes an enormous domain for postmodern technological imagination. The general animal urge to *gain information* from the environment has been enormously expanded for humans during the modern period by applications of technology that have changed the very meaning of "information" and "environment." Telescopes in many ways began the modern revolution, but now human beings can "see" and "hear" across distances that would have left Galileo gaping. Gamma-ray detection, X-ray and radio telescopy—these, and more, hugely increase the range and types of data available for human collection. Beyond explicitly scientific instrumentation, ordinary people now can "see" and "hear" events around the world through television; an endless profusion of other virtual environments are instantly available through the Internet. Likewise, the unassuming telephone, pervasively present, not only in homes but also in cars and on sidewalks, at the tables of restaurants, and even in concert halls, allows technologically equipped humans to "reach out and touch" and "be touched" by an indefinite range of "someones" at all hours and in all circumstances. Again we find an urgent need for discipline by internal norms, the logic of the art of life, pulled by aspiration to maintain optimum balance, "to live better," in the constant struggle against mentality's anarchical tendency.

Similarly, the universal animal urge to *move about* in the environment, as expressed through modern technology, is in need of critique and fresh, more creative advance under the logic of life. The age of the private automobile as we have known it, for example, needs deep reevaluation. Wonderful early human aspirations for private mobility, jointly harvesting the practical fruit of many successful theories—from those behind internal combustion engines to those making possible synthetic rubber—have been brutally hijacked and given ugly embodiment in the behemoths rumbling antisocially and antienvironmentally across the asphalt universe that modern civilization is rapidly becoming. New creative aspirations, retaining yearning for individual flexibility along with social and natural imperatives, need embodiment. Sitting in traffic jams, we can dream of public modes of mobility melded with personally directed destination-carriers. We may also aspire to ways of limiting the need for transport itself, through market decentralization and virtual conferencing. Such new aspirations will meld speculative Reason with innovative practical methods for the sake of "living better."

At the top of Aristotle's pyramid, and relating explicitly to the human species alone, are the technologies of Reason itself. Reason, we have seen, permeates and transforms all the earlier levels, giving fresh meaning to human issues of nourishment, reproduction, sensation, and locomotion. But Reason also has its own unique functions: calculation and reflection.

On *calculation,* the rule-governed manipulation of formal symbols, the world has greatly changed since Aristotle's time, in which the abacus was the most advanced available aid to calculation. Nothing has changed more spectacularly in our everyday technosphere than in the computerization of work and life. Not just the fact of change but its continuing acceleration is beyond easy comprehension or prediction. In many ways the computer is a superb example of what is involved in the urge to surpass every plateau of achievement with new achievements woven from the theoretical prowess of speculative Reason—which already yearns for newly imagined goals before the latest is fully embodied. But Whitehead would remind us that here, too, the need for a logic of mental self-restraint, serving the art of life, is also superbly illustrated. Before we know it, wider ethical issues surround life at countless levels. Questions of privacy, its importance and legitimate limits, problems of "identity theft," issues of human responsibility where computer "experts" can race ahead of human calculational capacities in diagnosing and treating illness, or in calling for a nuclear preemptive strike—all these and more overwhelm existing institutions, and our sense of self in them, faster than we can respond thoughtfully to the bombardment of unprecedented challenges. We are in need of a comprehensive world picture in which these issues can be made sense of, sorted, and put into perspective. We are in need, that is, of more than calculative rationality; we seek wisdom.

Wisdom involves thoughtful balance, a sense of proportion, judgment on what can be discarded and what is essential, grasp of connections through the clutter of mere information. Calculative speed may help, but it may not. It is hard to imagine what technologies could "produce" wisdom, though it is useful to reflect on what sorts of technology might embody wisdom's qualities. A creatively designed transportation system, facilitating freedom of movement without becoming snarled in aggressive ego trips, might offer one example. A beautifully proportioned building, fitting its natural and social location, resting easy on demands for power, filtering its waste to make its output no more burdensome than its input, and dedicated to constructive uses in advancement of the urge to live, live well, and live better, would provide another example. Medical advances, in relief of pain and in support of good health, could offer still more. Public health projects, for the sake of clean air and water, suitable not only for rich countries but also for the desperately poor—all these could be embraced as postmodern "wise" technologies.

But sometimes, in a world trying creatively to live by the logic of the art of life, wisdom will call for voluntary renunciation of technology. Speculative Reason, if true to its restless, gadfly nature, will criticize not only specific instances of technology but also under some circumstances the quest for a "technological fix" itself. The quiet values of the hospice are sometimes more appropriate than the hectic clamor of the hospital. This may sound odd to those who imagine Whitehead to be a meliorative activist under all circumstances. But such an image leaves out of account Whitehead's embrace of Peace, the experience of that form of wisdom that penetrates beyond present possibilities and rests in the recognition that tragic beauty is its own final justification (AI, 366–81). Every event starts with unbounded aspiration, guided by subjective aim, and ends with only finite achievement. Technology is always the instrument of purpose, subjective aim, always the means to something more. Peace, however, goes beyond purpose and leaves all means behind. It appears as Zest realizes its own finitude and takes comfort, beyond all instruments, in the final goal: Beauty.

Notes

1. Alfred North Whitehead, *Adventures of Ideas* (New York: The MacMillan Company, 1933), 60. Hereafter referred to as AI.

2. Alfred North Whitehead, *The Function of Reason* (Boston: Beacon Press, 1958), 18–24. Hereafter referred to as FOR.

3. Alfred North Whitehead, *Process and Reality* (corrected edition, edited by David Ray Griffin and Donald W. Sherburne; New York: The Free Press, 1978), 105. Hereafter referred to as PR.

Contributors

GEORGE ALLAN, Professor of Philosophy Emeritus at Dickinson College, has authored three books exploring the ontological foundations for social value. *The Importances of the Past, The Realizations of the Future,* and *The Patterns of the Present.* A former President of the Association for Process Philosophy of Education, he is the author of a book titled *Rethinking College Education.*

LISA BELLANTONI is Assistant Professor of Philosophy at Albright College. She is the author of *Moral Progress: A Process Critique of MacIntyre,* published by SUNY Press.

JOHN B. COBB JR., Avery Professor Emeritus at the Claremont School of Theology and the Claremont Graduate School, is the author of thirty books, the Co-director of the Center for Process Studies, and Co-founder of Mobilization for the Human Family. His books, and his many articles, have dealt with Process Theology and with issues in ecology, particularly the issue of sustainability.

FREDERICK FERRÉ is Professor of Philosophy Emeritus at the University of Georgia, where he served as Research Professor and was Co-founder of the Interdisciplinary Graduate Faculty of Environmental Ethics. Of his eight books, two focus on technology and the three most recent are expansions of his Gifford Lectures.

DAVID L. HALL, recently deceased, was Professor of Philosophy at The University of Texas at El Paso. An early book was titled *The Civilization of Experience: A Whiteheadian Theory of Culture* and in 1994 SUNY Press published his *Richard Rorty: Prophet and Poet of the New Pragmatism.* In a series of collaborations with Roger T. Ames he used Whitehead's metaphysics as a vehicle for comparative studies of Chinese thought.

WILLIAM S. HAMRICK is Professor of Philosophy at Southern Illinois University, Edwardsville. A book, *Kindness and the Good Society,* was published by SUNY Press. His many articles deal with both Whitehead's thought ("Whitehead and Merleau-Ponty: Some Moral Implications") and phenomenology ("A Phenomenological Critique of Hart's Concept of Rules").

ROBERT CUMMINGS NEVILLE was for many years Dean of the Boston University School of Theology and Professor in the Departments of Religion and Philosophy at BU. He is the author of seventeen books, including titles such as *Reconstruction of Thinking, Recovery of the Measure,* and the most recent, *Religion in Late Modernity.* He is currently Dean of the Chapel at BU.

JANUSZ A. POLANOWSKI, a native of Wroclaw, Poland, is teaching at Nashville State Technological Institute while completing his doctorate at Vanderbilt University. In 1997 he co-authored a book, with John Mills, titled *The Ontology of Prejudice.*

PATRICK SHADE is Associate Professor of Philosophy at Rhodes College. His recent book is titled *Habits of Hope: A Pragmatic Theory* and was published by the Vanderbilt University Press.

DONALD W. SHERBURNE is Professor of Philosophy Emeritus at Vanderbilt University. He is author of *A Whiteheadian Aesthetic, A Key to Whitehead's PROCESS AND REALITY,* and, with David Ray Griffin, co-editor of Whitehead's *Process and Reality: Corrected Edition.*

Note on Supporting Center

This series is published under the auspices of the Center for Process Studies, a research organization affiliated with the Claremont School of Theology and Claremont Graduate University. It was founded in 1973 by John B. Cobb Jr., Founding Director, and David Ray Griffin, Executive Director; Margorie Suchocki is now also a Co-Director. It encourages research and reflection on the process philosophy of Alfred North Whitehead, Charles Hartshorne, and related thinkers, and on the application and testing of this viewpoint in all areas of thought and practice. The center sponsors conferences, welcomes visiting scholars to use its library, and publishes a scholarly journal, Process Studies, and a newsletter, Process Perspectives. Located at 11325 North College, Claremont, CA 91711, it gratefully accepts (tax-deductible) contributions to support its work.

Index

SUNY Series in Constructive Postmodern Thought
David Ray Griffin, series editor

David Ray Griffin, editor, *The Reenchantment of Science: Postmodern Proposals*

David Ray Griffin, editor, *Spirituality and Society: Postmodern Visions*

David Ray Griffin, *God and Religion in the Postmodern World: Essays in Postmodern Theology*

David Ray Griffin, William A. Beardslee, and Joe Holland, *Varieties of Postmodern Theology*

David Ray Griffin and Huston Smith, *Primordial Truth and Postmodern Theology*

David Ray Griffin, editor, *Sacred Interconnections: Postmodern Spirituality, Political Economy, and Art*

Robert Inchausti, *The Ignorant Perfection of Ordinary People*

David W. Orr, *Ecological Literacy: Education and the Transition to a Postmodern World*

David Ray Griffin, John B. Cobb Jr., Marcus P. Ford, Pete A. Y. Gunter, and Peter Ochs, *Founders of Constructive Postmodern Philosophy: Peirce, James, Bergson, Whitehead, and Hartshorne*

David Ray Griffin and Richard A. Falk, editors, *Postmodern Politics for a Planet in Crisis: Policy, Process, and Presidential Vision*

Steve Odin, *The Social Self in Zen and American Pragmatism*

Frederick Ferré, *Being and Value: Toward a Constructive Postmodern Metaphysics*

Sandra B. Lubarsky and David Ray Griffin, editors, *Jewish Theology and Process Thought*

J. Baird Callicott and Fernando J. R. da Rocha, editors, *Earth Summit Ethics: Toward a Reconstructive Postmodern Philosophy of Environmental Education*

David Ray Griffin, *Parapsychology, Philosophy, and Spirituality: A Postmodern Exploration*

Jay Earley, *Transforming Human Culture: Social Evolution and the Planetary Crisis*

Daniel A. Dombrowski, *Kazantzakis and God*

E. M. Adams, *A Society Fit for Human Beings*

Frederick Ferré, *Knowing and Value: Toward a Constructive Postmodern Epistemology*

Jerry H. Gill, *The Tacit Mode: Michael Polanyi's Postmodern Philosophy*

Nicholas F. Gier, *Spiritual Titanism: Indian, Chinese, and Western Perspectives*

David Ray Griffin, *Religion and Scientific Naturalism: Overcoming the Conflicts*

John A. Jungerman, *World in Process: Creativity and Interconnection in the New Physics*

Frederick Ferré, *Living and Value: Toward a Constructive Postmodern Ethics*

Laurence Foss, *The End of Modern Medicine: Biomedical Science Under a Microscope*

John B. Cobb Jr., *Postmodernism and Public Policy: Reframing Religion, Culture, Education, Sexuality, Class, Race, Politics, and the Economy*

Catherine Keller and Anne Daniell, editors, *Process and Difference: Between Cosmological and Poststructuralist Postmodernisms*

Timothy E. Eastman and Hank Keeton, editors, *Physics and Whitehead: Quantum, Process, and Experience*

Nicholas F. Gier, *The Virtue of Nonviolence: From Gautama to Gandhi*

George Allan, *Higher Education in the Making*

Timothy Walker Jr., *Mothership Connections*